THE EVERGREEN STORY

I want you to know how truly impressed I am by what you have done with your life. The business success properly speaks for itself. You are universally admired for that. But your being one of a "thousand points of light" says even more.

— *George Herbert Walker Bush*
41st President of the United States
(In a note to Evergreen Founder Del Smith)

What really sets Del Smith apart from other aviation entrepreneurs is the breadth of his success in this industry, and the fact that this success is a product of his own initiative, ingenuity and determination. Del did not inherit his wealth, and he did not walk into an established corporation; he built this global, diversified aviation group from the ground up.

— *Senator John McCain*
R-Arizona; US Navy (Retired)

Delford M. Smith

THE
EVERGREEN
STORY

BILL YENNE

WITH A PREFACE AND EPILOGUE BY

DELFORD M. SMITH

CHAIRMAN AND FOUNDER,
EVERGREEN INTERNATIONAL AVIATION

Evergreen International Aviation, Inc.
3850 Three Mile Lane
McMinnville, Oregon 97128 USA
(503) 472-9361
Fax: (503) 472-1048
http://www.evergreenaviation.com

ISBN: 0-9776374-1-7

Printed in China

Produced by AGS BookWorks, Inc.
PO Box 460313
San Francisco, CA 94146
(415) 285-8799
www.agsbookworks.com

About the Author:
        Bill Yenne is the San Francisco-based author of numerous books on historical
topics, from Lewis and Clark to the Second World War, and of course, aviation history. *The Wall Street Journal* recently said of his work that it "has the rare quality
of being both an excellent reference work and a pleasure to read."
        The author of *The Story of the Boeing Company*, Mr. Yenne has also writ-
ten histories of America's other great planemakers, including Convair, Lockheed,
McDonnell Douglas, and North American Aviation — as well as histories of many
of their greatest aircraft. He has also penned histories of the US Air Force and the
Strategic Air Command. Of the latter, Major Michael Perini wrote in *Air Force
Magazine:* "This book deserves a place on any airman's bookshelf and in the stacks
of serious military libraries."
        He is a regular contributor to *International Air Power Review,* and he
has been a contributor to encyclopedias of both world wars. He worked with
the legendary US Air Force commander, General Curtis E. LeMay, to pro-
duce *Superfortress: The B-29 and American Airpower in World War II,* which
Publisher's Weekly described as "An eloquent tribute."
        Mr. Yenne is a member of the American Aviation Historical Society and the
American Society of Journalists & Authors, as well as a graduate of the Stanford
University Professional Publishing Course.

TABLE OF CONTENTS

Introduction

A PORTRAIT OF EVERGREEN

EVERGREEN INTERNATIONAL AVIATION IS A GLOBAL AVIATION service company founded in 1960 by Delford M. Smith. He started with two helicopters, several dedicated pilots and one guiding principal. That motto, "Quality Without Compromise," still remains, while the company has long since grown into an international fleet of helicopters and fixed-wing aircraft that have provided safe and reliable service for customers in over 170 countries. Based in McMinnville, Oregon, 50 miles southwest of Portland, Evergreen is a world leader in air freight, aviation services and global humanitarian relief operations.

Evergreen is a family of synergistic subsidiary companies that make it the most diversified aviation services provider in the world.

Two of the subsidiary companies operate aircraft on a contract basis. Evergreen International Airlines, Inc. (EIA) provides global air cargo transportation and charter services for major airlines as well as freight forwarders. Evergreen Helicopters, Inc. (EHI) conducts specialized helicopter services, and offers complete helicopter component repair and overhaul services. Evergreen Aviation Ground Logistics Enterprises, Inc. (EAGLE) provides airport logistics and ground handling services. Evergreen Trade (formerly known as Evergreen Aircraft Sales & Leasing or EASL) buys and sells both helicopters and fixed-wing aircraft and engines, as well as aircraft parts and components. Evergreen Systems Logistics provides global air and surface transportation services. The Evergreen Maintenance Center (EMC), located in Marana, Arizona, is one of the most comprehensive and diversified maintenance facilities in the Western Hemisphere, including the world's largest storage and preservation facility for private and commercial aircraft. The Maintenance Center also has an on-site engineering department to support routine maintenance, modification and conversion work.

On the non-aviation side of the business, Evergreen Agricultural Enterprises (EAE) is a diversified farming operation that manages a nursery and over 8,000 acres of farms in the heart of Oregon's Willamette Valley. The crop varieties range from grass seed and hazelnuts to wine grapes, Christmas trees and organic blueberries.

Philanthropy, or "giving back," has always been an important part of Evergreen's corporate profile, and reflects Delford Smith's philosophy of doing business. To build on that philosophy, Del Smith created Evergreen Humanitarian & Relief Services, Inc. (EHRSI), a non-profit organization that expands upon a history of such activities that is as old as the company. The Michael King Smith Kid's Fund, better known as the "Kid Bank," was founded in 1983 to provide financial help for children under 18 to start or expand businesses. The Evergreen Aviation Museum and Captain Michael King Smith Educational Institute is a major American aviation museum that houses many historically important aircraft, including the Howard Hughes HK-1 flying boat, better known as the "Spruce Goose."

Though all the Evergreen corporations are mutually independent, synergy is built into the organizational structure. For example, Evergreen Trade, the Evergreen Maintenance Center, and EAGLE supply services to Evergreen International Airlines and Evergreen Helicopters. Throughout the United States and around the world, the marketing people at all of the Evergreen companies "cross-sell" the services of one another.

Each of these components strive for diversification, each learning more about the others each day to broaden their horizons. It has been said countless times throughout the company that everyone hired at Evergreen — regardless of which title he or she may have — is to be a salesperson, which is why everyone tries to learn more about each of the Evergreen companies every day.

This has been Evergreen's strength through the years. The marketplace is always changing, so it is important that everyone is working to get into new markets. Del Smith's philosophy is that you have to think outside the box. "If you're not growing, you're not building," he says, "and you're not going to achieve maximum success."

THE FOUNDER

The founder of Evergreen International Aviation, Delford Michael Smith, is a tough-minded, perfection-driven, compassionate and patriotic man who possesses a keen sense of humor and an uncanny ability to see worldwide opportunities for Evergreen's unique aviation services. He rewards the loyalty and dedication of his employees, and projects his personal work ethic values throughout the entire organization.

""He's a tough-minded optimist," Evergreen Trade President Mike Hines says, describing Del Smith. "He truly is a remarkable person. He possesses every quality one would want to see in a great leader. Day in and day out, Mr. Smith leads his team with a 'can do' attitude — motivating, teaching, and showing his people how to achieve success."

Evergreen's early success was due to Smith's extraordinary ability to envision opportunities to use the helicopter's distinctive flying and lifting capabilities when competitors didn't. Through the ensuing decades, that same vision has been applied to all other Evergreen enterprises. Evergreen's continued success is a direct result of Smith's management style.

Del Smith also has a sixth sense about people, and he surrounds himself with dedicated, talented staff and managers. He gives all employees as much opportunity and responsibility as they are willing to assume. They soon learn that there is no such word as "can't" in the Evergreen lexicon and that the word "opportunities" is always preferable to the word "problems."

Throughout his career, Del Smith has received numerous honors and commendations, including aviation's Humanitarian of the Year Award, the Boy Scouts of America Silver Beaver Award, the National Defense Transportation Association's 1993 Man of the Year Award, the Bell Helicopters Leadership Award, the Kaman Heroism Award, and the World Vision Contributor Award.

Del Smith has served on the boards of the Air Transport Association, the National Air Carrier Association, the National Defense Transportation Airlift Committee, and Helicopter Association International (HAI). While participating in HAI, he served as both president and chairman. He has served on the boards of directors for the Museum of Flight in Seattle, and the Linfield College Board in McMinnville, Oregon. He was inducted into the Pratt & Whitney Pathfinder Hall of Fame at the Museum of Flight in Seattle.

One of Smith's most prestigious honors came on December 17, 1999, the 96th anniversary of Wilbur and Orville Wright's first four powered flights near Kitty Hawk, North Carolina. The Wright Brothers Memorial Trophy was awarded to Del Smith by the prestigious National Aeronautic Association in Washington, DC. Since 1948, the trophy has been presented annually for significant public service of enduring value to aviation in the United States. The National Aeronautic Association is the National Aero Club of the United States and the nation's oldest aviation organization, founded in 1905.

In his letter nominating Smith for the trophy, former naval aviator, and United States Senator from Arizona, John McCain penned what is certainly one of the best one-paragraph descriptions of the spirit of the man behind Evergreen:

"What really sets Del Smith apart from other aviation entrepreneurs is the breadth of his success in this industry, and the fact that this success is a product of his own initiative, ingenuity and determination. Del did not inherit his wealth, and he did not walk into an established corporation; he built this global, diversified aviation group from the ground up."

As a recipient of the Wright Brothers Memorial Trophy, Smith joined a fraternity of aviation greats that include Charles Lindbergh, Lieutenant General James "Jimmy" Doolittle, and Senator Barry Goldwater, as well as a who's who of industry giants, including Clarence "Kelly" Johnson of Lockheed's legendary "Skunk Works," John Leland "Lee" Atwood of North American Aviation and Donald Wills Douglas, founder of Douglas Aircraft. Smith was unanimously selected by the National Aeronautic Association committee for "exceptional achievements in the creation of worldwide aviation enterprises, lifelong commitment to national security and humanitarian concerns, highest integrity and leadership standards, and preservation of aviation history for future generations."

The Wright Brothers Memorial Trophy selection board cited his humanitarian accomplishments, including his 1999 donation of two 747 flights of relief supplies to Kosovo refugees in Tirana, Albania; Evergreen's key role in rushing a five-year-old boy from Ghana to the United States for emergency treatment for a gangrenous infection; and his company-sponsored speaking engagements in Oregon schools for a quadriplegic motivational speaker.

"Distinguishing Del Smith from so many other successful entrepreneurs are the myriad measures that can be applied to his success," wrote Stephen Munro, publisher of *Aviation Week* Newsletters, of Smith's having been awarded the 1999 trophy. "There are financial measures, anchored by his development of Evergreen International Aviation into a diversified business with annual revenues exceeding $500 million. There also are measures of his commitment to humanitarian pursuits, national security and business development. It is those achievements that Smith would cite as the fundamental metrics of his success, and they are the reasons why the industry convened to celebrate his receipt of the Wright Brothers Memorial Trophy."

"Orville, Wilbur and Del," read the headline in a full-page advertisement that General Electric's GE Engine Services component placed in various publications. The ad went on to read "We join in honoring one of the great pioneers of aviation — Del Smith, CEO and Founder, Evergreen International. We've known for a long time that you have the 'Wright stuff.' Congratulations, Del."

In 2002, Smith received the prestigious Horatio Alger Award, which pays tribute to distinguished Americans who share beliefs of dedication, purpose, perseverance, and patriotism.

In recognition of Smith's achievements, W. Clement Stone, president of the Napoleon Hill Foundation Board of Trustees and the founder and chairman of Combined International Corporation, presented Del Smith with the Foundation's prestigious Gold Medal for Entrepreneurial Achievement. A major element in Del Smith's success through the years can be traced to his having embraced the principles advocated by Dr. Hill, the noted author of *Think and Grow Rich*. In the preface to a follow-on book entitled *Succeed and Grow Rich Through Persuasion*, Samuel A. Cypert paid special tribute to Smith:

"He so successfully applied the principles," Cypert wrote in 1991, "that he built Evergreen International Airlines into a billion-dollar private company and became a multi-millionaire himself. More important, he helped countless others along the way. His family, friends and employees all have a favorite Del Smith story. The thread that weaves through all of them is how Smith gave them an opportunity and encouraged them to achieve things they thought were beyond their reach. His quiet generosity has helped many more who have no idea who their benefactor may be."

"This is not to suggest that Smith is a soft touch," Cypert continued. "Nothing could be further from the truth. He is a tough negotiator and a demanding boss, but for achievers who share his fundamental values, he is a tireless mentor. His beliefs permeate his business, his family, and his recreation. They are so closely linked that it's difficult to tell where one ends and the other begins."

As Samuel Cypert observed, "Del Smith has been a positive influence on countless people whose lives he has touched. By believing in them, he has helped them to believe in themselves and encouraged them to become achievers. He has accumulated great financial wealth, but he has also found the true riches of life: the respect of his family, his friends and his business associates. He has made the world a better place for his having been a part of it."

Throughout the company, one is constantly crossing paths with Evergreen personnel who have not only learned from Del Smith, but who have been inspired by him. "Any day that you can spend with Mr. Smith is worth months in overall business education, entrepreneurship, leadership and friendship," observed David Rath, a board member and president of Evergreen Helicopters, Inc.

Within Evergreen, one is struck by the fact that the company is often perceived as being less of an organization and more of a family. In 2002, Evergreen was nominated by the Austin Family Business Program at the Oregon State University College of Business as one of the best large family owned and operated Oregon businesses. "At first glance, I wondered how Evergreen would receive the award because our understanding was that this award was based on families who have owned and operated a business from one generation to the next. Once again, as does happen quite often, I was pleasantly surprised when we learned that Evergreen International Aviation, Inc. was selected! Through discussion with others, I realized all of us working at Evergreen are a family who help run the business. We collectively presented to Oregon State University that although there was no 'direct' relative running the business, many Evergreen employees are family in that they grow up within the company and alongside Del Smith. He treats the employees as family and in return, we all do our best to watch out for the best interests of the company as though it was our own."

"Del is a mentor to so many at Evergreen," Rath continued. "But to a lot of us he is much more than that, he is also a father figure."

Del Smith's "Six M" Philosophy

In discussing Evergreen operations and the successes of his companies, Del Smith often says that "If you can't measure it, you can't manage it," and the yardstick by which he measures the operations and the successes of his companies, are the "Six M's." These are management, money, men and women, machines, materiel and market.

Each of the Six M's means something different for each of the operating companies, and each of the Six M's has evolved over time. This philosophy is discussed in detail in the chapters which follow. It is impossible to discuss the evolution of the Evergreen companies without doing so against the backdrop of the Six M philosophy.

The "management" aspect describes the Evergreen leadership team and their relation to customers and to the Evergreen assets that are their responsibility.

When "money" is discussed, it is in the context of revenues and the cost of doing business, and the profit derived from that business, which is the cornerstone of expanding capabilities and the growth of the business. Evergreen International Aviation President Tim Wahlberg put it succinctly when he said: "The money side makes sure payables are current and that receivables are *really* current."

The phrase "men and women" is a term that encompasses the broad scope of Evergreen's most important asset. Throughout the Evergreen story, and as we will see throughout this book, Evergreen's people have been — and continue to be — the key and indispensable component in the company's successes. As Tim Wahlberg said, "Our people are Evergreen's greatest asset, while selection can be a most difficult task. Growth can be limited by the time and energy that it can often take for the proper selection of leaders, but Evergreen is proud of the leaders that it has chosen by taking the time."

"One of the things I am most proud of is that Evergreen, through Delford Smith, employs, educates and invests tirelessly in the younger generation," explains Evergreen Trade President Mike Hines. "For the good of everyone, Evergreen grows young, eager students into exceptionally qualified future business leaders. These young people are given opportunities that are rarely found elsewhere; their education is beyond the classroom, and the investment only makes the company and our community stronger."

The terms "machines" and "materiel" are similar, but distinct. The former refers to the tools that Evergreen personnel use to do their work. A "machine" may be as simple as the agricultural tools used by Evergreen Agricultural Enterprises or as complex as the multi-million dollar 747 aircraft operated by the aircrews of Evergreen International Airlines. It may also be the ground handling equipment used by Evergreen Aviation Ground Logistics Enterprises, or the vast array of machine tools at Evergreen Maintenance Center.

When "materiel" is discussed in the context of Evergreen's business, it may refer to the parts needed by any of the Evergreen companies or the parts bought and sold by Evergreen Trade. For example, Evergreen Trade's "materiel" is the inventory that flows through it, while its "machines" are "its aircraft that are used in sales, leasing or part outs."

In general, "market" describes the relationship between one or more of the Evergreen companies and specific customers, and to the marketplace. This is usually seen as the most important of the six. As Tim Wahlberg explains, "The market is the key to everything. If you don't have a market, you're finished. You have to recognize what your markets are, and then stay ahead of the market. With our large sales and marketing team, we are way ahead of the other operators."

The Six M's are never considered independently, but rather in the context of how they are all integrated into the total company operations. As Tim Wahlberg puts it: "On the management side, the important thing is to recognize the work opportunities. On the manpower, machines and materiel side, the key is to develop the capability, special tools, and training necessary to take advantage of those work opportunities."

The parent company, Evergreen International Aviation (EA) is very much involved in the "money" dimension of the financing activities of the "machines" for all the component companies. The latter, in turn are more closely involved with hands-on operations relating to "machines" and "materiel" than is the parent company.

In the case of "market," EA will provide general corporate marketing in terms of administrative support. Evergreen International Aviation is involved in setting overall corporate strategy and following through on the administrative activities related to it. This might include advertising and marketing at major trade shows, such as the Paris or Farnborough International Air Shows.

Liane Kelly, vice president for administration at EAGLE in Indianapolis, has explained how the Six M's gradually caught on with her. "When sitting in initial orientation for Evergreen over some years ago," she recalls, "I found the Six M philosophy to be 'catchy' but wondered how it applied to running a company. As each 'M' was explained, it became apparent that the discipline represented by each 'M' was an integral part of a successful business. To this day, I've found the Six M philosophy a valuable tool, even in my personal life. Whenever contemplating a new project, a move, an investment or even something as simple as a vacation, using each 'M' on my personal checklist has allowed me to make sure that everything is covered. After all, it's definitely proven to be Mr. Smith's key to success!"

QUALITY WITHOUT COMPROMISE

MANAGEMENT MEETING MENTORING:
WORDS OF WISDOM FROM THE CHAIRMAN

DON'T COME HOME WITHOUT A DEAL.

SALES SELLS; FINANCE COSTS;
AND MANAGEMENT PRICES.

YOU CAN'T TAKE HOPE TO A BANKER.

IT'S BETTER TO GET PERMISSION THAN ASK
FOR FORGIVENESS.

TO ERR IS HUMAN, BUT FORGIVENESS IS NOT
OUR COMPANY POLICY.

IF YOU CAN'T MEASURE IT,
YOU CAN'T MANAGE IT.

OPTIONS ARE TO GET — NOT TO GIVE.

GOAL SETTING IS GOAL GETTING.

SAFETY IS OUR TOP PRIORITY.

SAFETY IS A FUNCTION OF QUALITY PERSONNEL,
TRAINING, PROVEN TECHNOLOGY, GOOD JUDGMENT,
HARD WORK AND DOLLARS.

A CLEAN SHOP IS A SAFE SHOP.

THE ONLY THING WORSE THAN NO WORK IS CHEAP
WORK, AND WE WON'T DO IT.

FIRST GET THE WORK — THEN BUY THE IRON.

IF YOU TAKE CARE OF YOUR MACHINES, THEN YOUR
MACHINES WILL TAKE CARE OF YOU.

CAPTURE COSTS DAILY.

LEARNING IS DOING.

ON REPORTING — THE WORST IS AUTOPSY. BETTER
IS CURRENT. BEST IS FORECAST.

WE ARE IN BUSINESS FOR TWO REASONS — FUN
AND PROFIT. IF THERE'S NO PROFIT, IT AIN'T NO
FUN.

PUT A NAME AND TIMELINE ON ACCOUNTABILITY.

NOBODY IS AS SMART AS EVERYBODY.

MANAGEMENT IS TO BE DONE BY CONSENSUS.

QUALITY PEOPLE WORKING IN A QUALITY ENVIRONMENT

WILL GIVE QUALITY SERVICE.
OUR EMPLOYEES ARE OUR GREATEST ASSETS.

IT IS NOT WHAT YOU EXPECT IN LIFE BUT WHAT YOU INSPECT THAT TURNS OUT RIGHT — "REVIEW RESULTS REGULARLY."

WE MUST CONTINUE TO HAVE A HEALTHY DISCONTENT FOR THE PRESENT.

PERFORMANCE IS THE ONLY THING THAT COUNTS.

RESOLVE WHAT YOU OUGHT AND PERFORM WITHOUT FAIL WHAT YOU RESOLVE.

THERE IS NO SUBSTITUTE FOR HARD WORK AND HONESTY.

PRIOR PREPARATION PREVENTS POOR PERFORMANCE.

GOD GAVE US LIFE; WE OWE HIM OUR BEST PERFORMANCE.

WHAT THE MIND CAN CONCEIVE AND BELIEVE, IT CAN ACHIEVE.

COMMIT TO PROFIT IN OPERATIONS.
SALES IS THE ENGINE THAT RUNS THE COMPANY.

FIXED-PRICE CONTRACTS WILL BURN YOU EVERY TIME.

STAGGER CONTRACT TERMINATION DATES.

EVERY EMPLOYEE IS A SALESMAN AND EVERY EMPLOYEE IS A MANAGER.

IF YOU THINK YOU CAN'T, YOU CAN'T.
IF YOU THINK YOU CAN, YOU CAN.

ADVERSITY CAN BE A LAUNCHING PAD FOR SOMETHING BIGGER AND BETTER.

SUCCESS HAS MANY PARENTS.

SUCCESS IS NINETY PERCENT ACTION AND TEN PERCENT TALK.

THE BEST IS YET TO COME.

Preface

by

Delford M. Smith

THIS BOOK IS INTENDED TO BE AN HONEST HISTORY OF THE Evergreen companies, and it is my hope that it will also serve as a learning tool, especially for young, ambitious people who want to do something worthwhile with their lives.

I hope that the reader will gain some useful insights through reading of our experiences in the first decades of Evergreen's history and evolution. I would like them to learn — through sharing some of what we've accomplished — things about running a company that aren't necessarily properly taught in academic colleges. These include the fundamental elements of management, the fundamental disciplines of money, and the practical management of human resources, not to mention leadership and common sense.

I would also like to express my heartfelt appreciation to Evergreen's workforce — both past and present. Employees are Evergreen's greatest assets. There would be no history to write about if it were not for their untiring efforts in support of this family of companies. Evergreen's growth and many accomplishments are the direct result of a sincere team effort. All recognition is to be shared among this team of employees. It is their time, enthusiasm, dedication and talents that have enriched and made Evergreen the successful corporation it is today. My sincere thanks to all of them.

> **THE EVERGREEN PHILOSOPHY**
>
> ON ANY GIVEN DAY, AT ANY EVERGREEN FACILITY, AN EMPLOYEE OR VISITOR WILL BE ABLE TO VIEW PRESENTATION PLAQUES THAT PROMINENTLY DEFINE THE CORPORATE PHILOSOPHY, STANDARDS, AND BASIC CULTURE UPON WHICH EVERGREEN WAS BUILT. THEY READ:
>
> **OUR CUSTOMER IS OUR PURPOSE**
>
> **SAFETY IS OUR TOP PRIORITY**
>
> **QUALITY IS OUR ONLY STANDARD**
>
> **STABILITY IS OUR ABSOLUTE RESPONSIBILITY**
>
> **RELIABILITY IS OUR FINE REPUTATION**
>
> **AGILITY IS OUR GROWTH OPPORTUNITY**
>
> **TOTAL CAPABILITY IS OUR VAST RESOURCE**
>
> **PROFITABILITY IS OUR FUTURE**
>
> **OUR EMPLOYEES ARE OUR GREATEST ASSETS**
>
> **QUALITY WITHOUT COMPROMISE**

I was raised with Benjamin Franklin's Virtues for Living, the Ten Commandments and the Napoleon Hill philosophy. Hill was born in 1883 in a one-room cabin on the Pound River in Wise County, Virginia and started his career as a reporter for small town newspapers. He lived to be 87 and became one of the best-loved of American motivational authors by teaching that your potential for success is limited only by your own ambition and desire.

At Evergreen, we have made Hill's principles part of our culture, principles such as Definiteness of Purpose, the Mastermind Principle, Quiet Faith, Believing in Yourself and Your Maker, and Going the Extra Mile. That willingness to go the extra mile for the customer is part of what has made Evergreen stay strong, while other companies have fallen by the wayside.

NAPOLEON HILL'S
17 PRINCIPLES FOR SUCCESS

1. DEFINITENESS OF PURPOSE IS THE
STARTING POINT OF ALL ACHIEVEMENT

2. THE MASTER MIND ALLIANCE

3. APPLIED FAITH

4. GOING THE EXTRA MILE

5. PLEASING PERSONALITY

6. PERSONAL INITIATIVE

7. POSITIVE MENTAL ATTITUDE

8. ENTHUSIASM (THAT INSPIRED FEELING)

9. SELF-DISCIPLINE

10. ACCURATE THINKING

11. CONTROLLED ATTENTION

12. TEAMWORK

13. LEARNING FROM ADVERSITY AND DEFEAT

14. CREATIVE VISION

15. MAINTENANCE OF SOUND HEALTH

16. BUDGETING TIME AND MONEY

17. COSMIC HABITFORCE –
THE LAW WHICH FIXES ALL HABITS

WHATEVER THE MIND CAN CONCEIVE
AND BELIEVE,
THE MIND CAN ACHIEVE.

– NAPOLEON HILL

THE TEN COMMANDMENTS

1. I AM THE LORD THY GOD, THOU SHALT HAVE NO OTHER GODS BEFORE ME.

2. THOU SHALT NOT MAKE UNTO THEE ANY GRAVEN IMAGE.

3. THOU SHALT NOT TAKE THE NAME OF THE LORD THY GOD IN VAIN.

4. REMEMBER THE SABBATH DAY, TO KEEP IT HOLY.

5. HONOR THY FATHER AND THY MOTHER.

6. THOU SHALT NOT KILL.

7. THOU SHALT NOT COMMIT ADULTERY.

8. THOU SHALT NOT STEAL.

9. THOU SHALT NOT BEAR FALSE WITNESS AGAINST THY NEIGHBOR.

10. THOU SHALT NOT COVET THY NEIGHBOR'S WIFE.

One of the principles that has served us especially well at Evergreen is definiteness of purpose. This is the notion that goal-setting is goal-getting. To use an aviation analogy, it's like flying with a compass. If you don't have a compass, you don't know where you're going. If you don't set goals, you can't achieve as much as if you do set goals. The other necessity in goal setting is creating a time line. If your project doesn't have a deadline, your goal is nothing more than an idle wish.

We have a management meeting every Monday morning where we regularly focus on goal setting. We set goals that can be measured, because you can't manage something if you can't measure it, and we review our goals on a very regular basis.

It always pleases me to see leaders who are able to articulate the goals or the mission statement to their staff. Those leaders or managers who set goals achieve much more than those who drift without a compass or a commitment. It stretches people and makes them grow.

Leaders who can articulate their goals are excellent motivators, and keeping people motivated is an important tool in the tool chest of leadership. In our society, we need to motivate our young people

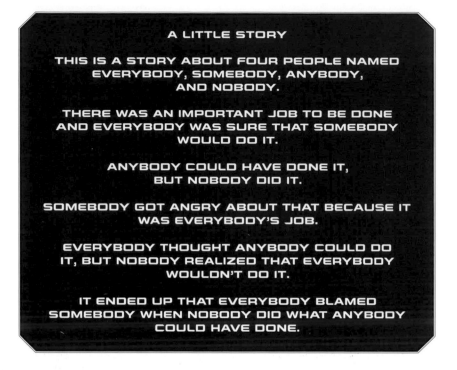

A LITTLE STORY

THIS IS A STORY ABOUT FOUR PEOPLE NAMED
EVERYBODY, SOMEBODY, ANYBODY,
AND NOBODY.

THERE WAS AN IMPORTANT JOB TO BE DONE
AND EVERYBODY WAS SURE THAT SOMEBODY
WOULD DO IT.

ANYBODY COULD HAVE DONE IT,
BUT NOBODY DID IT.

SOMEBODY GOT ANGRY ABOUT THAT BECAUSE IT
WAS EVERYBODY'S JOB.

EVERYBODY THOUGHT ANYBODY COULD DO
IT, BUT NOBODY REALIZED THAT EVERYBODY
WOULDN'T DO IT.

IT ENDED UP THAT EVERYBODY BLAMED
SOMEBODY WHEN NOBODY DID WHAT ANYBODY
COULD HAVE DONE.

and teach them to believe in themselves. At Evergreen, we motivate people with praise, and with positive reinforcement.

We also need to teach young people the value of a good day's work. When I was in grade school, I was delivering two paper routes, one in the morning, and one in the evening. I learned to work. We also always stress the importance of teamwork and accurate thinking at every level of Evergreen operations.

Another principle that has served us well is that of the master-mind alliance. An important part of success in business is surrounding yourself with the people best suited for the task. Nobody is as smart as everybody. By this, I mean moral, honest people who are specialists in their fields, and who are professional in every sense of the word.

These philosophies are applied to Evergreen every day, in every transaction. A deal is a deal. We don't rethink jobs. If we put in a bid and get the job, we do the job, whether or not we bid it quite right. It's performance that matters.

One of my favorite quotes from Napoleon Hill is "What the mind can conceive and believe, it can achieve." That thought has guided us into the twenty-first century, as we have built Evergreen into what it is today.

The Six M Philosophy

We use the Six M's of "management," "money," "men and women," "machines," "materiel" and "market" to describe all the aspects of our business and to measure all aspects of our operations. You can't manage what you can't measure, and we use the Six M's as the yardstick with which to measure Evergreen's performance.

Management

The first commandment in a manager's handbook should be to build your own succession. The idea is to become a mentor to your own successor. Seamless succession builds a strong, self-perpetuating organization.

The second commandment would be to create what Napoleon Hill calls a mastermind alliance, and surround yourself with quality people. A good leader must surround himself with a competent group. This is true when you are a kid growing up with the right selection of friends, or in business where you need the right management team and the right board members.

For example, in the bidding process, we may want five salesmen to tell us the market situation, but we also may want five accountants to tell us the costing situation. Costing includes items such as depreciation, the cost of money, the cost of human resources, the cost of machines, and — if it's overseas — the tax implications and the type of currency to be used. But, at the same time, we need our production people involved. We may be sitting in a comfortable board room when the job that we are discussing is in the Arctic, where it is 20 degrees below zero, or in the desert where it's 130 degrees.

A third lesson would be to follow the "Three R's" and to "Review Results Regularly." It's not what you *expect,* but what you *inspect,* that turns out the way you want it to. We need to accurately forecast revenue generation, to budget and to maintain discipline on expenses. After a manager commits to the revenue goal, as well as the pre-tax goal, the result is the only thing that counts.

The manager also has the responsibility of recruiting and training quality people, growing them, having as much interest in their individual development as in the company development, building their strengths and helping them — to paraphrase Napoleon Hill — to conceive, believe, and achieve.

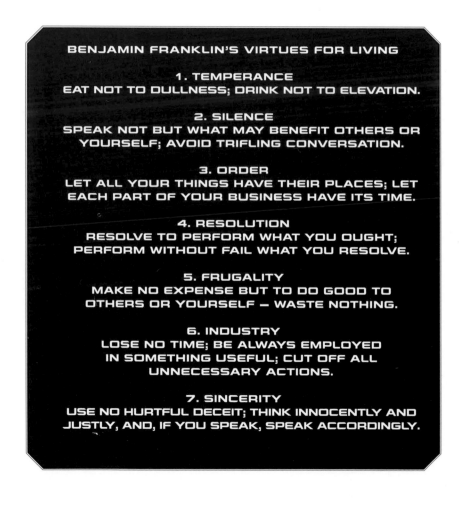

BENJAMIN FRANKLIN'S VIRTUES FOR LIVING

1. TEMPERANCE
EAT NOT TO DULLNESS; DRINK NOT TO ELEVATION.

2. SILENCE
SPEAK NOT BUT WHAT MAY BENEFIT OTHERS OR
YOURSELF; AVOID TRIFLING CONVERSATION.

3. ORDER
LET ALL YOUR THINGS HAVE THEIR PLACES; LET
EACH PART OF YOUR BUSINESS HAVE ITS TIME.

4. RESOLUTION
RESOLVE TO PERFORM WHAT YOU OUGHT;
PERFORM WITHOUT FAIL WHAT YOU RESOLVE.

5. FRUGALITY
MAKE NO EXPENSE BUT TO DO GOOD TO
OTHERS OR YOURSELF — WASTE NOTHING.

6. INDUSTRY
LOSE NO TIME; BE ALWAYS EMPLOYED
IN SOMETHING USEFUL; CUT OFF ALL
UNNECESSARY ACTIONS.

7. SINCERITY
USE NO HURTFUL DECEIT; THINK INNOCENTLY AND
JUSTLY, AND, IF YOU SPEAK, SPEAK ACCORDINGLY.

Finally, there is leadership. It is the spark of the individual that moves mankind. It is the ability of the leader to impart to others his or her energy, desire, and determination. A leader must create a culture of invested work habits, keeping the whole team fresh and enthusiastic.

Leadership is one of the rarest talents on earth, but, with few exceptions, such as with some coaches, I don't see it being taught in primary or secondary school. I see it being taught in families, in scouting and in the military. Most of the people I meet who have had a military background, have had a leadership training course.

8. JUSTICE
WRONG NONE BY DOING INJURIES, OR OMITTING THE BENEFITS THAT ARE YOUR DUTY.

9. MODERATION
AVOID EXTREMES; FORBEAR RESENTING INJURIES SO MUCH AS YOU THINK THEY DESERVE.

10. CLEANLINESS
TOLERATE NO UNCLEANLINESS IN BODY, CLOTHES, OR HABITATION.

11. TRANQUILITY
BE NOT DISTURBED AT TRIFLES, OR AT ACCIDENTS COMMON OR UNAVOIDABLE.

12. CHASTITY
RARELY USE VENERY BUT FOR HEALTH OR OFFSPRING, NEVER TO DULLNESS, WEAKNESS OR THE INJURY OF YOUR OWN OR ANOTHER'S PEACE OR REPUTATION.

13. HUMILITY
IMITATE JESUS AND SOCRATES.

There is a difference between managers and leaders, but a team should have both good managers as well as good leaders. All sales teams should have depth, because if you don't have depth, you will miss opportunities.

One of the differences between management and leadership is creative vision. Management is a team of competent people managing a process, but it's up to leaders to have a creative vision.

At Evergreen, we integrate our aircraft into a coherent system. For example, in the Pacific Northwest, the lumber companies used to buy the timber and the haulers were just a lifter with a hook, and the work went to the cheapest bid. I would bid against the lumber companies because Evergreen had a helicopter that did the lift work. We bought heavy-lift helicopters before our competition, so our approach was to put the helicopter into the timber package as a yarding vehicle. We bought the timber because I knew that Evergreen could lift the wood out more economically, so instead of the mills paying to have *their* wood hauled, they were having to buy the wood from us, and we sold to the highest bidder. We were the biggest lumber exporter in Oregon for about eight years in a row.

At Evergreen, we strive to build character in our leaders, and sometimes it happens the hard way. We have seen that adversity and defeat build character and ultimately create winners. We saw this in the cyclist, Lance Armstrong, who overcame cancer to win the Tour de France seven years in a row. I must confess that the trials we went through during the recession of the early nineties made me even more motivated and determined for the company to progress and succeed.

REVIEW
RESULTS
REGULARLY

We faced a tough situation, but we always paid our debts. We took the moral high road and earned the respect of our lenders. The bankers realize what we accomplished, so lending comes easy for us.

MONEY

A business can have everything else, but if it lacks credibility with its lenders, it lacks a future. In business, you have to have that credibility, and the way that you earn that credibility is through performance. As with your customers, performance counts. The lenders demand total honesty and full accountability. The lenders look for accurate forecasts that are consistently met. We're loyal to our customers, but we are also loyal  to our lenders. We are honest with them, and they have been loyal to us. The lenders require the Three C's: Cash, Collateral and Character. Evergreen has consistently met all three.

We apply good discipline and make commitments to our lenders. When our management team commits to the banks that they are going to do $60 million of revenue and have 20 percent growth and a 15 percent pre-tax profit, they've got to live by their word. It's a good way to help the company be better than its competition.

One way to avoid cheap work is to not get overbought with hardware, which is a concept that dovetails into the "M's" of machines and materiel. Any transportation company management team will want to keep upgrading its fleet to keep consistent with the industry, but they  must be careful to keep things balanced. You're matching the machines to the mission, but you're also matching the machines to the market.

We teach Evergreen leaders that excess inventory costs them 36 cents on every dollar every year. If you buy $100 million worth of spares that are unnecessary, it's costing $36 million a year. It's 10 percent for the cost of money, 10 percent for the human resources to manage that inventory, and the balance for insurance, theft and obsolescence. A leader must constantly be asking himself whether he is buying more inventory than is necessary.

MEN AND WOMEN

In personnel leadership, Evergreen has "Three S," "Three P" and "Four D" philosophies. The first three are the Selection, Salary, and Supervision of personnel. We have to make the right selection, hire the best, and provide them with the very best training. In selection, we want to know that we are getting the right people in terms of work ethic and character. We go back to the high school principal, the ball coach, and the scout leader. Character is more important than the technical capability, because technical skills can be taught.

THE THREE S
PHILOSOPHY:
SELECTION,
SALARY, AND
SUPERVISION

After hiring good people, our next goal is to do our best to retain them, and Evergreen is good at that. Our management has an average of 25 years with us.

Napoleon Hill gave us the "Three P" philosophy, which I have applied to managing Evergreen. These are Positive thinking, Personal initiative, and Pleasing personality. At Evergreen, our philosophy is that every individual is a marketing person. It's not just the sales force. I also want the technicians to be fighting for these people, and I want everyone to be a marketing force for the entire Evergreen organization.

THE THREE P
PHILOSOPHY:
POSITIVE THINKING,
PERSONAL
INITIATIVE, AND
PLEASING
PERSONALITY

We believe in the "Four D's," which are Determination, Desire, Discipline, and Dedication, all of which are expected of Evergreen employees. It is the responsibility of the Evergreen leadership to maintain a sense of discipline, but also to inspire self-discipline in the team and to maintain a feeling of enthusiasm.

Evergreen management also teaches accountability, commitment and responsibility. Our managers and our employees are not only committed to their departments, their operating company and the holding company, but to their fellow employees and to themselves.

MACHINES

Evergreen has always prided itself by the selection of trained and capable technicians who can work in remote and extreme environments. The Engineering Department constantly strengthens our maintenance programs to enhance reliability at the most economical cost. Maintenance control is an extension of the Maintenance Team that provides for fast recovery of Aircraft On Ground (AOG). Evergreen's trained flight crews are an integral part of the Reliability Team and can get more life out of an aircraft than the industry average. They are an integral part of the reliability and on-time performance.

> **THE FOUR D PHILOSOPHY: DETERMINATION, DESIRE, DISCIPLINE, AND DEDICATION**

At Evergreen, we have always said that "If you take care of your machines, your machines will take care of you." This is not rhetoric, it is deed, action and honest practice.

Safety is Evergreen's top priority. We have never compromised safety. Regardless of the economic trials and tribulations that we have experienced, we have never passed that cross to be borne by the maintenance people. Evergreen has never dealt with counterfeit parts or bootleg parts, or anything that has a questionable history.

We keep our material rotation current. If something expires or needs to be overhauled, we don't just leave it in a materiel hangar or a warehouse. Time-expired engines stacked in a hangar won't keep the airline reliable. You've got to get them overhauled in a timely way. We have always gone to quality shops. We don't go to blacksmith shops. I don't want somebody putting one of our engines on an anvil and pounding on it.

We always work in a conscientious way to match the machine to the mission. This is especially true with helicopters, because you really have to tailor the aircraft to the mission. For example, you've got to have a hot and high aircraft for the Mount McKinley rescue missions. For harvesting timber, you have to have a heavy-lifter. We use the McDonnell Douglas (Hughes) 500 in Africa because the rivers are narrow and there is always a thick jungle. For that job we need a small and maneuverable helicopter with a narrow rotor blade diameter.

MATERIEL

With respect to materiel, Evergreen works energetically at keeping a balance between too much and too little. We need to have enough logistical support to accomplish the mission without compromise, but at the same time, having too much inventory means having your money tied up in non-performing assets. If you aren't prudent in materiel management, you are really handicapping the well-being of the company. At Evergreen, we really believe in inventory measurement, and we measure inventory frequently.

Evergreen has the best warranty program in the world and that takes cooperation. The mechanics have to give performance data on the components from different vendors to the materiel people and the warranty administrator. Our track record is about eight percent warranty adjusted, and we process about 2,000 claims

annually. Some are denied, most are granted. Some that are denied
are reprocessed with more supporting data. We don't try to get
something for nothing.

We also involve our finance people in this process. We pay
attention to the balance sheet as well as the income statement. The
income statement tells us our revenues, expenses and pre-tax profits. The balance sheet tells us whether our inventory is increasing
beyond what is necessary for a safe and reliable operation.

We also barter a great deal, and we require our vendors to agree
to take offsets in the amount of 25 percent before we enter into a
vendor relationship. If Evergreen is buying something, we expect
the vendors to be able to help us maintain a balance with our
inventory by taking some portion of inventory that is compatible
with their business. For example, working with certain subcontrac-
tors will help us balance our inventory level by taking some offset
if we have excess inventory, or if we have some core engines that
we want to phase out of our system. With our major vendors, we
insist on a buy-back provision. Once a year, excess parts that are
still in cosmoline, and in the original package, are returned with a
minimum restocking charge.

Reliability of parts and components is a maintenance and a
materiel issue. Materiel uses it as much as maintenance. At Evergreen, we really focus on the integrity of reliability reports. We
can tell you what's going to break on an aircraft before it happens,
because we measure everything. A good reliability department
helps us overhaul or buy exactly what we need, so that we don't
end up with a warehouse full of left shoes. The materiel people
are constantly running a statistical analysis of reliability to prevent
overbuying in any area.

An important thing to remember about the materiel situation at
Evergreen is that we have a global operation. We have decentralized
operations, and we don't have the luxury of 300 flying machines
within a 500-mile radius, as do many airlines; or within a 50-mile

radius, as is the case with many petroleum helicopter companies. Some of our aircraft are in New Guinea, some are in Australia, some are in the Arabian Gulf, some are in Alaska, and some are in West Africa. As we come and go from those jobs, there will be situations where we have to carry extra heavy inventory because we are so decentralized and so dispersed.

For example, in Africa, where we have been working with the United Nations' Onchocerciasis (River Blindness) Control Program for more than a quarter of a century, we carry heavy inventories. This is to insure absolutely that our helicopters are always airworthy, because if the cycle of insecticide applications is broken, that can create a major problem. For this reason, we established major parts depots at Odienne in the Ivory Coast, and elsewhere in West Africa. In most helicopter operations in the world, 20 percent of the helicopter's total value is considered to be an adequate supply. In Africa, we probably carry 40 to 50 percent, because that is what is necessary to accomplish the mission.

MARKET

Our purpose at Evergreen — and at every truly successful company in the world — is to serve our customers. Our customer is our purpose. A good lesson for young people would be to study and make an accurate evaluation of marketing. They've got to make the right selections. They each have a finite amount of time, talent, and treasure. As we get older, we realize that the decisions we made early in life have really determined our success.

It is essential to do the proper amount of honest research. As we implement a plan or put an organization together, we have to build a market and build team spirit within a marketing organization that is both well-organized, and is staffed with the right people. By this, I mean people who are of outstanding, virtuous character and who also possess persuasive selling skills. These people are representing the company, and we don't get a second chance to make a first impression, so they have to be good.

A good marketing team is composed of people who believe in themselves, set goals, go the extra mile, and demonstrate a lot of personal initiative. A good marketing person must be a positive thinker, a team player, and have a pleasing personality. Such a person must also be able to articulate, write, and prepare. And obviously, the most important traits of a salesman are persistence and perseverance.

There is no substitute for hard work and honesty. When we go to the trade shows, we're not there for the social events. We're there to be productive and achieve our business goals.

A marketing team should be creative and think outside of the box. They should not allow themselves to be limited. If we don't have the equipment for a particular job, we'll lease it or buy it upon receipt of a contract. If it's a capital expenditure, and the job is sound, that justifies it.

While we are building a marketing team, one of the most important things to remember is that it is performance that counts. It is the sales force that generates the work opportunities for the technicians, the maintenance personnel, the pilots, and all the others who generate the revenues. This, in turn, must be backed with a good public relations group and a good administrative team.

The work of the marketing team must be done in harmony with the financial teams, so that the costing of the jobs is done accurately and sensibly. Accountants tend to think that sales and marketing people will bid too cheap because of their enthusiasm to get the job, while the sales and marketing people feel that accountants are so cautious they would never get any work. We must maintain a balance in this process. We let the accountants do the costing, the management do the pricing, and the sales people do the selling. We need a balance and an insistence that everyone measure costs accurately. Nobody should bid jobs without the proper study and management approval.

OUR CUSTOMER IS OUR PURPOSE

A sales force should not focus to the extreme on low prices. As I have always said, "cheap work" is worse than no work at all, because it is energy expended for no return or for negative return. It is a very serious responsibility for sales and marketing people to maintain responsible pricing because they are putting the future of the company and the well-being of the employees at risk. If the sales and marketing team underbids the cost of the work, we have to cut pilots, mechanics and administrative personnel. If the sales force isn't performing, they are putting many employees and their families at risk.

The entire Evergreen organization is taught to be resourceful for the capital needs. All the people within the organization owe the salesmen sound operational performance. In effect, we are constantly saying that everybody in the organization is a salesman. Everyone is

---

PERSISTENCE PAYS

80 PERCENT OF ALL SALES ARE MADE AFTER THE FIFTH CALL.

48 PERCENT OF SALESPEOPLE GIVE UP AFTER THE FIRST CALL.

25 PERCENT GIVE UP AFTER THE SECOND CALL.

12 PERCENT MAKE THREE CALLS AND THEN STOP.

5 PERCENT QUIT AFTER THE FOURTH CALL.

10 PERCENT KEEP ON CALLING AFTER THE FOURTH CALL, AND TO THIS PERSISTENT 10 PERCENT GOES 80 PERCENT OF ALL THE SALES.

made aware of their own responsibilities, and told that each person, in his or her own way, and in his or her particular capacity, is a salesman for the company.

Our outlook is that it takes five times as much time, talent, and treasure to get a new customer as it does to retain an existing one. Customer retention is everyone's job, because the customer is our purpose.

SUMMARY

As I have said, we use the Six M's as the yardstick with which to measure Evergreen's performance on an ongoing basis. The units of measurement are five priorities. The first priority at Evergreen is always *safety* because the rewards of safe operations are beyond measure, and because there is simply no acceptable alternative to a safe operation. Next are *profitability,* because it is our here and now, as well as our future; *reliability,* because that is our reputation; and, of course, there are the *customers,* because they are our purpose. Finally, there is *agility,* because it is only through agility that we are able to capture the future.

THE BEST OF THE BEST: EVERGREEN PILOTS.

Chapter 1:

DELFORD MICHAEL SMITH, THE EARLY YEARS

(1930-1960)

THE EVERGREEN STORY BEGINS WITH AN IDEA, REVOLUTIONARY for its time, about exploiting the potential of helicopters in agriculture and in the timber industry. From that idea came first the success, followed by the vision to build upon success and to turn the idea of that first helicopter operation into a regional, then national and ultimately international, company. Today, Evergreen is the most diverse aviation company in the world.

But before there was the idea, there was the man behind that idea.

Delford Michael Smith was born on February 25, 1930 amid tragedy. His father, Michael King, an English businessman and former Royal Air Force pilot living in Canada, was driving with his pregnant wife beside him when a train struck their car. Michael King was killed instantly, but Mrs. King lived long enough to give birth to her baby and to name him Michael. Handed over to the Sacred Heart Orphanage in Seattle, the boy was adopted at the age of 20 months by Emory and Mabel Barbara Smith, who gave him the name Delford. Shortly thereafter his adoptive father abandoned the family, and Mabel Smith was left to raise the youngster on her own.

"She was a saint," Smith says of his adoptive mother. "She had a great capacity for love and was the most powerful force in my life.

She taught me the value of honesty, hard work, good study habits, Christian values, and to be responsible for my actions. As an adoptive mother, her purpose in life was to give me a start. She taught me the basics."

Del Smith grew up during the Great Depression in Centralia, Washington, then a town of 3,500 in the Chehalis River Valley. Times were tough for Mabel and her son during the Depression years. Their house was the smallest and least endowed with creature comforts of any on the poor side of Centralia. The drafty little home was heated only by an old cast-iron cook stove. To get coal for heat in the winter, "Buddy," as Mabel referred to her son, would throw cow chips at the men on the freight trains as they passed through town to induce them to throw coal at him which he could take home for fuel.

The house lacked indoor plumbing, but the worst thing about the place was its location immediately across the road from the bank of the swift-flowing Skookumchuck River. Every spring, the river would rise and cover the floor of the meager home.

"Grandma," as Del called his adoptive mother, was not in good health, but she worked long hours at low pay in a chocolate factory during the day and did laundry at night in order to pay the rent and keep them clothed and fed. She would walk the eighteen blocks to this second job to save bus fare, knowing that the bus fare could buy a loaf of day-old bread.

"In those days I did all the household chores, chopped a lot of wood, built the fire in the stove, and prepared the meals," Del Smith recalls. "To earn money, I shoveled snow, picked berries, and set pins at bowling alleys. I did it with a real intensity and worked many hours at low pay."

Against the backdrop of these horrible economic times, nothing dulled Mabel's cheerful, optimistic spirit, which she reinforced with regular church attendance and what she called "uplift" books from the public library. She read these aloud to her son every evening after supper, before she left for work. Some of the titles,

WINTER IN CENTRALIA, 1930S.

along with texts from the Bible were *Self Help* by Samuel Smiles, *Acres of Diamonds* by Russell H. Conwell, and the works of Orison Swett Marden.

It was his mother who first introduced Del Smith to the works of Napoleon Hill, which would be among the greatest inspirations in his life. Del learned from his mother the rewards that came from putting the values she taught into practice through independent enterprise. She believed in teaching, and in passing on her values and her experience at every opportunity. As he recalls, "I was taught that what I could conceive and believe, I could achieve."

"You learned to enterprise at an early age in those days and reap the rewards for hard work," Smith says. "That's probably why many of the kids of our age grew up to have an intolerance for laziness or excuses."

THE EMERGING ENTREPRENEUR

Mabel Smith encouraged her son to earn his own way and always to give a day's work for a day's pay. She also taught him the fundamentals of credit and the interest that must be paid when money is borrowed.

Del Smith's history of success in business dates back to his first venture in free enterprise when he was in the second grade. Shortly after his seventh birthday, Mabel encouraged him to go to a local bank and borrow a few dollars to buy a Defiance lawn mower from

Sears & Roebuck. She accompanied him to the bank, but he had to approach the loan officer and explain that he would work hard mowing lawns to repay the debt. The loan was approved, and Del set to work lining up mowing jobs, for which he charged ten to twenty-five cents a lawn.

At the rate he worked, he could have paid off the loan in one summer, but Mabel advised him to "develop a reputation for reliability with more than one bank." So he went to a second bank, borrowed four dollars, and used that money to pay down the first loan. Soon, he had a growing savings account as well as good credit with both banks.

A YOUNG FISHERMAN.

When the autumn brought an end to his lawn mowing income, Del Smith took on a paper route for the *Tacoma News Tribune*. More territory became available as other boys quit when winter weather made the task of newspaper delivery unpleasant, and Del took every opportunity to expand his route. He also got his first course in receivables management — the hard way. One lady who agreed to take the paper from him was a member of a wealthy family that owned a great deal of timber land. When he went to collect payment from her after the first month, she said she'd decided that she did not want the paper and refused to pay. Del took the loss, but he resolved not to let that happen again. He asked all new customers to sign their orders and told them when he would be around to collect his money.

The following spring, he picked up paper routes for the *Centralia Daily Chronicle* and the *Portland Oregonian* and hired other boys to help him service his expanding territory. In three years' time, he and his employees were delivering papers to what seemed to be nearly every address in town.

To facilitate his newspaper deliveries, Del acquired a bicycle. How he did so illustrates the innate business acumen and entrepreneurial spirit that came to define his life and career. He had been given a jackknife by his Uncle Cliff, who taught him woodcraft, how to handle a saw and ax, and took him fishing on weekends. Del used the knife to initiate a series of swaps, trading one thing for the next, that culminated in his acquisition of a sturdy Hawthorne bicycle.

With his new bike, he was able to deliver papers much faster. He also made a wagon for his bike by nailing the axle and wheels from an old tricycle to the bottom of an apple box and rigging a tongue to the bike's back carrier. He also began soliciting customers for ice deliveries. He would go to an ice plant near his home and pay fifty cents for a hundred-pound block of ice. He would then chop the block into five twenty-pound chunks, which he'd wrap in gunnysacks and place in his wagon, two at a time, for delivery. He charged twelve cents a chunk, which he delivered to his customers' iceboxes. This netted him a dime on every hundred-pound block of ice. Del also used his bike to carry Mabel to and from her work places since they couldn't afford a car.

During the winter of 1941, Del supplemented his paper routes by working at a kennel that bred springer and cocker spaniels. For a ten-year-old, he had an uncanny knack for teaching dogs obedience and winning their devotion at the same time.

He also went to work chopping wood for the father of his Edison Elementary School classmate, Quay Jorgensen. The elder Mr. Jorgensen sold firewood as a sideline to his operation of a small sawmill, which was really just a circular saw powered by a belt from one back wheel of an old truck. Since he knew Del, he had no reservations about Del's ability to handle an ax. Like Quay, he'd been using one

A SUMMER JOB ON THE PEA THRESHER (DEL SMITH, SECOND FROM RIGHT).

since he was in first grade. The man's only instruction to him was: "Don't cut your foot off."

Among the principles of success outlined by Napoleon Hill, the first and most important one was that of having a definite major purpose. "Purpose is the touchstone of any accomplishment, large or small," Hill wrote. "A strong man can be defeated by a child who has a purpose. Shift your habits of thinking about the significance of your task and you can accomplish the seemingly impossible."

At the age of 11, Del Smith had defined a "major purpose." He would buy his mother a house!

By the summer of 1942, Del had saved $50 from his various business enterprises, and was ready to make his move. He approached Gene and Hazel Ragan, customers from one of his paper routes who had a house for sale for $1,500. He was able to work out a private sale, paying $50 down, and agreeing to pay $12 a month until the purchase price was paid off.

Heated by a Kalamazoo potbellied stove, the solid little white frame bungalow at 1217 G Street in Centralia had two bedrooms, a living room, a kitchen, a space heater in the living room *and* indoor plumbing. It was also situated two blocks west of his mother's former home, and thus well clear of any floodwaters from the Skookum-chuck River.

"It was a dicey risk at the time," Del recalled later of his first real estate venture. "But we both enjoyed watching the debt balance come down steadily until the mortgage was paid off."

It was not all hard work during Del Smith's high school years. He was active in school sports and the Boy Scouts. "It was automatic that you went to church on Sundays and that you got respectable grades," he says. "And it was a 'given' that you worked to earn money for your clothes and your school activities. You worked harder in the summers because more opportunities were available. At the same time, you had to do some career planning and think about the future."

When the United States had entered World War II in 1941, the resulting labor shortage afforded Del Smith an opportunity to expand his employment horizons.

"In the days when the war was on, you were allowed to work at jobs that the [child labor] laws would not permit today," he recalls. "You harvested crops, drove farm machinery and worked in the logging camps. One of my best friends was Allen Johnson whose mother was also a remarkable lady. Between Grandma and Mrs. Johnson, they taught us to work hard, to have worthy goals and to achieve."

During the summers between their years in high school, Allen and Del worked for the highway department, then the state forestry service, and next in the logging camps.

In the meantime, Del had learned how to handle draft horse teams from Floyd "Bub" Semft, a friend of the family, who was a teamster and pole peeler for a company that produced pilings and telephone poles. After teaching Del how to handle horses, he hired the boy to care for his teams when he went off on pole-peeling jobs. He also was willing to loan Del money from time to time.

While on the state highway department road crew, Del's group was assigned to install and paint guardrails and to erect standards for mailboxes in front of every farmhouse along the road. The farmers would ask the workers to paint their mailboxes at the same time the standards were being put in, but the crew boss would not allow it. Del saw this as an opportunity. He approached the farmers with an offer to come back after working hours, paint their mailboxes white or silver for a dollar and stencil their names in black on the side for fifty cents more.

Del thought sure some of his crew members would want to share in his painting scheme, but they didn't. One summed up the group's feelings when he said "What? After

DEL SMITH GRADUATED FROM HIGH SCHOOL IN 1948.

working all day, you want me to go out and paint mailboxes? You have to be kidding!"

Del could not, of course, use the highway department's equipment for this moonlighting job (which quite often was done literally by the light of the moon) so he borrowed enough money from Bub Semft to purchase an old Model A Ford. After dinner at camp, when the rest of the crew turned their attentions to swimming or playing softball, Del Smith would drive back along the route they'd worked during the day. He'd pull up to a mailbox, remove one of the sparkplugs from the Model A's engine, and screw the nipple of his spraygun hose in its place. Then he'd restart the engine and quickly paint the mailbox.

Most of his customers also wanted their names stenciled on their box. In those cases he would follow another Napoleon Hill precept and "go the extra mile" by giving the little metal signal flag a free coat of red paint. Del Smith painted from three to five mailboxes each evening and from fifteen to twenty on Saturdays. By the end of the summer, he was able to repay the loan from Semft and put another $500 into the bank.

He tended his growing savings carefully, using his pocket diary to keep close account of all his income and expenditures, as well as how he spent each minute of his time every day. The idea for this personal record keeping came from his reading of the autobiography of Benjamin Franklin.

Meanwhile, his developing money sense came from Napoleon Hill's idea of forming a "Mastermind Alliance" in order to "attract money, which is shy and elusive." To Del, it made sense to enlist the aid of others and persuade them that they would benefit from helping him. He never hesitated to borrow money to finance a project rather than diminish his own savings.

In school, Del Smith did well academically, but the Napoleon Hill principles his mother encouraged him to follow included the advice that "The man who has been active on the campus, whose personality is such that he gets along with all kinds of people, and who has done an adequate job with his studies, has a most decided edge over the strictly academic student."

Del took this advice to heart. He was elected vice-president of his junior class and president of his senior class. He also played sports, lettering in football and joining the intramural baseball and basketball teams, and was active in Hi-Y, the YMCA-affiliated student service club. He admired Morrie Folsom, a florist who was the adult counselor of Hi-Y, because of his enthusiasm, a trait Napoleon Hill considered vital to success. "Without enthusiasm, one cannot be convincing," Hill wrote. "Moreover, enthusiasm is contagious and the person who has it, under control, is generally welcomed in any group of people."

Among the activities for which young Del Smith showed particular enthusiasm was music. He had learned to play the drums in grammar school music classes, and during his freshman year, with some help from Bub Semft, who had once played trombone with Bob Crosby's Bobcats, he organized a dance band. The six-piece group included Semft and three of Del's teachers. They played on Saturday nights at places like the Oakview Grange Hall, the Centralia Elks Club, and the Masonic Lodge. After paying the

Del Smith on Drums!

members of his band, Del would pocket about $150 a week.

Having achieved local prominence as a drummer, Del was encouraged by friends who thought he might follow a musical career. He wasn't sure. Another career path beckoned. He had been attracted to airplanes since he first built balsawood models in Cub Scouts and memorized the silhouettes of the fighters and bombers of World War II. It was natural that he would be drawn to the Chehalis Airport, which was not far from the kennels where he had one of his many part-time jobs. He became a "ramp rat" in the fall of his junior year in high school, polishing planes and running errands in exchange for occasional flying lessons.

After school started that year, Del paid a visit to the office of Longview Fiber, a large timber company in the area, and made arrangements to thin any trees under ten feet tall from selected stands of fir. He hired a group of his fellow students to cut the trees, pile them onto a rented truck, and bring them to Centralia and Chehalis, where he had set up four Christmas-tree lots. He grossed nearly $1,000 on sales of the trees and used some of his earnings to pay for more flying lessons. Shortly before his seventeenth birthday, he made his solo flight in a Piper J-3 Cub. He received his pilot's license in 1948 at age 18.

COLLEGE YEARS

By the end of Del's high school years, Grandma Smith had not only firmly implanted the value and rewards of the work ethic in him but had also instilled in him an intolerance for lateness and excuses, and the meaning of a deadline for completion of a task. He learned from her the benefits of an education and the belief that true success in life was possible only through honesty, integrity, performance and quality workmanship. Thanks to her, the word "can't" never became a part of his vocabulary. He also learned that success does not come easily and that which is achieved by hard work usually will flourish.

One of Del Smith's favorite sayings that originated with Grandma Smith is, "God gave us the gift of life. We owe God our best performance."

After graduating from high school in 1949, Del Smith could not afford to follow his friends, the Johnson brothers, to the University of Washington in Seattle. Instead, he enrolled in Centralia Junior College, a two-year school that stressed sciences and engineering. He then went on to the University of Washington for his final two years. He financed his education from his own savings, supplemented by two loans, one from a family friend and the other one borrowed against the equity in the family home.

Years later, he would reflect that he probably studied harder and learned more during those two years in Centralia than after he transferred to the more prestigious campus in Seattle. He quickly established a pattern of attending classes all morning and spending the entire afternoon, until 5:30 p.m., in the library. After preparing

DEL SMITH AT THE U OF WASHINGTON, FRONT ROW, THIRD FROM LEFT.

supper, eating with his mother, and washing the dishes, he would go back to the library to study from 7:00 to 11:00 p.m. The result of this effort was clearly evident in his grades, and his mother would view them with satisfaction, saying, "The harder you work, Delford, the luckier you get."

In the summer of 1950, as his freshman year came to a close, the Long Bell Timber Company hired Del and his best friend at college, Don McIntosh. The pay was good, but the work was brutally hard. When the wake-up call came at 4:30 a.m., the young lumberjacks would wolf down a big breakfast and head for the woods. Their shirts would be drenched with sweat from 6:00 a.m. to 6:00 p.m.

Long Bell's operation was an industrialized form of logging called highballing, in which a long cable, the skyline, was suspended from reinforced beams. It would be run across a valley to the cutting area from a huge electric "donkey" engine that sat on railroad tracks. Six or eight big logs would be coupled together with chokers, which were heavy cables about an inch in diameter and 40 feet long. The logs were hoisted into the air by the skyline like matchsticks, and carried across to the tracks, where they would be loaded onto flatbed cars. The lumberjacks would have to pick the right logs from a group piled up jackstraw fashion in order to tightly set the chokers around them.

Running up a hill with a choker was a tough job, although running with the 80-pound hook that was shoved under the choker was harder. One end of the choker had a welded nubbin that had to be slid into a retaining bell. If it was done correctly, the bell would hold the choker cable fast when slack was taken up by the donkey engine. A "whistle pump" operator communicated with the man running the donkey engine by means of a complex system of signals. Sometimes the logs were hoisted before a man could get clear of the pile, or a choker might let go and drop logs on him. Accidents of this type were not uncommon and were often fatal. When a fatality occurred, the victim would be laid on a tree stump until quitting time, so as not to waste precious working time in taking him out of the jobsite.

GOD GAVE US THE GIFT OF LIFE.

WE OWE GOD OUR BEST PERFORMANCE.

At the end of that first summer, Del and Don were the only two remaining of the group of eight young college men who had gone into the woods together. One was killed, and the others decided that the job wasn't for them.

The two Centralia boys worked at Long Bell again the following year before transferring to the University of Washington.

When classes were finished following his junior year, Del went back to work for Long Bell. This time, he became a topper or high-climber, which was the highest-paid job in the woods, as well as being the most arduous and the most dangerous. The topper climbed trees selected for their height and favorable location with respect to other trees to be felled. After being topped and trimmed, these trees would be rigged with booms and used to skid the bucked logs into piles to await highballing. Del carried a short-handled ax and a saw on his belt and lopped off interfering branches as he ascended. When he reached the desired height, usually 175 to 200 feet above the ground, he would cut the top off the tree and hold fast as it toppled free, setting the trunk to swaying crazily. Then he'd descend like a monkey on a string and climb right back up in the role of rigger. About 20 feet from the ground, he would fasten heavy steel plates to hold the boom, then he would attach a block and tackle, through which he would run the skidding cable.

Reflecting on that work years later, he told an interviewer, "I used to pray each morning that I'd last until noon. Then I'd pray to last until quitting time."

At the University of Washington, Del Smith decided to major in psychology, while Don McIntosh entered the pre-med program. One of the major events of Del's first year at the University of Washington was being rushed by Phi Gamma Delta, the fraternity to which both Alan and Irwin Johnson belonged. The "Fijis" were a rich fraternity, and belonging provided an opportunity to socialize with men from families of great wealth and power. Del felt drawn to these young men, and he was at ease with them.

Adjusting to the new academic climate was more difficult. Del found the larger classes less intense than he had been accustomed to at Centralia Junior College, and some of the professors seemed remote from their students. The real problem, however, was his economics professor who, on the first day of class, announced that students should consider his course the most important activity in their lives. "I will not excuse absences for any reason other than a death in your family," he said. "Anyone who misses a class will get an F for the semester."

Having to be at every class session threw a kink into Del's plans. He had intended to cut classes for a day or two in order to buy a patch of timber near Longview that he had spotted. He thought he could get the timber for a good price. It was situated on a waterway that could be used to float it to a sawmill and it stood right between lands owned by Weyerhaeuser on one side and Georgia Pacific on the other. The choice between following the professor's rules and taking the opportunity to do a big-time timber deal was not difficult for Del Smith to make. A few days after classes started, he was on his way to Longview, where he managed to buy the timber for $40,000.

The economics professor was upset by his absence, but Del informed him that he had already made arrangements to drop the class and switch to an insurance course.

Two weeks later, Del got an offer of $45,000 for his timber from Weyerhaeuser. He took Weyerhaeuser's letter to Georgia Pacific and dangled it in front of the purchasing agent, who was well aware of the value of the timber. The Georgia Pacific man upped the ante to $50,000. Next, Del appeared in Weyerhaeuser's office and explained why he could not accept their offer because Georgia Pacific wanted his timber so badly. Then he cooled his heels in the waiting room while the Weyerhaeuser purchasing agent and other executives conferred.

Finally, the purchasing agent called Del back into his office and said, "Mr. Smith, we'll give you $60,000 for your rights, and that's our final offer."

"Sold," Del said, and he drove back to Seattle richer by $20,000 (more than ten times that amount in today's dollars).

He was tempted to call on his former economics professor and tell him about the deal — he had probably made more in that single transaction than the professor made in a year — but he decided that it would be uncharitable.

As he was driving between Longview and Seattle, Del Smith had noticed a huge pile of pulpwood waste outside a Crown Zellerbach paper plant along the Columbia River. On one trip, he took time to drive up to the plant and ask the manager what was being done with the waste.

"Nothing," was the answer. "It's stuff we can't use. We just let it pile up. Eventually we'll have to get rid of it."

A few days later, Del paid a visit to the US Army's Fort Lewis, near Tacoma, Washington. He learned from the contracting procurement officer that bids would be let on toilet tissue in three weeks. He asked for the specifications on the army-issue tissue, copied them, and the next day, he drove back to the Crown Zellerbach plant to consult with one of its chemists.

"Would that pulp waste you have piled out back conform to this spec?" he asked.

"Oh sure," the chemist answered. "That's a cheap grade of paper you are looking at there."

Del then went to the plant's disposal department and arranged to buy the waste at what was virtually a giveaway price. After classes the following day, he paid another visit to Fort Lewis and obtained a history of bidding on toilet tissue at the post. It showed, as he had suspected, a substantial margin for the suppliers. He entered a bid five-percent under that of the low bidder on the previous round and won a two-year contract to supply toilet tissue to Fort Lewis.

During these activities, Del Smith had been spending a lot of extra time in the forestry section of the University of Washington library, doing research on paper making. He'd also been scouting for used wood-chipping machinery and knew where he could buy the equipment he needed from the Badger Paper Company near Green Bay, Wisconsin. Next, he revisited Crown Zellerbach's plant and shared his plan with the man who was said to be the company's best chipping-machine operator. The man agreed to moonlight for him. Del then made arrangements to lease a small warehouse for his paper-making operation. When his bid was accepted by the US Army, he closed the deal with Badger, paying $10,000 down on the $50,000 chipping machine with his two-year contract as security. He had the machine shipped west, signed the lease agreement for his warehouse, and within two months he was in business making toilet tissue.

"Learning is doing," Mabel Smith had often told her son, and he put the homily into practice at the university by taking a part-time job selling insurance for General of America to augment his insurance class. The following semester, when he took a course in money and banking, he took on a second part-time job as a teller for the Queen Anne Bank.

At one point Del Smith had three outside jobs — insurance sales, banking, and washing dishes in a school cafeteria. This was in addition to supervising operations of his tissue-manufacturing plant and going to school!

Del was able to do well academically despite his work commitments, because he had learned to concentrate when he studied. He did not make Phi Beta Kappa, but he came close enough for his own satisfaction, reinforced by what he had learned from reading the works of Napoleon Hill.

The only competitive sport in which Del Smith participated at the University of Washington was golf, and he was a mainstay of the Huskies' team. Also during his years at the University of Washington, he participated in the Air Force Reserve Officers' Training Corps (AFROTC) program.

When Del Smith graduated from the University of Washington in 1953 with a Bachelor of Science degree in Business and Psychology, he was also commissioned as a second lieutenant in the US Air Force. He had graduated with top honors as a Distinguished Military Student out of a group of more than 1,600 AFROTC cadets.

MILITARY SERVICE

Second Lieutenant Del Smith had entered the US Air Force flight school with dreams of becoming a fighter pilot. This ambition was dashed when an exacting physical examination revealed his color blindness. He had long been adept at compensating for this condition, and it had not interfered with his having earned his pilot's license when he was in high school, but the Air Force disqualified him.

He couldn't fly an Air Force aircraft, but he was determined to pass the stiff requirements to qualify to jump out of one. He became a paratrooper assigned to the US Air Force's Tactical Air Command at Pope Air Force Base, North Carolina, where he com-

LIEUTENANT
DELFORD MICHAEL
SMITH,
US AIR FORCE
(1953).

manded a combat "Pathfinder" team that operated in conjunction with the US Army's 82nd Airborne Division. His team was trained to parachute into a war zone and set up ground-air communications for Air Force attack aircraft in support of Army troops. He made 52 parachute jumps while on maneuvers during exercises in Europe and Korea, as well as Central and South America. He enjoyed the leadership challenges of combat training and the exhilaration of jumping out of airplanes.

Off base, Del Smith shared a house with another lieutenant named Slade Gordon. Thirty-four years later, Gordon, who had gone on to become a United States Senator from Washington, told a reporter for the *Portland Oregonian* that Del Smith had been "the best junior officer I ever knew, but he was totally frustrated with not being right at the center of things."

Another man, Leonard A. Sheft, who also had been a young lieutenant then, told the reporter that Del Smith stood out as "intense, patriotic, and dedicated. His troops liked him and he was a good officer."

Sheft's wife, Monique, remembered Del as "a quiet man with little money but with charm and an enigmatic smile." He impressed her as "a tiger waiting to come up. But he was very polite, a 'Yes, Ma'am,' 'No, Ma'am' type."

Some of his Air Force acquaintances believed that Del was so well cut out for the service that he would stay in and become a general one day. Given his entrepreneurial bent, it seems unlikely he would have considered a military career, but if he did, the notion probably was dispelled by incidents such as the one that occurred when he was stationed in Germany.

The general in command of the base wanted to build a powerful radio transmitter so his men could talk to their parents at Christmas. The idea had been thwarted by bureaucratic fumbling, and Del Smith, now a first lieutenant, was assigned to cut through the red tape. As it turned out, he knew some avionics experts in Pennsylvania who had the necessary equipment. He also was able to arrange with the base's airlift squadron for C-119 cargo planes to bring the materiel and five technicians to Germany.

Within three weeks, Del Smith's radio station and antenna tower were up and running, and the troops were able to talk with their parents that Christmas. Letters of appreciation from happy parents began piling up on the general's desk and he ordered a full-dress parade to honor Lieutenant Smith's outstanding performance.

Only one week after he had stood on the reviewing stand to have the general pin a meritorious service medal to his tunic, Lieutenant Smith became the subject of a barrage of angry memoranda from higher headquarters. His actions in acquiring the radio equipment had violated the chain of command and had expended military funds without authorization. At the next unit parade, the general sheep-ishly stripped the medal from Lieutenant Smith's chest and gave a pained lecture to the troops about the necessity of following the military chain of command. This experience showed Del that the military style of leadership was not going to mix well with his way of doing things.

Del Smith completed his military obligation and left active duty in 1955. He was eager to get back to civilian life and start carving out a career for himself in business. He wasn't sure what he wanted to do, but he knew it would be in some aspect of commercial aviation, and he knew it would be big.

BEGINNING A CAREER IN AVIATION

While he was in the service, Del Smith had seen military heli-copters at work and was convinced that they were going to be what he called "the industrial workhorses of the future." He foresaw many possibilities for their vertical lift potential that had not yet been uti-lized commercially and he was sure there would be a future for him in some way connected with them. He became a true believer in a world filled with skeptics.

"In the early fifties and sixties, pioneering vertical flight was very exciting, much as fixed-wing flying was in its early years," he observed. "I thought the helicopter was an angel of mercy and a remarkable industrial tool that could be exploited and had a potential that few realized."

To follow his hunch about helicopters, Del Smith scouted out the early pioneering helicopter companies such as Okanagan in British Columbia, Carl Brady in Alaska and the Dean Johnson Helicopter Company in McMinnville, Oregon.

After he left the service, Del had returned home to Centralia, Washington, and one day, while driving through the neighboring town of Chehalis, he spotted a helicopter on a trailer. He did a fast U-turn, pulled in beside the rig, and struck up a conversation with the truck driver. He said that he was hauling the machine back to McMinnville, Oregon, 300 miles south, after completing a spraying job in northern Washington. He mentioned that his boss was offering ex-servicemen a chance to learn to fly helicopters in exchange for work. That was all Del Smith needed to hear. By noon the next day, he was knocking on Dean Johnson's door.

"Dean had a big heart and was willing to help a kid get a start," Del said. "So I got my helicopter training from him, and from some other old-timers like George Carlson, Joe Soloy, and Bob Tremble."

Dean Johnson was a fun-loving pilot who had flown F4U Corsair fighter planes from US Navy aircraft carriers during World War II. After the war, he flew briefly for United States Steel Corporation in Alaska, where he got to know Joe Soloy, a pilot for the Humble Oil and Refining Company. Joe would later become famous for his aircraft engine conversions and for founding the Soloy Corporation of Olympia, Washington in 1970.

Johnson and Soloy were about the same age, and although Dean had much more air time, he was impressed by Soloy's skill. He was especially intrigued by the fact that Soloy was flying one of the first helicopters to work commercially in Alaska.

The vertical lift industry was in its infancy in the late 1940's, but Dean Johnson's imagination was inspired by the business possibilities he saw in Soloy's machine. Only a few years before, in 1942, Igor Sikorsky had delivered his first R-4 to the US Army. Helicopters quickly proved their value in daring rescue missions and in operations that would have been impossible for fixed wing aircraft. In the years immediately after the war, manufacturing companies such as Sikorsky and Bell, as well as Stanley Hiller — the boy genius from Menlo Park, California — began producing helicopters for the civilian market.

In 1950, Dean Johnson returned to McMinnville, his hometown, and began raising capital for a helicopter company and flying school. His major backer was Uri S. Alderman, a prosperous farmer, who was known as the "Potato King of the Willamette Valley." Like Johnson,

Alderman was convinced that there was a great need for helicopters in agriculture.

Johnson went to the Hiller production facility for a course in flying helicopters that was tied to his purchase of a Hiller A-Model. In 1951, Joe Soloy left Alaska and went to work for Johnson as a crop duster and future instructor in the flying school Dean intended to open. The school never really got off the ground, but over the next four years Soloy did independently teach a number of people to fly helicopters. One of them was George Carlson, a young man from Portland who had such a natural touch at the controls that Dean asked him to hire on as a pilot. Another was Del Smith, fresh out of the Air Force in the late summer of 1955.

"I joined the Air Force because I wanted to be a fighter pilot, but I couldn't pass the vision test because I was color blind," Del told Dean Johnson. "So I did the next best thing, I jumped out of airplanes as a paratroop officer in the Pathfinders. I still want to fly, and I'm sure I can pass the physicals for flying a helicopter."

"You're on," Johnson said. "We have four helicopters here that need a lot of work and a fifth we've been using for spare parts. We have a lot of paint stripping and other things to do during the winter months. We hope to get that fifth ship built up and operational by spring. So you'll learn the mechanical side of helicopters while you're learning to fly them. Come summer, you'll be loading planes and maybe flying a few dusting flights. How much air time you get will depend on how hard you work at the other jobs."

"All I want is a chance," Del told him. "I'll show you I know how to work."

As Dean Johnson learned in the weeks and months that followed, that was an understatement. Del Smith not only knew how to work, he was fanatic about it. His constant hustle around the shop and the determination with which he attacked the arduous tasks of paint stripping and parts cleaning caused the older hands to exchange smiles and raise eyebrows. Some of them kidded him for his diligence by hanging a tin sign over his stripping bucket, christening it Del's

Gunk Tank. He took the ribbing in good part, and he was so likable and polite that none of the guys could really get down on him.

George Carlson and Del Smith became good friends, and in the summer of 1956 they decided to move into the same rooming house in McMinnville. This seemed a convenient arrangement, because Del was assigned to load Carlson's helicopter with pesticide "dust." In practice, however, the pair made an exceedingly odd couple. Like most of the men in Dean Johnson's organization, Carlson had an easy-going attitude toward work. If he didn't get his flying machine into the air until 9:00 a.m., that was OK. He'd work a little later at the end of the day to make up the difference. This approach rubbed Del the wrong way.

"It's inefficient, George," Del told him. "You know you get more out of your flying machine and the dust lays down better early in the morning before the air warms up and the humidity gets high. We ought to have everything ready the night before, and we ought to get out there at daybreak so we can get you in the air by seven o'clock."

"Come on, Del," Carlson replied. "The ten o'clock dust kills the bugs just as dead as seven o'clock dust."

"But you're not as productive then. You burn more fuel on the same amount of coverage!"

And so it went all that summer, with Del pounding on Carlson's door at 5:00 a.m. and Carlson grumbling and burrowing back under the covers until Del came in and dragged him out, both laughing and cursing with mock savagery.

The cement that bound this curious pair was a love of flying and Del's admiration for Carlson's skilled touch on the controls of his helicopter. Carlson could get the machine off the ground and take it through transition to lift faster than nearly any other pilot except Joe Soloy or Dean Johnson himself.

On Carlson's part, the cynicism of many Johnson employees toward Del's compulsive drive to work harder and more efficiently than anyone else was tempered by respect. He never had to worry

DEL SMITH (LEFT) WITH MR. AND MRS. DEAN JOHNSON IN 1956.

about the readiness of his flying machine or wonder whether his partner would have dust ready to load when he landed.

On weekends, Del drove home to Centralia, where he would play drums in a dance band on Saturday nights and go to church with his mother on Sundays. He sometimes borrowed $20 from Carlson on Friday night, promising to repay it on Monday morning, which he invariably did. Carlson never resented the loans, for he felt certain, despite Del's habitual shortage of pocket money, that his friend had unusual talent in financial matters.

Though his slight color-blindness had disqualified him from a career as a US Air Force pilot, Del Smith received a waiver on his commercial pilot's license. Already qualified in fixed wing aircraft, he received his commercial helicopter license in 1957.

"I wanted to do something honestly and I didn't want to fudge on my flying physical exam and possibly endanger someone else," he said about getting the helicopter license despite his disability. "But I never believed that the color limitation was a problem."

In the spring of 1957, Dean Johnson finally got his fifth Hiller A-Model helicopter built up to airworthy condition, and on Memorial Day, he and his pilots flew all five ships in proud formation over the City of McMinnville. He was elated. He believed his little company was close to turning the corner financially, and that he and his wife, Eileen, soon would be able to take a little more out of the business for themselves and their two children.

It was not to be.

A few weeks later, in mid-June, Dean was piloting his Piper Supercub when it went down near McMinnville. George Carlson and Ralph Grow, one of the helicopter mechanics, saw it happen. Johnson was flying at low level, where the tree line periodically obscured the Supercub, but it would always come back into view. As they watched, the plane dropped out of sight again. This time it did not reappear. The long moment it took for the onlookers to realize something was wrong was punctuated by the distance-delayed sound of a deadly thud.

As a plume of black smoke rose above the trees, Carlson and the others leaped into a car and sped toward where the plane had disappeared. The Supercub had crashed in the trees at the edge of a field and was on fire when the group from the hangar arrived. They pulled Dean free of the wreckage, and as they leaned him against the sloping trunk of a tree, the plane exploded.

At the same time, Del Smith was coming from Dayton, driving in the opposite direction with his truckload of crop dust. He arrived on the scene in time to watch Dean being loaded into a McMinnville Fire Department ambulance, and he followed the ambulance to the hospital in a car with Carlson. When they entered the emergency room, they learned that Johnson had died of his injuries.

Dean's passing deeply affected the personnel at the helicopter company, but Eileen Johnson did her best to pick up the pieces. One of her first moves was to drop the Alaska operation, feeling it was too remote and difficult to handle. Joe Soloy took it over himself, renaming it TEMSCO Helicopters, an acronym for Timber Exploration Mining Surveying & Cargo Operations.

Eileen tried to find someone who could manage the McMinnville operation. One of the people she approached was Del Smith — apparently Dean had told her about the young man's business acumen — but Del declined, saying he really wanted to get more flying experience. He had already made arrangements to go to Alaska and work with Soloy.

EARLY BUSINESS VENTURES

After Dean Johnson's unfortunate accident, Del Smith went up to Ketchikan, where he would pile up hundreds of hours of flying time, while gaining priceless experience. He returned to McMinnville in the summer of 1958 and hired on as a pilot for Johnson's old company, which was now being operated by Uri Alderman, as executor of his estate. On his first day on the job, Del recalls walking into the hangar to see some of the crews loading rifle shells and others sitting around chatting idly. Apparently little work had been lined up for the helicopters. He could see no future for himself in the remnants of the Dean Johnson Company, so he began looking for other opportunities.

Del Smith thought about buying the company from Alderman in 1958, but instead, he went to work flying helicopters for Vernon Geil, the owner of a veneer company in Sweet Home, Oregon. Geil had served in the US Army in Italy during World War II, and had purchased a 92-acre farm, which he managed to work while holding down a job at a sawmill five miles away. Geil's fledgling helicopter operation blossomed, thanks in large part to Del's efforts in lining up new work projects with the US Forest Service and the Bureau of Land Management.

Working with Geil, Del gained more experience in diversified flying which included crop dusting, timber spraying, logging and firefighting operations. Many of these jobs came about through Del's personal sales initiatives.

Meanwhile, Del was intrigued by Geil's penchant for what he called "horse trading." Geil would send for bid lists on government auctions of excess and obsolete goods and buy lots that included major items such as automotive parts, large generators, or other equipment. Geil usually paid far less than he knew he could get from someone in the industry who had a need for such things. While Del was teaching Geil to fly helicopters, Geil was coaching him in horse trading. It became a game with them, as they delighted in turning government castoffs into cash. Once they were notified by mail that their bid had won a certain lot, they'd take turns driving a tractor-trailer rig to pick it up in Texas, Oklahoma, or wherever the goods were warehoused.

Del's focus in bidding was on acquiring Hiller helicopter parts. The Army had a large fleet of Hillers, and he found there were some good deals to be had on surplus engines, rotor blades, tail booms, and even basic bodies. He acquired some of the latter for between $250 and $300, spent $400 having them reconditioned, and then sold them back to the Hiller factory for between $8,000 and $10,000. He and Geil did the same sort of deals on time-expired helicopter engines, which they would trade in to the manufacturers. They also assembled enough parts to enable Geil's mechanic, Bill Jones, to build a fourth helicopter from scratch.

Sometimes, however, there were unpleasant surprises among the goods they acquired. For example, Del once accepted the contents of 330 long wooden cases, sight unseen, because the lot included some helicopter parts he wanted. He eyed the sealed cases hopefully, thinking they might contain something such as ski poles, but when he and Geil finally opened them, they found 8,000 wooden crutches. "What the devil are we going to do with 8,000 crutches?" Geil muttered.

Having paid three cents each for the crutches, Del managed to sell the entire lot for two dollars apiece to a furniture manufacturer, who used them for chair backs.

In 1959, Geil and Smith recovered a Hiller C-Model helicopter that had sunk in the ice-flecked waters of Stephens Passage near Juneau, Alaska. It had been purchased new from the manufacturer by Alaska Coastal Airlines, a predecessor of Alaska Airlines, for $60,000, and had very little time on it. Someone had failed to calibrate the ship's carburetor correctly, and the engine suddenly coughed and conked out. The dismayed owners watched their investment crash into the water and sink. The pilot got out safely, but any vestige of interest the owners had in the helicopter business went down with their ship.

Del heard about the accident the following day, and he urged Geil to mount a salvage attempt.

"We can rebuild it perfectly," he said. "The sea water won't start to corrode it until the air hits it again, and the only things we won't be able to clean up and save will be the magnesium parts."

They arranged with the insurance adjuster to buy the sunken craft for $4,000, and Del personally led the crew that recovered it. As soon as the crane winched the hulk, streaming water and seaweed, aboard the recovery barge, Del went to work with wrench and screwdriver, pulling the magnesium parts out of his prize. A crew was hired to strip the hull down to the metal, apply a coating of zinc chromate to inhibit corrosion, and repaint it. The bill for the recovery operation and restoration, including engine work, came to $16,000. Geil had acquired a fourth helicopter, one that had flown only a few hours, for about a third of its original cost.

Del Smith recalls that he enjoyed working with Vernon Geil, but by 1960, he was ready for something bigger. His vision for a helicopter company went far beyond Geil's modest plans. Del had seen the tremendous potential for helicopter operations and he was eager to explore it.

"He told me that he didn't have an interest in building a bigger company." Del Smith recalled. "So I bought his two Hiller UH-12E helicopters and immediately went to work."

Del Smith hit the ground running in pursuit of his dream of a bigger company. It would be a daunting task, but nobody who was aware of his background, or who had known him while he was growing up in Centralia, would have bet against him.

Chapter 2:

EVERGREEN HELICOPTERS, THE EARLY YEARS

(1960-1967)

WHILE HE WAS STILL WORKING WITH VERNON GEIL, DEL Smith reconnected with his boyhood friend, Quay Jorgensen, who had coincidentally also become a helicopter pilot. He had flown in the Army, and was intrigued by the verbal pictures that Del now painted of the helicopter as a modern workhorse. He also was excited about the type of work that Del was doing for Vernon Geil. Each time Del and Jorgensen got together, the idea that they should join forces in setting up a new helicopter company seemed more reasonable.

On July 1, 1960, Smith and Jorgensen officially incorporated Evergreen Helicopters in Corvallis. The following morning, Evergreen landed its first commercial job, a sagebrush-spraying contract.

Almost immediately after Evergreen Helicopters was founded, Del Smith and Quay Jorgensen picked up the threads of old boyhood rivalries, transferring them to flying performance. As a result, the two drove themselves harder than they might have otherwise done. Each wanted to spray more sagebrush, fly more hours, or go farther and faster than the other.

All the while, Del was dreaming of bigger things for Evergreen. He told Jorgensen about Dean Johnson, Inc. and how its operation must be suffering.

"Uri Alderman isn't able to manage it properly and he can't afford to shut it down, so I'll bet he'd be happy to sell it," he told Quay. "One of these days when work slows down here, we really ought to go up to McMinnville and buy that outfit."

Work did not slow down, however. The pair flew steadily throughout the year. One day in the spring of 1961, he told Quay, "We've really been ringing the till. I'm going to pay off both of our machines and we'll soon be able to buy another E Model."

That plan was abandoned in August 1961, when Quay was injured in a helicopter accident while he was flying on a forest fire in the Wallowa Mountains of eastern Oregon. Del was working at the headwaters of the Columbia River in Canada when he learned about the accident, and he immediately turned his helicopter south and headed for the hospital where Quay was being treated.

As Quay was recuperating, Del proposed that instead of buying a new helicopter and continuing to operate Evergreen on the same basis, they go to Alderman's headquarters and make an offer for Dean Johnson, Inc. Quay agreed, and they drove to McMinnville one autumn morning in Del's battered 1946 Chrysler. The car broke down about ten miles short of their destination, so they hitched a ride with a passing farmer.

Alderman was skeptical at first about the disheveled pair who appeared in his office that morning, but Del made a persuasive presentation. He described Evergreen's successful operation in Sweet Home and said, "We have to make a deal today, because every hour our flying machine isn't working is costing us a good amount of revenue."

He paused as though mustering his strength and added, "We can offer $60,000 for the Dean Johnson company."

Alderman was visibly moved. He said, "I think we have a deal," and asked his visitors to meet him later that afternoon in the office of his attorney in McMinnville.

Del and Quay hitchhiked to McMinnville and spent the next several hours sleeping under a big oak tree on the campus of Linfield College. Then they walked downtown to the office of

PHOEBE HOCKEN WITH DEL SMITH AND HIS SON MIKE.

Alderman's attorney, who had the purchase agreement ready for Del's signature.

The deal was $20,000 down with the balance to be paid out of operating profits. Del was confident that there would be operating profits and that he would be able handle the commitment. Anyone who had known Del Smith during his business career that began when he was a seven-year-old in Centralia could easily predict that there would, indeed, be operating profits.

PHOEBE HOCKEN, THE FIRST LADY OF EVERGREEN

When he had finished with the corporate paperwork on July 1, 1960, Del Smith asked his lawyer to recommend a good accountant for Evergreen. The lawyer introduced him to a woman named Phoebe Hocken. She was given the five-minute-old corporation's account because it was well known around the office that she loved flying.

"We were blessed with Phoebe Hocken," Del Smith remembers. "She was a big contributor to the start of Evergreen. She was the administrator and the financial leader. We never had contract

DEL SMITH (RIGHT) WITH ONE OF EVERGREEN'S FIRST HILLER UH-12S.

problems, never had banking problems, and never had customer problems. As a matter of fact, she was also well respected by all the helicopter manufacturers. Other than my adoptive mother, she influenced my life more than anybody. She really taught all of us the basics of business. We were operationally good, we could fly and maintain an aircraft, but she was the one who kept the bank relations positive. Everybody loved her."

"She gave us good financial discipline," Del said of Phoebe. An Evergreen publication credits her with "an ability to accommodate the company's growth and maintain good relations with the financial community" during the expansion years.

"Someone has to shuffle the paper and mind the store," Phoebe Hocken said modestly. "One of my jobs was to send parts on the bus to wherever they were needed, and I also had to contact the men in the field and send them their pay. I got to be very well known at the Western Union office."

Phoebe Hocken's father had been an accounting professor, and she had worked with him, managing finances and doing accounting work for small, independent sawmills in the little logging towns on or near the Oregon coast, such as Coos Bay, Toledo, and Newport.

During World War II, she married a former military pilot who later worked his way through Oregon State as a cropduster. After several years, they decided that he should settle down to a less dangerous job, but they agreed that he would cropdust for one more year because the pay was quite good. He was killed in a crash, leaving Phoebe with two children and another on the way. She married a second pilot who also was killed, but she persevered and raised the kids well. The boys graduated Phi Beta Kappa and went on to receive PhD's.

Although Del Smith was continually flying, he always arranged his schedule to return to McMinnville one day a week and work with Phoebe on the bids for future Forest Service work. He recalls Phoebe as having been a genius at keeping track of company financial matters. She kept the operation going on the business side at McMinnville while he flew and kept the Evergreen crews busy working in the field. This continued even when Del moved his family to Anchorage, Alaska between 1966 and 1968. She would travel up there periodically to check the books.

Phoebe Hocken's indispensable contributions to Evergreen's early achievements are second only to those of Del Smith. She was with Evergreen at its inception, and her key role in finance and administration formed the foundation of Evergreen's initial and continued success. Her exceptional organizational, human relations, and financial disciplines are still taught today.

She retired in October 1983, but for these accomplishments, she is still referred to respectfully as the "First Lady of Evergreen."

SOLE OWNERSHIP

After his crash, Quay Jorgensen left the company, and in 1962, Del Smith became the sole owner of Evergreen Helicopters. By this time, through Del's initiative, the company had grown rapidly from its two original Hiller helicopters to seven. Within a year the company was working those seven helicopters hard as opportunities increased throughout the Pacific Northwest and in Alaska. The roster of pilots now included men such as Elton Eby, Al Cole, Dale Hill, Don Knechtges and Jerry Harchenko.

Under Del Smith's leadership, Evergreen proved that his machines could do an accurate job of placing seeds, herbicides and pesticides where customers wanted them. Evergreen was also demonstrating that helicopters could tackle many jobs that fixed-wing aircraft simply could not perform. As Del and his mechanics gained more experience, they designed and patented spray nozzles and devices for the helicopters that improved the various applications required.

"We found uses for helicopters that no one had ever thought about," Smith says. "Logging proved to be one of those jobs. We could get into areas where there were no roads, drop the loggers off and then pick up the logs later for delivery to trucks at the bottom of the mountains. We not only saved time in a logging operation but the environment wasn't disturbed by having to build roads to each site. Those were exciting years as we proved that the helicopter could harvest timber safely and profitably."

Smith saw "work opportunities" (a favorite phrase) in strange places. Possessed with a rare combination of vision, persistence, and sense of timing and optimism, he saw opportunities for profit where others saw only risk. He quickly learned financial discipline and with his emphasis on quality performance, Evergreen prospered.

Evergreen's early success was due in large measure to Smith's intuitive understanding of the timber industry. When he was growing up in Centralia, Smith had a great deal of contact with the timber industry through people he knew, through his seasonal work in the timber industry, and especially from working with men who persevered in such a demanding work environment.

As much as he knew, he realized that there was even more to be learned in order to keep Evergreen competitive within the logging industry. He and Phoebe Hocken attended a forestry class one day a week for about three months in order to understand the industry better, and to help them in the bidding process. They learned about log scaling, how much the various types of timber weigh, and the significance of knowing upon which side of the mountain trees were growing.

By the fifties, the industry realized that timber was a renewable resource if managed properly. At the turn of the twentieth century, when the Pacific Northwest was being pioneered, the timber industry was harvesting trees with little or no thought of conservation. Trees were cut, and when more lumber was needed, the loggers just went a bit deeper into the forest. By the fifties, the big lumber companies realized that the supply of trees was finite, however, unlike minerals mined from the earth, trees could be replanted. All the timber land that had been logged had a potential for a second growth of trees — and more.

The problem that the timber industry faced in turning the idea of renewed forests into reality was one of accessibility. The areas that had been logged over the previous decades were now covered with a virtually impenetrable jungle of brush. The most efficient way to work most of the land that needed to be reforested was to fly over it.

This was where Del Smith and his helicopter came into play. He remembers that, "it was an exciting opportunity, because it seemed like it was a market that would never vanish."

Indeed, he could see that there were numerous opportunities for helicopter work in the forests of the Pacific Northwest. Seeding was the obvious one, but before that, there was site preparation. As with a farm, the ground needed to be readied for planting. In this case, chemicals had to be applied to eradicate the undesirable brush. Only then could the seeds be planted. Helicopters were the only practical way to do either of these jobs on most of the land in the Northwest.

Del Smith was especially excited with the prospects of applying helicopter operations to the timber industry because there would be four seasons of work. This was unique. During the fifties, many helicopter operations didn't have four seasons, but in lumbering, helicopters could work year-round. In the spring, there was dormant spraying — the application of herbicides. In the summer, there would be fire-fighting, and the seeding would begin in the fall and last into the winter.

When it came to seeding, the timber industry wanted roughly 500 trees to the acre, so a typical application was about a pound of timber seed per acre. More than 500 seeds were needed — because some wouldn't sprout and birds and small animals would eat some as well — so it was calculated that a pound of seeds per acre would yield the desired number of trees.

The standard practice in Evergreen's early days was for Del and his team of pilots, drivers and mechanics to move from job to job at night in a caravan of flat bed trucks hauling the helicopters, a batch truck or two with the chemicals, and fuel trucks. Upon arrival at a site, everyone would catch what sleep they could so that they would be ready at dawn for the day's flying if the weather and the winds permitted.

At the end of Evergreen's first year of helicopter seeding operations, the Bureau of Land Management acknowledged that Smith and his helicopter crews could do the work of replanting burned-out or logged-over areas at a third the cost of reseeding by hand.

Today's second and third growth timber in the Pacific Northwest is the result of this realization and subsequent emphasis on nurturing the growth of timber. Much of this success would not have been possible without Del Smith's understanding of the helicopter's vertical lifting, seeding and fertilizing capabilities.

BUILDING THE FLEET

Del Smith built the Evergreen fleet up from the two original UH-12E's to a fleet of seven. Modest by today's standards, this fleet was actually the largest of its kind in the Pacific Northwest in the early 1960's.

The helicopters that Dean Johnson and Del Smith operated were Hiller two-seat machines, a mix of Models UH-12A, UH-12B and UH-12C aircraft, which dated back to a 1948 design, and were, as Smith recalls, underpowered for the tough demands of forestry and agricultural work that they were doing. This would change, however, with the introduction of the Hiller Model UH-12E, known to the pilots simply as the "12E." Powered by a 360 hp Lycoming V-540 engine — compared to the 180 hp Franklin engine of the earlier UH-12's — the Hiller 12E had a greater top speed and a range of 215 miles. The 12E would also later incorporate an anhedral stabilizer on the tail boom.

The UH-12 series had been created by the brilliant young designer Stanley Hiller, Jr., who had designed and built his first helicopter in 1944 when he was just 18 years old. This helicopter, designated XH-44, was the first efficient American helicopter with coaxial, contra-rotating rotors. He would abandon this feature, however, when he created the more conventional UH-12 series. It was the latter type that would become the first helicopter to make a commercial flight across the continent. Hiller's UH-12 series was selected by the United States military for acquisition as an observation helicopter and purchased under the US Army designation H-23 and the US Navy designation HTE. Given the name "Raven," this helicopter became the standard military training helicopter for the United States armed forces, and for Britain's Royal Navy.

With his helicopters, Del Smith was able to pick up some large brush eradication and reforestation contracts for timber companies and government agencies. Evergreen was hired by International Paper to eliminate myrtle brush on its property in Oregon, and by Weyerhaeuser for similar work. Another of Evergreen's big 1961 contracts was reseeding logged areas in western Washington and the vast Tillamook Burn area in western Oregon. It was work that would have been economically impossible without the use of helicopters.

Meanwhile, the Montana Fish and Game Department contracted with Evergreen Helicopters to count moose in the Upper Ruby River country in the Madison-Beaverhead area of southwestern Montana. This was another project that would have been extremely time consuming without the use of helicopters. The results of the Evergreen census showed that there were twice as many of the big animals than previously estimated.

In the beginning, Del Smith steered Evergreen Helicopters, Inc. toward work in the timber industry because of his experience, and the scope of the work on projects that often involved as much as 250,000 acres. Gradually, though, he began to add subcontracts on agricultural work to the Evergreen Helicopters, Inc. repertoire. Crops required application work and this translated into work opportunities for Evergreen helicopters. During 1962, Evergreen bid on the big budworm eradication projects in Idaho and Montana.

Meanwhile, Smith was working hard to establish increased credibility with the banks. His business plan would always involve maintaining the support of the company's commercial lenders.

EARLY EVERGREEN PROJECTS

By 1962, Evergreen Helicopters, Inc. was seeding and spraying from Washington to California, and was doing fire control work on Oregon's Mt. Hood. During 1962, Evergreen even used helicopters to restring powerlines for Pacific Power & Light. Evergreen's helicopters also helped the US Army Corps of Engineers in an operation involving a three-million-pound dredge. This saved the Army time and resources, and resulted in a savings of 56 percent.

In 1963, Evergreen Helicopters, Inc. completed a huge brush-spraying project in Oregon's Umpqua National Forest and helped to attack the Douglas fir tussock moth across 64,000 acres in central Oregon. Involving a total of 18 helicopters, this operation was the largest of its kind in United States history, and it resulted in a 100 percent success. In 1964, the US Forest Service awarded Evergreen a 56,000-acre contract for tussock moth eradication in the Malheur and Ochoco National Forests.

By the mid-sixties, Evergreen was rapidly becoming the destructive tussock moth's worst enemy. In 1965, the company participated in "Operation Bugout," the spraying of 500,000 acres in Idaho's rugged intermountain region. Similar efforts continued, and by 1974, thanks to Evergreen's efforts, the tussock moth had been eliminated in the state of Oregon.

Yet the tussock moth was not the only harmful pest that had Evergreen's helicopters to fear. Not even inclement weather kept the dreadful insects safe from Del Smith's Hillers. In July 1963, despite the worst weather on record for that month in the state of Washington, Evergreen accomplished a successful aerial assault on the hemlock looper. The project turned out to be the largest aerial insect eradication project ever attempted in the United States.

It was in 1963 that Evergreen was called upon to help to combat a yellow aphid attack on the sugar cane fields in Puerto Rico. Ultimately, the project turned into a long-term contract with the Plata Sugar Company in which thousands of acres of nutrient-starved cane fields were treated with a half-ton of fertilizer per acre to restore productivity. As its business expanded globally in the seventies, Evergreen would continue with pest eradication projects to aid the timber industry in the Pacific Northwest. A decade later, in 1974, Evergreen eradicated Washington's damaging spruce budworm.

In response to the requirements of agricultural projects, Del Smith and Evergreen maintenance supervisor Norman McGrew developed a helicopter spray system known as the "PaceSpreader." It permitted a fast and economical application of granular chemicals — including fertilizers — with unprecedented precision. The Evergreen PaceSpreader permitted high-volume application at relatively high helicopter speeds. The best system then in use would move 150 pounds per minute, while the Evergreen system could spread up to 800 pounds in the same amount of time.

In addition to the speed, the Evergreen system had a uniform broadcast pattern that would ensure a more even application, thus avoiding crop damage and chemical waste. The earlier systems dropped too much fertilizer at the center of the spreader swath and too little at the edges. At the same time, the Evergreen PaceSpreader had a 120-foot swath, nearly five times that of the existing systems. This made the work faster and it cut down on the possibility

An Evergreen Hiller 12E with a PaceSpreader.

of overlapping swaths. In summary, a helicopter equipped with the Evergreen PaceSpreader could do in a day what another helicopter required a week to accomplish.

Developed for fertilizer and agricultural chemicals, the Evergreen PaceSpreader was easily adapted to seeding applications. This was to be revolutionary for the timber industry, because, at the time, the seeds cost $20 a pound, and waste or damage through mishandling was a nagging problem.

If the PaceSpreader was important to the timber industry and to agricultural concerns, it was also a benefit to helicopter operators. As Del Smith said at the time he began marketing Evergreen's unique system, "Reliable operators are now forced to turn down many potentially profitable contracts because of the lack of a spreader equal to the task."

By the time that Evergreen was granted its patent on the system in December 1965, there were a dozen of them in service with companies in Canada and the United States, as well as in South America. For Evergreen itself, 75 percent of its revenue flying hours in the mid-sixties were devoted to application work, and the PaceSpreader dramatically increased the productivity of the Evergreen helicopters.

Another use of helicopters pioneered by Evergreen was brush eradication around electrical power lines, which had been the cause of up to 90 percent of the power outages in the Pacific Northwest. To do this by hand had cost between $800 and $900 an acre. Evergreen could do the job from the air with $40 worth of chemicals and $30 worth of flying. All the lines in the Bonneville system, as well as those of Pacific Power & Light, Portland General Electric, and the Rural Electrification Administration, were cleared of brush from the air, with Evergreen as the leading player.

During the sixties, the Evergreen helicopters were also used for salvage work off the Oregon coast with ships that had run aground or were in danger of sinking. The insurance companies would pay 50 percent of the invoice of what was salvaged because it was cheaper than paying the claim.

"We were always the first to respond," Del Smith remembers. "I remember one ship loaded with timber products — such as cedar shakes — with several yachts bound for Hawaii sitting on top. We off-lifted all the yachts, and then we off-lifted all the shakes. We got down to the larger timber and we off-loaded that too. We put in our claim, but the insurance company said it was less timber than we had said. They didn't know that we had it scaled beforehand, and they thought they could get away with this. I said 'Why don't we scale it. If we're right, you'll pay for it, and if you're right, we'll pay for the scaler.' I knew what the scale was going to be. We collected all our money from the insurance company — and they paid for the scaling."

MEDICAL APPLICATIONS

The capabilities of helicopters revolutionized many aspects of everyday life in the fifties and sixties. They revolutionized agriculture and other industries, because they could do what was impossible for land vehicles or airplanes. It would be the same with emergency medicine. Here, the helicopters became the "angels of mercy" that Del Smith knew they could be.

Emergency medical evacuation — later known as "medevac" — had originated with the United States armed forces during the Korean War (1950-1953), and the idea came stateside soon afterward. The military medevac operations in Korea had demonstrated an enormous life-saving capability. These operations showed that if a trauma patient arrived at a medical facility within the first hour after an injury — referred to as the "golden hour" — the chances for survival exceeded 90 percent. Although the "angels of mercy" were often the only means available to do this, the civilian market was surprisingly reluctant to implement this service at first.

"We had matched the helicopter with forestry," Smith recalls, "but medevac took a lot of pioneering, because we had to build a rapport with the police and the local Federal Aviation Administration authority, as well as with the fire department and hospital management."

Evergreen Helicopters, Inc. was one of the original companies to develop medical applications for helicopters in the civilian market. In fact, Evergreen was conducting medevac operations in the civilian market for several years before the United States military developed its comprehensive, successful and well-known system for the Vietnam War.

Medevac operations would begin for Evergreen in 1962, but in April 1961 Evergreen had already gained some notoriety transporting 29 pints of blood from McMinnville to Portland for an urgent open-heart operation.

Del Smith remembers that medevac flying presented some unique challenges. "In forestry work, you could always land on the top of a hill where the tail rotor wasn't a risk to anybody. At hospitals, we found ourselves landing where there were people closing in on the tail rotor, and there was a higher risk of someone being injured. We also had to land in pretty tight areas. The Evergreen pilots were called out at all hours of the night to go into locations that were strange to them. It was some serious flying."

As Evergreen Helicopters President David Rath points out, "Evergreen pioneered the medevac industry and continues to have more than 35 in Alaska working for various hospitals."

HELICOPTER RESCUES

Often, when Del Smith speaks of helicopters as "angels of mercy," he is referring to one of their most dramatic uses — rescue work.

Whether it is a situation of difficult terrain, stranded flood victims or people lost at sea, helicopters are usually able to make impossible rescues possible. But, as with many other helicopter applications, helicopter rescues were revolutionary in the fifties and sixties.

Two early rescue efforts involving Evergreen helicopters illustrate both the capabilities of the hardware and the determination of the pilots. In December 1962, Evergreen pilot Jim Klotz was working a job for Puget Sound Dredging Company near Coos Bay, Oregon, when he was advised of an emergency situation. The lumber ship *Alaska Cedar* had run aground offshore from the entrance to Coos Bay Harbor in high seas.

A veteran pilot and a member of the Washington National Guard, Klotz responded to the emergency immediately. He reached the ship, but found that there was no place to land, so he and his assistant, Elton Eby, landed on the harbor entrance jetty. In consultation with United States Coast Guard officials on the jetty, Klotz determined that he would carry a line out to the stricken ship and rig a sling on a block and tackle that the crew could use to escape the ship. This would mean that Klotz would have to fly low and slow across the treacherous wave tops.

"Crashing waves were breaking so high that at one time, they completely covered the chopper's bubble [flight deck]." Klotz recalled. "After the crew fastened the line, I flew it back to the jetty — a distance of 200 feet. It was pretty rough."

By the time he was done, Klotz was soaking wet and the flight deck was full of sea water, but 24 crewmen and their captain were saved. For his efforts, Klotz received a commendation from the Coast Guard, and was named Helicopter Pilot of the Year by the Helicopter Association of America.

Through the years, Evergreen pilots have been responsible for numerous harrowing helicopter rescues. In fact, these heroic pilots have come from all levels of Evergreen's chain of command, all the way up to the chairman himself.

It was on December 27, 1965, that Evergreen chairman Del Smith made a mercy flight into gathering darkness to rescue a young woman from the raging floodwaters of the Yamhill River. Mary Lou Boyer, 18, and her friend, 19-year-old David Hughes, had been thrown from their rubber raft, but had managed to reach a small island. As the waters rose, Hughes was able to swim ashore, but Boyer remained stranded. When Hughes was able to report her predicament, the Yamhill County Sheriff Bud Mekkers put out a call for help.

"The sheriff reported that there was a good chance that her life would be lost," Smith remembers. "We volunteered to help. Two or three of the pilots didn't want to fly in the dark and the driving rain over that river, but I felt that I could and do it safely."

Using only a small landing light to illuminate the search area and help him dodge the utility lines that criss-crossed the river, he began to look for the stranded teen. "I spotted her where I didn't want to see her," Smith said. "She was tucked into a bank that was overgrown with brush, but I was able to get a skid in there and I got her out."

For his daring, Del Smith received the Frederick L. Feinberg Award in Washington, DC and Evergreen Helicopters, Inc. was cited by the Federal Aviation Administration for their outstanding safety record.

THE SIX M'S IN THE EARLY YEARS

Del Smith developed his "Six M Principle" — management, money, men and women, machines, materiel, and market — early in the formulation of his philosophy for running the company. Evergreen had good management and it developed good financial stability. In terms of "machines," helicopter manufacturers such as Bell and Hiller were always eager to have Evergreen launch a new make or model.

As for the market part of the formula during the early years, Smith has said that he felt from the beginning that his team had "a natural ability to go hustle work."

"We were organized and persistent." He continued, "We knew we'd be properly prepared if we knew how to write proposals, if we knew how to scrub up and visit the utility company, the timber company, or the oil company. We wanted quality, but we also wanted quantity. We were advocates for the potential uses of the helicopter, whether it was the mining industry, or the oil industry, or even with the canneries that owned a lot of the agricultural lands."

Evergreen also made frequent sales calls on government agencies. They worked closely with the Bonneville Power Administration, the federal agency that managed the big hydroelectric dams on the Columbia River. Bonneville needed helicopters to patrol their lines. Evergreen also worked with the United States Department of the Interior's Bureau of Indian Affairs and Bureau of Land Management. They worked for the state forestry and highway departments of Oregon and Washington and other states in the West.

"We didn't get caught up in carrying movie stars," Del Smith laughed. "We wanted to build powerlines."

Del Smith genuinely enjoyed exploring the industrial potential of aviation and his enthusiasm spilled over into selling people on this idea. This enthusiasm helped Evergreen get the biggest and the best jobs. "We would get the big government projects," he said, "and we would subcontract to our competition."

Men, women and materiel were also important from the beginning. "We believed in proper training of the maintenance men," Smith said. "We took pride in making sure they all went through the airframe school and the engine school. They were familiar with the equipment that we were working on. There was a lot of spirit. In the early years, the maintenance guys were excited and enthusiastic about proving the value of the helicopter. They were willing to travel a lot, which was essential."

Of course, the pride in the people who make up Evergreen is a two-way street. "Mr. Smith has always remembered where I started, where I've been and will brag about it to everyone that we come in contact with," said Tammy Lewers, Manager of Inventory and Tech Data at Evergreen Trade Fixed Wing. "That always makes me feel truly appreciated. I will forever be grateful to Mr. Smith for his generosity and unmatched kindness throughout the years. His gracious demeanor, personal recognition and much-appreciated compliments will never be taken for granted or forgotten. I have enormous respect for him."

THE SIX M'S:

MANAGEMENT, MONEY, MEN AND WOMEN, MACHINES, MATERIEL, AND MARKET

Evergreen invested a great deal of money in training the pilots and maintenance crews in the sixties. Mountain flying was more difficult in the early years when the helicopters had less power than the models introduced in later decades. "The pilots were, by and large, pretty rugged guys," Del Smith remembers. "In those days, it was not a vocation for the fainthearted. It took a lot more skill to fly the equipment than it does today. As the industry matured, the helicopters became more reliable."

Chapter 3:
EXPANDING THE SCOPE

(1968-1973)

B Y 1968, THE INDUSTRIAL HELICOPTER MARKET HAD BEGUN TO change, and it became, as Del Smith described it, "a new level of experience. It was all very exciting." Evergreen made the transition from the small utility ships — such as the Hiller UH-12E — to medium-size, turbine-engined helicopters, specifically the Bell 205, the commercial version of the ubiquitous military UH-1 "Huey," which was being used at that time in large numbers in the war in Southeast Asia. In Del Smith's words, "Our dream was to own a helicopter with a turbine engine that had a lot of thrust and a lot of horsepower."

In 1968, Evergreen Helicopters, Inc. acquired the first commercial Bell Model 205 turbine helicopter. Between then and 1972, Evergreen would purchase 11 turbine-powered Bell helicopters, as well as Fairchild Hiller FH-1100's. The company would also begin to acquire true heavy-lift helicopters. These would include the Sikorsky S-61, the first of which joined the fleet in July 1972 at a cost of $700,000. The S-61 was the commercial version of the military H-3 that was known by Americans serving in Southeast Asia as the "Jolly Green Giant." In its first five months of operation, the Evergreen S-61 had logged four million board feet of timber.

In March 1973, Evergreen would also begin operating the amazing Sikorsky S-64 Skycrane, the commercial version of the military H-54 Tarhe. The larger S-64 was much more expensive — at $2.8 million in 1973 dollars — but it had a lifting capacity of 20,000 pounds, compared to 8,500 for the S-61. The Skycrane had a range of over 200 miles and was powered by two Pratt & Whitney Model JFTD 12A-4A turbine engines. By the end of the year, Evergreen would announce the acquisition of two more. By the end of the decade, Evergreen would be operating a fleet of three Sikorsky S-64 Skycranes.

The equipment changes coincided with a different way of doing business in the forests of the Pacific Northwest that were Evergreen's home turf. The growing environmental movement of the mid-sixties had raised concerns about protecting the forests, and this led to the timber industry improving its logging methods. For Evergreen, it meant the start of experimental log harvesting with helicopters. These were tasks that were tailor-made for the S-61 and the S-64 Skycrane. With the Skycrane, Igor Sikorsky was 40 years ahead of his time.

Historically, commercial helicopter logging began back in December 1970, when Bob Brown — later chief pilot of Evergreen's heavy-lift division — first lifted a log in the Plumas National Forest near Oroville, California. In its early years, no company would exploit its potential more than Evergreen.

The US Forest Service had always made timber sales available, but by the early seventies they began to restrict the bidding to those who had the right equipment. This was ideal for Evergreen, because the big Sikorskys could get to logs that were in areas that were inaccessible, or where it would be too costly to build a road.

The common denominator of cost is the cost per hour of operating the helicopter. The operator must cover hourly expenses to earn a profit, and convert that figure to acre prices and pound prices, and these numbers to linear board feet prices. It was a new learning process for anybody who threw their hat in the ring of helicopter logging.

As Del Smith put it, "You had to come in with the right machine to match the size of the timber. You had to cut the wood for merchantable value. You couldn't come in with a small helicopter. Even in Canada today, they're splitting logs with dynamite so a smaller helicopter can lift them. This is a terrible waste."

In April 1973, shortly after taking delivery of the first Skycrane, Evergreen had it at work on a remote, 250-acre site near Frissell Creek in the McKenzie Ranger District of the Willamette National Forest in Oregon. Working continuously, except for 40-minute refuelling breaks, the Skycrane was able to lift an average of 200,000 board feet of lumber every day.

During the fall of 1973, Evergreen assigned an S-61 to logging operations near Ketchikan, Alaska. Alaska was just the third state (after Oregon and California) where helicopter logging had been attempted, and Evergreen was in on the ground floor. Two years later, Evergreen flew into the Allegheny National Forest to become the first company to conduct helicopter logging operations east of the Mississippi River.

By the early seventies, Evergreen was bidding on timber sales itself. "We were the best when it came to harvesting timber, and we became very good at buying timber," Del Smith said. "We could sell to the timber company, but if we *owned* that wood, we were in a much better business position. If we bought it where there was an abundance of sawmills, we could always get a decent price for the wood, but if we bought at a timber sale where there might be only one sawmill within 75 miles, we could never get a good price. Our only choice was to truck the wood 200 miles to another mill, which created an economic problem." In 1976, with this in mind, Evergreen bought its own sawmill in Gardnerville, Nevada, and ran it for three years.

Evergreen bought a tremendous amount of timber, employed a lot of cutters, had a fleet of over 75 logging trucks, and ultimately produced an average of 30 million board feet per Skycrane per year. Each of the Skycranes could fly eight hours a day and get 250,000 board feet of lumber, as much as a logger with a truck could do in an entire summer. The goal in the mid-seventies was to make at least $5,000 per hour to keep the Skycrane operations profitable, but Smith remembers one job where Evergreen was grossing about $50,000 an hour with the big helicopter.

Meanwhile, the Evergreen S-61's were also being used extensively for PaceSpreader operations in the Pacific Northwest. For example, in

AN EVERGREEN S-64 SKYCRANE LIFTING A STEEL TRANSMISSION TOWER.
(PHOTO BY RON MAY)

the winter of 1973-1974, an Evergreen S-61 and five Evergreen Bell 205's were used on a vast, 200,000-acre Weyerhaeuser tract in the largest aerial fertilization project in history. Operating from altitudes ranging from 2,000 to 6,000 feet, the Evergreen S-61 was distributing between 35 and 40 tons of nitrogen urea fertilizer every hour.

Weyerhaeuser researchers had determined that if urea was applied to growing trees in a reforested area, the trees would be mature and ready for harvest in about half the time that would be required without it. Application of urea would improve the cycle of production. As Del Smith remembers, Weyerhaeuser was a smart timber manager.

By the second or third time that urea was applied, there was less of a road network, and more of a need for helicopters. Aerial application was the only solution. Because Evergreen had pioneered this process, they were the logical choice. With the PaceSpreader, the Evergreen crews could accurately calibrate and identify the air speed and the spread exactly for the amount that Weyerhaeuser wanted per acre.

"This is where we really learned to work with granular materials," Del Smith said, "And that led to a new dimension in world forestry. We had been spraying herbicides and fighting fires and planting aerial seeds. We came in with our big Sikorskys and it was roughly equivalent to the volume of 50 trains with 100 cars each. The only thing we had to worry about there was the snowcap. They didn't want the fertilizer to dissolve and run off the top of the snow into the creeks and the rivers. So we hit it in the fall, right after fire season."

TO ALASKA WITH TURBINE POWER

The pivotal event in the economic history of Alaska occurred in 1968. It was to result in a greater impact on both the state and the nation than the Klondike Gold Rush more than half a century earlier, and it would permanently reshape the relationship between the rest of the United States and the place that had been the forty-ninth state for less than a decade. It was an event that would provide immense opportunities for Del Smith's Evergreen Helicopters, Inc.

On March 13, 1968, the Atlantic Richfield Company (ARCO) and Humble Oil & Refining Company (later Exxon) announced that oil had been discovered on Alaska's remote North Slope, overlooking Prudhoe Bay, far north of the Arctic Circle.

Less than four months later, on July 4, Evergreen Helicopters took delivery of its first commercial turbine-powered Bell Model 205. Del Smith flew it to Fairbanks, and turned it over to Ward Eason, Evergreen's operations man for Alaska, and he, in turn, took it to the Arctic.

In looking at the business potential surrounding the oil drilling operations, and foreseeing the construction of the trans-Alaska pipeline, Del Smith observed tersely, "We knew that this was going to be huge. There was a fever. It was going to be the biggest oil sale in the history of America, maybe even in the history of the world."

Del Smith could see that the Alaska terrain was better suited to helicopters than any other form of transportation. Alaska had virtually no roads outside the Anchorage-Fairbanks corridor, so fixed-wing aircraft had always been the key form of transportation. Helicopters provided even more versatility than fixed-wing aircraft because they could land or take off from virtually any patch of ground.

This would be a useful convenience for those crews who were doing the drilling, but helicopter versatility proved to be essential during the exploration phase as well. During the spring ice breakup in Prudhoe Bay, the North Slope oil drilling area was accessible *only* by helicopters.

In most of the world's "oil patches," crews doing exploration and drilling can get to their work in four-wheel drive vehicles. In Alaska, however, the tundra was hard to traverse because it was largely quicksand, and because environmental rules restricted vehicular access to the tundra. The tundra is so fragile that if a heavy truck with a drilling rig is driven across it, a canal is created and the tundra will never heal. Thus, everything had to be airlifted. Helicopters were not just convenient, they were essential.

"We were smart enough to see that," Del Smith laughed, "And we got in ahead of the rest of the pack with the first Bell 205."

In Alaska, Evergreen Helicopters, Inc. bought Johnson Helicopters and operated under the name Evergreen-Johnson for several years until the name became Evergreen Helicopters of Alaska, a name which remains today. Meanwhile, both Eason and Smith bought homes in Alaska, and started construction of a hangar and other facilities for a base in Anchorage. Evergreen also set up hangar facilities in remote Deadhorse and Yakutat, with living quarters for personnel at Yakutat.

Evergreen's center of gravity shifted northward with the oil rush, but a strong Evergreen team — including Phoebe Hocken and senior test pilot Fred Snell — remained in McMinnville, and McMinnville remained as the Evergreen headquarters. "Our competition wanted to give the impression that we left Oregon," Smith would say later, "But we didn't."

Between 1970 and 1973, the company invested a million dollars in the construction of a permanent headquarters facility on Three Mile Lane in McMinnville, which is still in use and which has been greatly expanded over the ensuing years.

The first work that Evergreen would do in the Alaska "oil patch" was seismic work related to surveying the pockets of subterranean oil. Seismic data was the best tool for determining where the oil was located. The way it works is that the exploration engineers put little, sound-detecting geophones into the ground and run wires back to a communications center called a "doghouse." Then a drilling machine drills holes next to the geophones and a dynamite charge is packed into the holes. When the dynamite is detonated, a seismograph charts the shock waves from the blast and geologists can read the resulting chart and determine where large pockets of liquid exist in the ground. These could be oil or could be saltwater. In sixties technology — and even today — it's not absolute, but it was the best they had, and it worked. Of course, the work had to be done at many sites and the gear had to be airlifted.

One of the key Evergreen people in Alaska was future Evergreen International Aviation President Tim Wahlberg. He came to work with Evergreen in 1969 after having served three years in Vietnam with the US Army as a helicopter mechanic, working on Bell UH-1 Hueys. He had qualified for an A&P (Airframe & Powerplant) license and just stopped by the Evergreen headquarters in McMinnville one day.

"I met this gentleman named Del Smith. I had no idea who he was. We got into a conversation about what he was doing," Wahlberg recalls. "At that point, Evergreen had just expanded to the Bell 205 and Fairchild Hiller FH-1100 turbine-powered helicopters. I met him on a Friday, and the following Monday, I was on my way to Alaska."

Initially, the Evergreen Alaska fleet consisted of the new Bell 205's and Fairchild Hiller FH-1100's, but eventually, the company assigned one of its fleet of Sikorsky S-64 Skycranes to Alaska. This helicopter, with its 20,000-pound lift capacity, would be instrumental in the completion of the last third of the Alaska pipeline.

Evergreen quickly earned a reputation for being highly reliable. The fleet was new, and the team was experienced because most of the Evergreen technicians and pilots were Vietnam veterans with a great deal of flight time and maintenance training — especially in Hueys, the military version of the Bell 205.

In Alaska, Evergreen helicopters spent almost as much time carrying environmental ecology scientists as they did engineers and surveyors. The scientists wanted to gather data on such diverse subjects as where the caribou mate or how the caribou were going to get across the pipeline. Evergreen also did fire control work in Alaska, and, in 1971, flew seismographic equipment into the Aleutian Island chain for the US Atomic Energy Commission.

In 1972, the Aidjex Ice Floe Tracking Project was done by Evergreen. Evergreen also went up to Canada's Prince Patrick Island, 220 miles north of the Magnetic North Pole, doing seismic work in conjunction with British Petroleum and Okanagan Helicopters. In 1976, using the most sophisticated navigation system ever installed in a helicopter, Evergreen used its S-61 fleet in a major oil exploration effort for Shell, Arco, and Mobil in the Yakutat and Cape Yakataga areas of the Gulf of Alaska. Because of poor weather conditions, the helicopters had to fly under instrument flight rules (IFR) conditions most of the time. For Evergreen, the "instrument" that made the work possible was the VLF/Omega long range navigation system.

The pipeline construction was scheduled to begin in 1970 by the Alyeska Pipeline Service Company, a consortium consisting of Humble Pipe Line, Atlantic Pipe Line, British Petroleum Pipe Line — and later Amerada Hess Corporation, Home Pipe Line, Mobil Pipe Line, Phillips Petroleum and Union Oil. However, suits filed by environmental groups and others to block pipeline construction held up the project until 1975, but when work was resumed, things moved quickly.

The first pipe was laid at Tonsina River in March 1975, and by October 26, the pipeline project was 50 percent complete. On June 20, 1977, the first oil began to flow. It had been a busy winter for many people, including the Evergreen Alaska crews.

"We liked the oil patches." Del Smith said succinctly, "And the oil companies took us seriously. We were very safe. We went into Alaska with 15 turbine helicopters, we came out with 15 and didn't put a scratch on one of them."

AROUND THE WORLD WITH TURBINE POWER

Soon, Evergreen Helicopters, Inc. was branching out into other oil patches. In 1972, Evergreen established an office in Houston and began ferrying crews to the offshore oil platforms in the Gulf of Mexico. This activity continues to the present day. Evergreen then went to what was called the "South Slope" in Australia, where the company teamed with Broken Hill Proprietary in oil exploration activities.

That same year, Evergreen donated helicopters and pilots to fly volunteer physicians into the Himalayas, where they delivered health care services to people in isolated areas far distant from roads. In the process, an Evergreen Alouette III helicopter set a high-altitude landing record when it delivered pharmaceuticals to a remote village in Nepal.

Also in 1972, major oil projects were begun with such companies as Sun Oil, Total and ARCO in Peru and Bolivia. The business in South America came at a good time for Evergreen, because South America's summer coincides with the Arctic winter, where flying conditions become so hostile. There is no daylight, temperatures would fall to 70 degrees below zero, and the wind blew at 40 mph for days at a time. In the summer, with 24 hours of daylight, Evergreen could get 300 hours a month out of its aircraft in the Arctic, but in the winter — even with IFR (Instrument Flight Rules) capability — they were often grounded for days at a time.

When the work in Peru and Bolivia came on line, Evergreen could pull crews and equipment out of Alaska to work in South America. Evergreen established major satellite bases in Lima, Peru, and La Paz, Bolivia. From here, Evergreen conducted seismic work, as well as jungle surveys, through 1974. The fleet assigned to South America would consist of Bell 205's, 206's, Aérospatiale Lamas and Sikorsky S-61s.

The Evergreen helicopters went from the windswept Arctic to what Tim Wahlberg colorfully described as "the mushy, slimy jungles of Peru and Bolivia."

"The conditions were really remote," Wahlberg added. "But then, nearly every place that Evergreen helicopters went, the conditions are really remote. That's our specialty."

This was borne out in 1973, when Evergreen received an emergency call from the US Agency for International Development (USAID). The rice crop in Pakistan was threatened by blight, and quite simply, USAID needed a company with proven, no-nonsense agricultural spraying expertise to save it.

Tim Wahlberg got the call on a Friday. "Can you guys pack up five spray systems and go to Pakistan on Monday?" USAID asked.

"I told them that we could," Wahlberg recalled. "We had a reputation for application work from helicopters. We were already spraying thousands and thousands of acres of gypsy moths, California fruit flies, and all the nasty little insects that want to eat up all the trees and kill the fruit."

On Monday, the US Air Force flew a team of Evergreen pilots and mechanics to Pakistan to install the Evergreen spray system on military helicopters from Korea. The Evergreen team taught the military pilots how to fly like crop dusters. They sprayed about 500,000 acres in two weeks' time.

"It was a really fast operation," Tim Wahlberg recalled proudly. "It was highly reliable, everything worked, and we were successful. All of a sudden, Evergreen started getting a lot of calls from the United States government to go out and do these types of operations."

There would be much more to come.

Chapter 4:

BECOMING A GLOBAL AVIATION COMPANY

(1974-1980)

IN 1974, AFTER FIVE YEARS IN ALASKA AND MORE THAN A DECADE in the Pacific Northwest, Evergreen began to experience a dramatic cycle of growth and international expansion. "It was really exciting," Tim Wahlberg recalls with a chuckle. "All of a sudden, we're all over the United States. We're located down in South America, we're up in Alaska, in Canada, and in the Pacific Rim countries. We were heads above everybody else, but then the competition wasn't as fierce as it is today."

By 1974, the cornerstones of the Evergreen helicopter fleet were still the Hiller UH-12E, of which Evergreen now owned 25, and the Bell Model 205 turbine helicopters, which numbered 20. In addition, the helicopter fleet also included 10 Bell 206B's, 10 Aérospatiale 315 Lamas, three Bell 212's and three Aérospatiale Alouettes. In the heavy-lift helicopter department, there were now Sikorsky S-61's and S-64 Skycranes, as well as a Sikorsky S-58T. A major helicopter acquisition later in the decade came in 1979, when Evergreen purchased eight Alouette IIIs from Portugal. The following year, Evergreen began adding the new Messerschmitt-Bölkow-Blohm Bo-105CB helicopters to its fleet.

The world's "oil patches" continued to be important for Evergreen. During the early years of the seventies, Evergreen helicopters had gone from Alaska's North Slope to Australia's South

Slope, and into South America to begin oil exploration operations in Peru and Bolivia.

By the mid-seventies, Evergreen was doing oil exploration work on and off shore in Papua New Guinea, Brunei, Thailand, and, briefly, in Vietnam. Evergreen flight crews had gone to Vietnam to manage Sikorsky S-61 operations for Japanese operators working for the Royal Dutch Shell Group.

The operations in Vietnam ended abruptly and dramatically as one of great turning points in the history of the decade unfolded in Southeast Asia. After nearly two decades of militarily supporting the government of South Vietnam in its efforts to remain independent of communist North Vietnam, the United States had chosen not to intervene when North Vietnam launched a massive invasion of its southern neighbor in early 1975.

By the end of April, North Vietnamese troops were closing in on Saigon, the capital of South Vietnam, and the United States government launched a monumental, and well-documented, effort to evacuate Americans and Vietnamese people who had worked for the American government. The final stage of this effort came on April 30, as United States military helicopters landed on the roof of the United States Embassy in Saigon to remove the last of the Americans.

At the same time, in an equally dramatic — if not nearly so well documented — effort, Evergreen helicopter crews also flew into the dangerous skies of the war zone, evacuating hundreds of people, including the Shell Oil Company personnel who had remained on the ground.

The collapse of South Vietnam displaced a number of people, especially Vietnamese who had worked with the American armed forces and American companies. One such man was Toan Van Nguyen, who had worked from 1965 to 1975 as a helicopter mechanic for Air America, Inc. "At the Fall of Saigon I became a marked man on account of my ten years with Air America," Toan recalled. "The only option for me and my family was escape in a fishing boat.

Within a few months, thanks to several friends, I had a job at a Denver Airport."

After six months in Denver, Toan got a call from his old lead man of the Saigon days, telling of a job opening in Oregon for a helicopter mechanic. "On calling the toll-free number, I got Evergreen's perceptive Personnel Manager, Mr. Clark Field. After a few questions and some chatter, he wound up in good Evergreen style saying 'OK, Toan. Come on down and I'll give you the job!'"

In May 1976, the Nguyen family covered the 1,250 miles of interstate highway in 27 driving hours, in time for Toan to report to the McMinnville hangar, and to be welcomed by Ed Bridges, Director of Maintenance. A couple of weeks later, Toan met Del Smith. "He was showing some VIP's around," Toan recalled. "As he introduced them to the workers in our hangar, I got to shake his own hand for the first time. A few days later I was delighted to meet him again, together with his sons, Michael and Mark, after Sunday Mass at St. James Church. Soon after that I was amused to see all three of them out on bikes in the street. I had thought they would surely be too rich for that!"

"Let me give one example of his family spirit," Toan continued. "Mr. Smith once stepped into the shop and after watching me at my work for a while, he simply said: 'Toan, if you know of any friends in need of a job, bring them here and I'll put them to work.' I have taken him up on this several times, beginning with my eldest son after his graduation from Oregon State University in Chemical & Computer Sciences Engineering, and later with my third son after he got his degree in Engineering. Mr. Smith gave both of them jobs."

Throughout the 1970s, Evergreen helicopters were involved in numerous projects around the world. For example, Evergreen crews had gone to Pakistan at the behest of USAID to save a rice crop in 1973. The following year, John Kiesler, along with two maintenance men and three Evergreen pilots, took two turbine-powered Aérospatiale Lama helicopters and a Bell 206B3 to drought-stricken Africa to support a World Health Organization relief effort. They assisted the African people by bringing medical technicians and supplies to their aid. In 1978, Evergreen began a multi-year project with China Power & Light to build a power line from Hong Kong to Guangzhou in China.

JOHNSON FLYING SERVICE, A KEY ACQUISITION

It was in 1974 that Del Smith first began to look seriously at expanding Evergreen into an airline. However, in the years before airline deregulation, there were only a finite number of airline operating authorities, so the only way to "start" an airline was to buy an existing one that already had an operating authority.

Del Smith had been looking for a likely prospect, and he got a lead on one literally by overhearing part of a conversation while passing through an airport in April 1974. It was the Johnson Flying Service, headquartered in Missoula, Montana, with an additional base in McCall, Idaho. The company had been started in 1924 by Robert R. Johnson, who was one of the West's earliest pioneer aviators.

Over half a century, Johnson Flying Service had earned a stellar reputation for its work in the mountains of Montana and the West, fighting forest fires and conducting mountain rescue work under harrowing conditions. At its peak, during World War II, Johnson Flying Service had over 100 aircraft, ranging from durable old Ford Trimotors to state-of-the-art DC-3's, and was flying troops and cargo throughout the United States, including flights to Alaska and Hawaii.

Before World War II, Johnson Flying Service, in collaboration with the US Forest Service, had come up with an idea — later borrowed by the wartime airborne infantry and used effectively during the war. They pioneered the technique of dropping firefighters by parachute near fires in remote terrain. These firefighters — known as "smokejumpers" — revolutionized the way forest fires were battled.

THE FORD TRIMOTOR, USED BY SMOKEJUMPERS, WAS PART OF THE JOHNSON
FLYING SERVICE FLEET THAT WAS ACQUIRED BY EVERGREEN.

During the forties, when the United States Congress first established a certification procedure for supplemental air carriers — or
"charter" carriers — Johnson was one of the first. This gave Johnson Flying Service the operating rights to fly passengers and cargo
on non-scheduled, or charter, flights throughout the United States
and Canada. When the regulations were codified in the early fifties,
Johnson was given the first supplemental certificate, number WE-
103. Originally there had been 165 supplemental air carriers, which
were referred to as "large irregulars" in the early years. By the early
sixties, there were just 35. Because of a series of crashes during the
decade of the sixties, federal regulations for the supplemental carriers were tightened, and this further reduced the number of airlines
in the field to 10, including the Johnson Flying Service. Because the
certificates were no longer being issued, and they were difficult to
transfer through a sale, they had become a valuable commodity.

The scheduled carriers tended to look down — with some
degree of jealousy perhaps — on the non-scheduled carriers,

because the non-scheduled carriers could move their rates very quickly, fly into new areas, and fly large groups with guarantees of filled airplanes. They didn't have the mandatory route structures that the scheduled carriers had to maintain. However, the supplementals had very strict, restrictive rules on flying passengers. For example, prior to deregulation in the late seventies, supplementals could not sell individual tickets.

By 1974, Johnson Flying Service had acquired a pair of 94-passenger Lockheed L-188 Electra four-engine, turboprop airliners and had applied to the United States Civil Aeronautics Board (CAB) for an authority to expand its operations into Mexico and the Caribbean. Meanwhile, however, the 81-year-old Bob Johnson was ready to think about retirement.

After he overheard the rumor that Johnson Flying Service was on the block, Del Smith called a pilot whom he knew at Johnson, and this man confirmed that the airline, along with its supplemental airline authority, was, in fact, for sale. There was an interested party, but he was having trouble getting together the financing, so Smith arranged a meeting with Bob Johnson himself. The two aviation pioneers met and cut a deal.

The acquisition would not finally be consummated, however, until the Civil Aeronautics Board formally approved a transfer of the Johnson Flying Service authority and license to Evergreen. As this process unfolded, competition for Johnson began to emerge. Among the groups who also sought ownership of the Montana airline were United States Steel, which had been making overtures to Bob Johnson for some time, and Dick Lassiter's Executive Jet Aviation, with which retired US Air Force General Curtis LeMay and actor (and US Air Force Reserve brigadier general) Jimmy Stewart were board members.

Eventually, both of these bids were turned down because of involvement with railroads on the part of the bidders. At that time, because of fear of unfair competition, entities that controlled railroads were not permitted to control airlines, and vice versa. In the

case of United States Steel, they owned a proprietary railroad to serve
their own facilities, but Executive Jet had backing from the Penn
Central Railroad, a corporation that had been formed in 1968 by
the merger of the Pennsylvania Railroad and the New York Central,
once two of America's most powerful railroads. Ironically, the Penn
Central was financially troubled from birth, and it failed in 1973.

Evergreen's major competitor came to be Bud Rud, an air
service operator who had been hired by Bob Johnson to run his
airline during the sales process. Since he was already in place, he
assumed that he would ultimately control the Johnson Flying Service through osmosis.

As the approval process moved at glacial speed, Evergreen
opened a government liaison office in Washington, DC to lobby
for its bid. Eventually, as the Civil Aeronautics Board rejected the
other bidders because of conflicts of interest, the scales began lean-
ing toward Evergreen. Yet, it took a letter to President Gerald Ford,
dated September 24, 1975 and signed by Senators Robert Packwood
and Mark Hatfield of Oregon, and Mike Mansfield of Montana, to
nudge the deal to completion. The Civil Aeronautics Board approval
was finally forthcoming on October 11. The Civil Aeronautics Board
decision authorizing the acquisition of Johnson Flying Service by
Evergreen Helicopters, Inc. was a 5-0 vote. President Ford officially
signed the transfer into effect on November 25.

With the change of ownership, supplemental carrier certificate
number WE-103, converted to EIAA-103. By acquiring the Johnson
Flying Service certificate, Evergreen now had a great deal of power.
As Tim Wahlberg recounts, "A tremendous amount of authority
came with it. It was quite unbelievable for us at the time."

THE BIRTH OF AN AIRLINE

Evergreen International Airlines, Inc. was officially incorporated
in Oregon on April 16, 1975 as a subsidiary of Evergreen Helicopters, Inc. On November 25, with a stroke of president Gerald Ford's

pen, the supplemental airline operating authority previously held by Johnson Flying Service was officially transferred to Evergreen International Airlines. The headquarters for Evergreen International Airlines were, in turn, transferred to the campus of the Evergreen Air Center (Evergreen Maintenance Center since 2007, see page 109) in Arizona. They would be moved to Newberg, Oregon, a suburb of Portland, in 1979, and relocated to the Evergreen corporate headquarters campus in McMinnville in 1981.

Bill Clark, who had been the director of operations for the Johnson Flying Service, became an essential part of the team when Evergreen International Airlines began its passenger and cargo services. He was very knowledgeable in international operations.

When Evergreen started doing more and more international business, Clark would be instrumental in Evergreen's getting up and running. He had been under contract to Saudia (Saudi Arabian Airlines) while employed by TWA for a number of years, so when Evergreen started DC-8 operations with Saudia, Bill was already familiar with these parts of the world, he was invaluable in setting up the operation.

"Bill was a man of integrity and he was instrumental in all of the international operations that started," Tom Pitzer recalls. "You never knew where Bill was, or where he would be next. He always carried a smile and had a can-do attitude."

Later senior vice president for maintenance, materiel and engineering at Evergreen International Airlines, Tom Pitzer was hired at Evergreen Helicopters in 1974. Two years later he was assigned to Evergreen Maintenance Center to coordinate the maintenance of the EIA's fleet. He remained in Marana until 1983, when he returned briefly to the helicopter company in McMinnville before joining Evergreen International Airlines in 1984 as the West Area Maintenance Manger.

Another man who came to Evergreen International Airlines from the Johnson Flying Service was Penn Stohr, who would become one of Evergreen's longest serving pilots. Stohr grew up with the Johnson

Flying Service. His father, who had been Bob Johnson's first pilot, was killed in a Ford Trimotor accident when Penn was in high school, but Penn started working for the Johnson Flying Service shortly after that, in 1960. Eventually, he rose to the post of senior vice president with Evergreen International Airlines, but he left that job to return to the cockpit, and he was still flying for the company at the turn of the century.

In 1975, Evergreen had reached a turning point. It was no longer merely a helicopter company. For 15 years, it had simply been Evergreen Helicopters, Inc. Now Evergreen was moving into fixed-wing aircraft and was on its way to becoming a family of companies.

"It was a big step for Del Smith. It was very courageous." Penn Stohr said. "Johnson Flying Service was a wonderful purchase on his part. His own tenacity beat out the other companies, and now Evergreen was offering airline services. There was a lot to learning airline culture, but we did it."

Evergreen's early fixed-wing fleet, largely the legacy of the Johnson Flying Service acquisition, included the three Lockheed Electras, three Douglas DC-3's, seven de Havilland Canada DHC-6's and three Cessna C421's. Evergreen also now owned a World War II-vintage Boeing B-17 Flying Fortress, which had been converted for use in dropping fire retardant on forest fires. Except for the Electras, which were put to work on military charters, these new fixed-wing assets were not really the nucleus around which to build a modern airline in the last quarter of the twentieth century.

Soon after the Johnson acquisition was finalized, Evergreen International Airlines began to acquire jets. The first two jetliners owned by Evergreen Airlines were a pair of Douglas DC-8-52's that were purchased from Air New Zealand. Before the first year of airline operations was over, Evergreen purchased a third DC-8-52 directly from the manufacturer, the Douglas Aircraft Company component of the McDonnell Douglas Corporation, in Long Beach, California. This one had originally been part of an Air New Zealand

IN THE 1970S, EVERGREEN BEGAN OPERATING DC-8 FREIGHTERS.

order, but the airline had traded it back to McDonnell Douglas for a DC-10, and the manufacturer was leasing it to a third party while waiting for a buyer.

Penn Stohr recalls the dramatic circumstances surrounding the acquisition of the third DC-8-52. "I remember that night as the money was being transferred and the deal closed." He said. "Our new airplane was on television being shot up in a hijack attempt in Cypress. The airplane ended up with bullet holes all over it and it had to be ferried back to the United States by Douglas flight crews, because it was under Douglas ownership. We put the airplane into one of our hangers and the Douglas people came in and completely rebuilt it."

Within its first year, Evergreen International Airlines was flying passenger charters into Saudi Arabia from Libya and from East Africa for the annual Haj, the Islamic religious pilgrimage to Mecca. Meanwhile, Evergreen also operated a program that was called Nesher — the Hebrew word for eagle — flying ethnic Hasidic Jewish passengers between New York and Tel Aviv. Evergreen International Airlines also flew passenger charters within the United States, ranging from sports teams to casino junkets under contract to the Golden Nugget in Las Vegas.

The Douglas DC-8 had been one of the earliest jet-powered commercial passenger aircraft. During the sixties, it had established commercial transport world records for speed, altitude, distance and payload. The Series -30 and -50 aircraft were produced in passenger, freighter and convertible freighter versions.

In 1978, Evergreen added the Douglas DC-8-60 "Super 60" series aircraft to its fleet. Of these, the Super 61 could carry up to 259 passengers on high-density, transcontinental routes, and the Super 62, which was designed for long-haul operations, carried up to 189 passengers for distances of up to 6,000 miles.

"They were just gorgeous airplanes." Penn Stohr said of the Evergreen DC-8 fleet. "They were perfect mechanically, they were wonderful. They served us quite well. They were extremely long range airplanes, so they worked well in the type of charter market we put them into."

The DC-8-63, the Super 63, combined the fuselage extension and payload capacity of the Super 61 with the long-range, aerodynamic and power plant improvements of the Super 62, and carried a maximum capacity of 259 passengers and baggage for 4,500 miles, or lesser loads even greater distances. The DC-8 Super 63F/63CF (Freighter/Convertible Freighter) was able to carry up to 118,000 pounds of freight, accommodating 18 standard cargo pallets in the main cabin.

Evergreen International Airlines' first DC-8-63 was added in 1980. Meanwhile, in 1979, Evergreen International Airlines had begun operating its DC-8's with the GNS-500A system. This made the airline the only carrier anywhere to operate worldwide with the VLF/Omega long range navigation system on DC-8 aircraft. The DC-8-63's were subsequently converted to DC-8-73 standard with the retrofitting of General Electric/SNECMA CFM56 turbofan engines. As Penn Stohr has pointed out, Evergreen was one of the first operators of the DC-8-73's.

During 1976, Evergreen International Airlines continued to expand its fleet. Several Convair 580 propliners were purchased, but the main thrust of Evergreen International Airlines' fleet expansion would be in jet transports. In addition to the DC-8's, Evergreen was able to pick up the leases on several McDonnell Douglas DC-9's (the DC-8's smaller, "T-tailed," twin-engine sister ship) that had been operated by Overseas National Airways, another supplemental carrier.

Specifically, Evergreen International Airlines owned DC-9-32 and DC-9-33 aircraft. The Series 30 DC-9 is 119.3 feet long, providing seats for up to 115 passengers and 895 cubic feet of cargo space. A high-lift wing system of leading edge slats gave it excellent short-field performance. The Series 30 aircraft are powered by either Pratt & Whitney JT8D-7 or JT8D-9 engines. Others are equipped with the JT8D-11 or the JT8D-15, with 15,500 pounds of thrust. The DC-9's performed very reliably throughout the years, maintaining a better than 98 percent on-time performance.

During 1976, Evergreen International Airlines joined the National Air Carrier Association, and the following year, the hub for Transatlantic operations was set up at New York's John F. Kennedy International Airport. It was also in 1977 that Evergreen International Airlines established Detroit as its center of charter airline operations. One of the first of these was Alaska Arctic Adventure Tours, which Evergreen International Airlines began running for Wein Alaska Airlines later in 1977.

In 1979, Ward Eason moved over from Evergreen Helicopters and was made President of Evergreen International Airlines. As Tom Pitzer recalls, "he was a perfect pick for this position. With his creative skills and his having worked with Del Smith, he made the airline start-up a success. I still look at him as the 'Father of Evergreen International Airlines.'"

By the end of the seventies, the airline had expanded dramatically as the Civil Aeronautics Board awarded it a section 418 certification concurrent with grandfather rights for domestic scheduled cargo authority. In turn, Evergreen International Airlines opened bases at Seattle-Tacoma International Airport, Portland Interna-

PART OF EVERGREEN'S FLEET OF DC-9S.

tional Airport, Oakland International Airport, and Los Angeles International Airport, and inaugurated a West Coast cargo common carriage system.

The importance to Evergreen International Airlines of the international market, especially the air freight market, led to the decision in 1977 to open the London sales office. This office would be instrumental in establishing Evergreen's role in the lucrative North Atlantic market between the United States and Europe.

Two of the most important slices of new business that Evergreen International Airlines would land during 1978 involved its becoming a contract carrier for Emery Air Freight and for the United States military. The latter involved a US Navy contract to operate all passenger flights — using a Lockheed Electra — between Naval Air Station Point Mugu and Long Beach, and a much broader contract with the US Air Force which would evolve into one of the airline's most important accounts. In 1978, Evergreen International Airlines was selected as an air carrier for the US Air Force Military Airlift Command (MAC) under the LogAir (Logistics Air) program. Headquartered at Scott AFB, Illinois, the Military Airlift Command was the US Air Force's global air transportation service, responsible for carrying personnel and materiel for the Air Force — and all the United States armed services — to destinations around the world. This job was performed on a routine, scheduled basis, as well as on an emergency basis in times of crisis. To accomplish its task, the Military Airlift Command maintained a large fleet of its own aircraft, but it also contracted with civil carriers to handle excess routine traffic. Evergreen International Airlines was now one of these carriers. Evergreen has continued to perform these tasks for the US Air Force on an ongoing basis ever since. The Military Airlift Command was the contracting agency through 1992, when it was incorporated into the newly created Air Mobility Command.

The LogAir system provided overnight service or next-day service between operating bases in the field and maintenance depots located throughout the United States — especially the Air Logistics Centers at Robbins AFB, Georgia; Kelly AFB, Texas; Tinker AFB, Oklahoma; McClellan AFB, California; and Hill AFB, Utah.

It was much less expensive for the US Air Force to contract with a commercial carrier to perform this service than to do it themselves.

"The LogAir program for the military was a really tough program," Tim Wahlberg remembers, "because we were flying to probably 10 different remote military bases, operating 10 hours a day, seven days a week."

The operations for Emery Air Freight began in 1976 when Emery launched its Emery Express service. Emery Express was one of the first overnight courier operations to compete with Federal Express, who had defined the market for next-day delivery. The Emery Express activity began with two DC-9's, both leased from Evergreen, one based in Newberg, New York, and the other in San Francisco and each flying from one base to the other by way of Denver, Colorado and Smyrna, Tennessee.

In 1979 Evergreen International Airlines began scheduled passenger services from Philadelphia to Freeport in the Bahamas. The following year, Jamaica became another scheduled destination for the airline. In 1980, the Thomson Vacations organization named Evergreen International Airlines as its prime air carrier to the Caribbean from Chicago, and contracted with Evergreen for DC-8 passenger service from other gateways, such as Minneapolis, Cleveland, St. Louis and Philadelphia.

Evergreen also formed an entity known as Evergreen Tours, which arranged vacation tours and charter aircraft from Evergreen International Airlines to fly its customers to their destinations.

In 1980, because of the capability of the DC-8-52's, Evergreen International Airlines became the first approved carrier to the Hawaiian outer island of Maui, which was destined to become one of the most important tourist destinations in the state. Whereas tourism had been down in Hawaii since the energy crisis of 1973-1974, tourist traffic was actually up by four percent in Maui when Evergreen started its charter flights on March 8.

All 186 seats on Evergreen's DC-8-52 flights to Maui, which originated in Seattle on Saturday mornings with a stop in Portland, were usually full by the time they took off from the latter city. Despite objections from Aloha Airlines and Hawaiian Airlines — the state's two inter-island carriers — Evergreen managed to add a Friday morning to its schedule on May 9. The objections carried no weight because the two inter-island airlines were *scheduled* carriers, and Evergreen was a *charter* operator.

Service to Hawaii was regulated at the time, so Evergreen operated charters. The only distinction between Evergreen's charters and United Air Lines scheduled service was that Evergreen couldn't sell tickets in the last seven days — which is not generally done in the tour-travel business anyway — *and* Evergreen could fly directly to and from Maui.

Evergreen operated service from Seattle and Portland. With DC-8-52's, the airline could operate non-stop back and forth to Maui. United Air Lines could not. They had only the DC-8-61's, so they had to go through Honolulu on their return to the mainland. At the time, United Air Lines was operating long-range DC-8-60 series aircraft to Hawaii, but they could land only at Honolulu. The reason was that there was a weight limit on the runway at Kahului on Maui, and the DC-8-60 series aircraft would be overweight if they took off with enough fuel to reach the mainland.

On May 18, 1980, under a charter to Evergreen Tours, Evergreen International Airlines began a Seattle-Las Vegas service, and added Portland-Las Vegas service on August 14. In the case of both the Maui and Las Vegas charters, Evergreen International Airlines offered customers the choice of an airfare-only ticket or a package that included accommodations and ground transportation.

In 1979, under the airline regulation, the Civil Aeronautics Board extended airline authority to Evergreen International Airlines to engage in charter air transportation of mail. This paved the way for the airmail contracts with the United States Postal Service that were to be such an important part of the Evergreen story during the eighties.

AN EXPANDING CORPORATION

For the first three years of its existence, Evergreen International Airlines was a subsidiary of the original Evergreen company, Evergreen Helicopters, Inc. On August 3, 1978, the new parent company, Evergreen International Aviation, Inc., was formed with a 12-member board. From that point, both Evergreen International Airlines and Evergreen Helicopters, Inc. would be its subsidiaries.

On January 24, 1979, they were joined by a third subsidiary, as Evergreen Air Center (Evergreen Maintenance Center after 2007) was officially incorporated. Evergreen International Aviation and Evergreen Helicopters, Inc. moved into the present headquarters complex on Three Mile Lane in McMinnville in 1980, and, as noted above, the Evergreen International Airlines headquarters moved there the following year.

As discussed in detail in later chapters, three further Evergreen subsidiary companies were added during the eighties. These were Evergreen Aviation Ground Logistics Enterprises, Evergreen Aircraft Sales & Leasing (known as Evergreen Trade since 2008), and Evergreen Agricultural Enterprises.

THE FACILITY IN ARIZONA

At the same time that Evergreen was waiting for the Civil Aeronautics Board to approve the acquisition of Johnson Flying Service, the company was also looking to acquire other assets and facilities to support its worldwide expansion and its move into the airline business. One of the most important of these acquisitions would be the assets of Intermountain Aviation, Inc., which owned the Marana Air Park, a huge aircraft maintenance facility located 27 miles north of Tucson, Arizona on land leased from Pinal County, Arizona.

Marana Air Park also had two runways, 6,850 and 6,500 feet in length. Evergreen Helicopters, Inc. had always had facilities to maintain its helicopter fleet, but as the company moved toward the airline business, there was now a need for a facility to maintain heavy transport aircraft.

"It was a natural fit," Del Smith recalls. "Intermountain approached us and explained that they had a repair station with an unlimited, Class I through IV certification, which gives Federal Aviation Administration authority to work on any type of aircraft. We really bought Marana for our own planned needs, but as we grew, it would change into more of a third-party operation. Intermountain also wanted to sell several aircraft, including its remaining Lockheed Electra, an aircraft which had been previously owned by the Los Angeles Dodgers baseball team. We bought them."

Purchased by Evergreen for $2.5 million on March 1, 1975, Marana Air Park had originated during World War II as one of the largest military pilot training bases in the Southwestern United States. It was selected by the US Army Air Forces (USAAF) for

AN AERIAL VIEW OF EVERGREEN'S MARANA FACILITY.

pilot training because of its excellent climate and location, and was established in April 1942 as Marana Army Air Field. During the three years it was used, it became the largest basic training base in the USAAF, with more than 30 classes and a total of 10,000 cadets receiving instruction.

With the conclusion of the war in September 1945, the USAAF (which became the US Air Force in 1947) declared the base to be surplus for peacetime use, and ordered its deactivation. During the late forties, the movable equipment at Marana Army Air Field was either sold or transferred to other bases. The runways, hangars, and older buildings were allowed to remain and they gradually deteriorated.

When the Korean War started in 1950, the US Air Force once again had an urgent need for pilots and a place to train them. And once again, Marana was chosen as one of the first inactive fields to be brought back into use. Its excellent previous record as a training site made it a logical choice. Restoration began on August 1, 1951, under the direction of the Darr Aeronautical Technical Corporation. On October 2, 1951, the first group of cadets to return to Marana, Class 52-G, arrived at the base. The ensuing months brought many improvements, including pumice stone barracks, a chapel, a theater, a dining hall, a cadet club, and administration buildings.

The process of rebuilding the US Air Force for the Cold War reached a plateau in the late fifties, and many of the bases that had been opened during the Korean War were no longer necessary for ongoing activities. Against this backdrop, the base was closed again in the fall of 1958 and turned over to Pinal County. In 1962, now renamed Marana Air Park, it was leased to Intermountain Aviation, a regional passenger freight carrier that also engaged in aircraft maintenance.

There have always been persistent rumors, occasionally making their way into the media, that Marana Air Park had been a "secret base" for Central Intelligence Agency covert operations. The basis for these rumors is probably the fact that Intermountain Aviation did a great deal of contract flying for the intelligence service — as well as branches of the military services — during the Vietnam War era. Intermountain reportedly specialized in air drops of supplies to intelligence operatives in the field.

It was conjectured in 1974 by Arizona Congressman Morris Udall, and later stated in the report of the Rockefeller Commission on intelligence operations, that Intermountain Aviation had been an actual subsidiary of the Central Intelligence Agency. There were a number of well-known air carriers, such as Air America and Southern Air Transport, that were either Central Intelligence Agency subsidiaries, subsidiaries of subsidiaries, or which did extensive contract work for the agency. The fact that Evergreen acquired the Marana facility from Intermountain would later lead to speculation that Evergreen itself was a subsidiary of the Central Intelligence Agency, which, of course, is untrue.

On the heels of Senate hearings regarding Central Intelligence Agency operations chaired by Idaho Senator Frank Church, Congress passed legislation that compelled the agency to divest itself of its network of subsidiaries and affiliates. This, in turn, led to Intermountain's decision to sell its assets to Evergreen.

In the meantime, Evergreen had also been approached to acquire some of the assets of Air America, which had operated both fixed-wing airplanes and helicopters throughout Southeast Asia. "I went over there and looked at their activity," Tim Wahlberg recalled. "They spoke quite frankly. They could see that their whole program would collapse if Vietnam was taken over by the Communists, and they wanted to dispose of their equipment. We decided that Air America wasn't a good idea, but Intermountain Aviation was perfect. It had the unlimited maintenance capability, a large storage facility and the unrestricted runway."

After the Evergreen acquisition, the Marana Air Park facility would be known as the "Evergreen Air Center," although this entity was not officially incorporated as Evergreen Air Center, Inc. (EAC) until January 1979. In January 2007, the facility was officially renamed as the Evergreen Maintenance Center (EMC).

Tim Wahlberg, with Murry Vinson and Tom Pitzer, were reassigned to the Evergreen Maintenance Center to take over management of operations at the new facility. "What Evergreen tried to do was to employ all the capabilities of the Maintenance Center," Wahlberg said. "We found ourselves getting into the paint business, into the interior business, and into doing major cargo modifications."

Tom Pitzer remembers getting a phone call from Tim Wahlberg in late 1979. "He asked me to come to Marana and help with helicopter maintenance, and work to build the capabilities that he had visions of. I spent a couple of months working there and could see the potential that Tim was talking about. In February 1976, I called my wife and told her I would be home to take her to dinner. One week later, we had moved to Arizona. Starting with some 40 employees, we had a work force of 350 eight years later. Just as 'can't' was not in our vocabulary, neither was 'late' relative to completing aircraft. Reliability and on-time performance was critical. It gave me a great feeling to have been part of Evergreen Maintenance Center. Still today, it has a special place in my heart."

In the beginning, most of the work done at the Maintenance Center involved the Evergreen International Airlines fleet. Because he was with the airline, Tom Pitzer was assigned to coordinate the maintenance of the Evergreen fleet at Marana. A routine was quickly established. "Our DC-8's would arrive Friday evening for scheduled checks of about 1,200 man hours," Pitzer explains. "And they'd depart on Sunday morning for their next missions."

"On the management side, the approach was to recognize the work opportunities," Tim Wahlberg said, commenting on the Six M philosophy at Evergreen Maintenance Center. "On the machines side, it would be to develop the capability and the special tools, and train people to use them. On the materiel side, it would be to turn out certain types of components and have them available. Having the right technicians and the right management of the technicians is as important as knowing how to grow with the market. We looked at machines and markets, all at the same time. And then there is the process of developing the management teams and becoming competitive for jobs. We were using the same pattern as Evergreen had used on the other businesses, but instead, Evergreen Maintenance Center was a totally diversified maintenance business. We had customers who were interested in training, fuel services and aircraft storage, as well as repair and modification. We started with the capabilities that Evergreen Maintenance Center had internally, and factored in the demands of the marketplace. Of course, the key was to always provide a quality service and to finish as quickly as possible."

"Managing the Maintenance Center was all new to us," Wahlberg mused. "We really had to learn from scratch and pick it up. But we quickly learned that if we could turn out a quality aircraft on time, it is more valuable, it would save that customer an earning opportunity he loses if it's late. He also has to pay ownership costs on the aircraft every day. If he's not working the machine, he's taking a loss."

In the early days, many of the Evergreen Maintenance Center customers were leasing companies and banks who used the aircraft storage capability because the dry climate of the Arizona desert, high security and no state taxes. For example, the entire Pan American World Airways fleet of Boeing 707's was stored at Evergreen Maintenance Center. Some of the aircraft stored there were periodically taken out of storage, reconditioned by the Evergreen crews and leased to other airlines.

Fortunately, Evergreen Maintenance Center was a relatively low cost operation. The annual rent being paid to Pinal County was about $300,000, so Evergreen started out with a low base asset and could concentrate on payroll and market. Over the years, however, Evergreen would greatly enhance the capabilities and assets at the Maintenance Center.

Evergreen Maintenance Center painting capabilities and quality matched the best work anywhere, and the same remains true today. Tom Pitzer recalls that was instrumental in working with United Parcel Service in painting their first aircraft, and their very first logo.

Evergreen Maintenance Center also was doing military and government work for the United States and other countries. These projects included a contract for overhauling the transmission and rotor-heads of Peruvian helicopters and reconditioning aircraft that came out of long-term storage at the US Air Force's Military Aircraft Storage & Disposition Center at Davis-Monthan AFB south of Tucson. The proximity of Evergreen Maintenance Center to Davis-Monthan has always put Evergreen in a good position for military contracts.

Under its military contracts, Evergreen Maintenance Center was doing IRAN (Inspect, Repair As Necessary) work, which involved activities such as painting and reactivating stored helicopters, ejection seats from T-33 trainers to modifications of P2V Neptune patrol planes. As Tim Wahlberg puts it, "We were doing anything and everything we could to generate the volume of revenue we needed to support the facility."

EVACUATING THE SHAH

For all of its activities in the early years after its formation in 1979, the Evergreen International Airlines flight that garnered the most attention in the media was the one that occurred on March 23, 1980. Evergreen's medevac flight of Iran's Shah Muhammad Reza Pahlevi from Panama to Egypt filled the headlines around the world for weeks.

Muhammad Reza Pahlevi had become the shah, or emperor, of the Middle East nation of Iran in 1941 after his father, Reza Shah Pahlevi, was deposed by British and Soviet troops because of his collaboration with the Germans during World War II. The new shah was friendly to the West and to outside development within Iran. This led to improved literacy and an increased standard of living for his people, and his large public works projects benefitted Iran's infrastructure and its economy. Nevertheless, Iranians who were strict followers of Islam disliked him for steering Iranian society on a secular, rather than religious, path, and many people were unhappy with the hard-handed way that he dealt with political dissent. As this dissatisfaction increased in the seventies, the shah ordered his internal security forces to tighten down on this discord. It was too late, and in January 1979, he was forced into exile. He settled in Cuernavaca, Mexico after stops in Egypt, Morocco and at Paradise Island in the Bahamas.

In Iran, there was a great deal of anti-American sentiment because of the support that the Iranian people believed the United States had given to the shah. In October 1979, when the shah flew to New York City for cancer treatment, Iranian extremists stormed the American embassy in Tehran, Iran, and took 66 people hostage. Thirteen were released in November 1979, and one was released in July 1980. The remaining 52 hostages would remain in captivity for 444 days.

In December 1979, as the shah was ready to leave the United States after recuperating from his surgery, he had become such a politically sensitive issue that Mexico refused to allow him to return. He travelled instead to Contadora Island, Panama, where he remained for three months.

In March 1980, the condition of the shah's cancerous spleen had deteriorated to the point where immediate surgery was required. Renowned surgeon Dr. Michael DeBakey agreed to do the surgery, but refused to do it in Panama because of lack of the facilities. The shah could not return to the United States, because of fears that the 53 hostages would be murdered if he was allowed to do so. Egypt's President Anwar Sadat said that he would allow the shah into his country if DeBakey could perform the operation at a Cairo hospital. The surgeon agreed and plans were made to move the ailing monarch as soon as possible.

An aircraft that Sadat promised to send for the shah was delayed, so in Washington, President Jimmy Carter assigned the task of arranging emergency transportation to White House Counsel Lloyd Cutler, who, in turn, contacted Executive Jet Aviation in Columbus, Ohio. Because his fleet consisted of shorter range business jets, Executive Jet Chairman Bruce Sundlan went to a company that he knew had jets with adequate range to fly from Panama to Cairo.

Del Smith remembers that he got the call on Saturday morning, March 22, asking for Evergreen to undertake the charter. "We had a DC-8-52 available in Detroit, so I said 'Yes,' we would be airborne within an hour."

The Evergreen International Airlines DC-8-52 responded as Smith had promised, and reached Panama City before the deposed shah and his entourage had been airlifted in from Contadora Island. They left Panama the following morning and arrived in Cairo in the early morning hours of March 24. The surgery was performed, but with the advanced state of the cancer, it extended the shah's life by just three months.

Some of the news accounts of the flight to Cairo picked up on the thread of Evergreen's "secret" connection with the Central Intelligence Agency. The intelligence agency had played a role in restoring the shah to power in a 1953 incident, and Evergreen had purchased the Marana Air Park from a former Central Intelligence Agency contract carrier. For some headline writers and conspiracy theorists, this tenuous association implied that Evergreen had flown the charter on behalf of the agency, and that some mysterious, dark purpose was involved.

When Evergreen was asked to comment on this, Evergreen International Airlines President Ward Eason explained that Lloyd Cutler, by way of Bruce Sundlan, had actually arranged the charter, and said simply: "They called us because we have a reputation for reliable service on a very short notice to anywhere in the world."

To this, Del Smith added: "Our only regret was that we couldn't bring the hostages home."

The 52 people held hostage in Iran would not finally be released until January 20, 1981, the day that Ronald Reagan was sworn in as President of the United States.

A GROWING COMPANY

The dramatic expansion of Evergreen in the late seventies centered on global expansion and the acquisitions of key new assets, such as Johnson Flying Service and the Marana Air Park. The creation of Evergreen International Airlines and Evergreen Maintenance Center would set the tone for the future of the company. However, the late seventies also saw expansion of the company domestically, and growing opportunities for Evergreen's core helicopter business in the United States.

In 1974, Evergreen Helicopters, Inc. purchased a 100-acre facility in Roanoke, Virginia with a 14,000-square-foot hangar, and announced construction of operating bases in Prattville, Alabama and Redding, California. The main use for the Prattville base was in support of spraying operations. Additional bases were also opened in Pullman, Washington and Carmel, Indiana. Yet another base was announced for Galveston, Texas in 1978, which would serve the off-shore oil operations in the Gulf of Mexico. Galveston became a satellite base for Evergreen Helicopters, Inc. because of their instrument flight rules (IFR) certificate. Within a year, the Galveston base became the jumping off point for establishment of a series of satellite bases stretching along the Gulf Coast into Louisiana. These would eventually include Abbeville, Cameron, Patterson and Venice in Louisiana, as well as Corpus Christi, Port O'Connor and Sabine Pass in Texas.

Between 1974 and 1977, sales offices were opened in Dallas, Texas; Atlanta, Georgia; and Prattville, Alabama. The McMinnville headquarters complex was further expanded, and in Pullman, Washington, Evergreen established an agricultural operations base and a fixed-wing training center in cooperation with Washington State University.

Del Smith's original vision when he started out had been to use helicopters for tasks that were more difficult and time consuming for ground-based equipment. During the late seventies, Evergreen's Sikorsky S-64 Skycrane allowed the company to pursue a wider spectrum of such jobs. As noted previously, the Skycrane had helped Evergreen pioneer helicopter logging in the Pacific Northwest and become the first company to conduct helicopter logging operations east of the Mississippi River. Evergreen also earned numerous construction contracts in the eastern United States during the latter part of the decade, including $4 million worth of business in 1977 alone. At the same time, Evergreen brought techniques honed in the Pacific Northwest to help control the problem of gypsy moth larvae, which were wreaking havoc on timber stands in Pennsylvania.

One of the most dramatic jobs performed by Evergreen helicopters in the late seventies was the use of a Sikorsky S-64 Skycrane to install the roof of the Pontiac Silverdome — then known as Detroit Lions Stadium — in Pontiac, Michigan. On June 14, 1975, the project was behind schedule and a call was placed to Evergreen. A network of 18 three-inch cables for the air-supported roof was lifted by the Skycrane from the stadium parking lot. The cables joined glass fiber panels to form a 200-ton roof membrane. Fabricated by Aggressive

Erectors & Bridgemen of Englewood, California, the cables ranged in length from 572 to 747 feet in length and weighed up to 16,000 pounds. Bob Brown, chief pilot of the Evergreen Heavy-lift Division completed the task, which could have taken six weeks using a conventional crane, in just 16 hours.

Two months later, the Detroit Lions played their first game at the Silverdome. With the largest seating capacity (80,368) of any of the National Football League stadiums, the Silverdome also hosted the Cincinnati Bengals and the San Francisco 49ers in Super Bowl XVI on January 24, 1982. The 49ers defeated the Bengals, 26-21, before a crowd of 81,270 in the first Super Bowl ever played in a northern United States city. In 2001, the vast Pontiac Silverdome was replaced by a smaller facility in the city of Detroit that would be known as "Detroit Lions Stadium," which, coincidentally, was the original name of the Silverdome.

In November 1975, five months after the Silverdome job, an Evergreen Skycrane was used to remove a conventional construction crane from the roof of the 70-story Peachtree Center Plaza building in downtown Atlanta, Georgia. The 49-ton crane was lifted in sections weighing 8,000 to 15,000 pounds. As with the Pontiac project, the use of the Skycrane accomplished in less than three hours what it might have taken weeks to do any other way.

The following year, an Evergreen Skycrane was used to reconstruct a power line in Nebraska, and to install large transmission towers in Sweden and near Kamloops, British Columbia. Also in 1976, Evergreen's Sikorsky S-58T was used to assist RCA Communications in the installation of a microwave station in the remote Chugach Mountains of Alaska. Three years later, an Evergreen Skycrane crew successfully moved an entire oil rig on Pullen Island in Canada. Avionics for helicopters continued to improve, permitting heavy-lift helicopter operations, even in poor visibility, or IFR, conditions. After 1980, when IFR flights for heavy-lift helicopters within Alaska were permitted, Evergreen's Skycrane operations in the forty-ninth state would expand significantly.

THE EVERGREEN SKYCRANE AT WORK ON THE PONTIAC SILVERDOME.

Even as Evergreen was growing by the creation of new facilities, the company also grew by expansion. In 1977, Evergreen would acquire Rotor-Aids and HeliServices of Singapore, as well as Penn-Line and Condor Helicopters.

Evergreen Helicopters, Inc. had been involved in emergency medical evacuation ("medevac") operations since the early sixties, but in 1979, Evergreen Life Line, with dedicated emergency medical transportation services, was established. One of the first important Evergreen medevac contracts was with Hermann Hospital in Houston, Texas. As Del Smith recalls, Hermann had an occupancy of about 400, with a potential of 800 beds to fill. The Alouette III helicopters — converted and FAA-approved at the Evergreen Maintenance Center — and Learjet that Evergreen assigned to the project allowed them to serve a much wider area in a timely manner and to utilize their full capacity. Eventually, Evergreen Life Line would serve over 20 hospitals in Indiana, Alabama, California, Montana and Florida, as well as Texas.

Meanwhile, Evergreen also became involved with Life Flight, a service inaugurated by Emanuel Hospital in Portland, Oregon. Life Flight maintained a communications center staffed by doctors, and contracted with Evergreen to provide helicopter service, and with Flightcraft and Western Skyways — both of Portland — for fixed-wing support.

THE MEXICO SPRAYING AND TRAINING CONTRACT

From January 1976 through March 1978 Evergreen Helicopters received a series of contracts from the United States State Department to assist in drug interdiction efforts in Mexico. This contract began, as many Evergreen contracts do, with a rush request from the customer to be on the scene on very short notice. Evergreen pilots, and especially mechanics, spent many long hours assembling, testing, disassembling and packing for shipment spray systems to be installed on Mexican government Bell 212s.

Initially, five pilots and three mechanics were assigned to the contract. The pilots were to fly Mexican government Bell 212 spray and chase ships, and the mechanics to install, test, and maintain the aircraft and spray systems. The principal base of operations was in Culiacan in the state of Sinaloa. Smaller operations were also flown out of Choix, Mazatlan, Guadalajara, Uruapan, Chilpancingo, Acapulco and Oaxaca. The spray 212s were crewed by an Evergreen pilot and a Mexican Federal Police copilot. The chase ships, which flew cover for the spray ships, were similarly crewed, and carried a combination of Mexican Federal Police (Procuraduria General de la Republica), United States Drug Enforcement Agency (DEA) agents, and occasionally Mexican Army personnel. A typical mission began at 7:00 a.m. with a spray ship departing with 300 gallons of herbicide (Paraquat or 2,4,5T) to spray opium fields located by the chase ship or a DEA spotter plane. Flights would continue all morning with the aircraft refueling and reloading herbicide in the field. Marijuana fields were also sprayed, but the main effort was against the opium crop. The opium plots ranged in size from a tenth of an acre to 70 acres, and were found anywhere from sea level to 8,000 feet. There was some risk to the flying. The spray helicopters were shot at and hit a few times, but without injury to the crew. Of greater risk was life on the ground, especially in Culiacan, where the Evergreen crews and DEA agents, not being the most popular people in town, turned the Hotel Tres Rios into a semi-armed camp.

The United States and Mexican governments were impressed enough with Evergreen's flying and maintenance skills that the contract was renewed several times. The contract also evolved from doing the operational flying to training the Mexican police pilots in the Bell 212 and spraying techniques, and Mexican mechanics in helicopter and spray system maintenance, so that the Mexicans could run the program themselves. The contract ended in March 1978 with Evergreen having established an excellent reputation with the State Department, DEA, and the Mexican government.

THE RIVER BLINDNESS PROJECT

Through the years, Evergreen has been called upon to conduct humanitarian operations all over the world, especially in Third World countries. These have occurred from Ethiopia to Pakistan, but none have lasted longer than the one undertaken in 1974 for the United Nations World Health Organization (WHO).

Under this project, Evergreen began a successful, long-term effort aimed at the control of a disastrous plague in Africa known as River Blindness. This disease, known scientifically as onchocerciasis, is caused by the parasite *Onchocerca volvulus* and transmitted by black flies that breed in rapidly flowing rivers and streams. River Blindness is so-called because it mainly affects people living in isolated agricultural villages located near rivers, and causes chronic eye and skin disorders. River Blindness is reported in 37 countries, but about 98 percent of the infected people are in Africa, where the disease is most severe along the major rivers in a belt spanning the central part of the sub-Saharan portion of the continent.

Eradication of the black flies would evolve into the world's largest application project and continue into the twenty-first century. The lives of literally tens of millions of people were affected positively in a program that Evergreen pioneered. Pioneering is really the important word, considering that no more than one or two helicopters had flown in most of this vast region before Evergreen arrived. There were no maps.

Flying from a base at Bobo Dioulasso in the West African nation of Upper Volta, Evergreen became, and still remains, an integral part of the United Nations' Onchocerciasis Control Program (OCP). When the OCP was first launched in 1974, it was in an area that encompassed seven countries in West Africa. In 1986 the program was extended to include four additional countries, bringing the total of participating countries to 11, with a combined population of about 30 million people. The operational area covers 1.23 million square kilometers, an area where helicopters offer the only practical means of logistical support. Some of the important Evergreen personnel who spent many long days and nights making this a successful program included Ed Bridges, Sr.; Jose Carrollo; Ron Gorman; and John Kiesler.

OCP's principal method for controlling onchocerciasis has been to break the cycle of transmission by eliminating the black fly. Simulium larvae are destroyed by application of selected insecticides through aerial spraying of breeding sites in fast-flowing rivers by Evergreen helicopters. OCP was also using Evergreen's helicopter fleet to distribute the drug ivermectin, which kills the parasites.

Once the cycle of River Blindness has been interrupted for 14 years, the reservoir of adult parasites theoretically dies out in the human population, thus eliminating the source of the disease. By the end of the twentieth century, Evergreen and its United Nations partners had virtually eliminated the parasites in the original seven-

AN EVERGREEN MD-500 ON THE JOB FOR WHO IN AFRICA.

country operations area. At OCP's launch in 1974, more than a million people in West Africa suffered from onchocerciasis, of whom 100,000 had serious eye problems, including 35,000 people who were completely blind. By the end of the century, there were virtually no infected people within the original area of OCP operations. Some 1.5 million people who were once infected with onchocerciasis no longer had any trace of the disease, and 12 million children born in the operational area since the program's inception were free of risk of contracting the disease. It is a project to which Evergreen and the World Health Organization can definitely point with pride.

Chapter 5:

EVERGREEN IN THE EIGHTIES

(1981-1989)

ROM THE TIME THAT IT WAS OFFICIALLY CREATED IN 1975, Evergreen International Airlines has been primarily a freight carrier, but during the eighties, a major business segment involved passenger charters, especially carrying vacationers from the Northeast and the upper Midwest to the Caribbean, and from the Pacific Northwest to Hawaii. In the beginning, the passenger fleet had included three passenger-configured Lockheed Electras — two that had been owned by Johnson Flying Service and one that was acquired from Intermountain Aviation — and DC-8's in passenger configuration were soon added as well.

In 1980, with the onset of the recession of the early eighties, the tour business began to slide into one of its periodic slumps. It was during the 1980's that Evergreen International Airlines began shifting its emphasis from the passenger business toward freight operations. In 1976, Evergreen had started operating L-188 Electras as freighters on a common carriage basis in domestic operations, while at the same time operating passenger-configured Electras. After 1981, the remaining passenger Electras were also converted for use as freighters.

The focus of the airline's activities shifted dramatically in 1981 when it landed a major contract with United Parcel Service. The largest pick-up and delivery system in the United States, United

Parcel Service had developed a comprehensive ground system, but they were eager to establish a dedicated fleet to serve their second-day air courier business. Known officially as "UPS Blue," this service complemented their "UPS Red" overnight service.

Prior to this time, United Parcel Service had been buying all of their capacity from the scheduled service providers, but they had now elected to begin "wet lease" operations, with Evergreen providing not only the aircraft itself, but crewing, maintaining and insuring it as well. Eventually, Evergreen operated a fleet of aircraft for United Parcel Service that included Evergreen-owned aircraft as well as aircraft that belonged to United Parcel Service.

"They were the toughest task masters Evergreen ever worked with," Evergreen President Tim Wahlberg said of United Parcel Service. "They'd shake you down every month, and talk about every delay on every aircraft, about every departure and every person. United Parcel Service was just dotting every 'I' and crossing every 'T.' They still are, and we thank them for it. Evergreen learned a lot working with United Parcel Service. Evergreen grew with them and stayed with them. We became the best service provider they had."

The DC-8's and DC-9's were the first jetliners operated by Evergreen, but, beginning in 1980, Boeing 727's became an important part of the Evergreen fleet. The 727, a "T-tail" tri-jet, is in the same size and weight class as the Douglas DC-9 that had been in the Evergreen fleet since the mid-seventies. First introduced to the market in the sixties, the 727 had been designed with innovative, triple-slotted, trailing edge flaps and new leading-edge slats, that gave it unprecedented low-speed landing and takeoff performance so that it could be accommodated by smaller airports. The 727-100 series, which Evergreen International Airlines would acquire, included the 727-100C (convertible/cargo) with a large cargo door, a strong floor and freight handling systems for switching in less than two hours between passenger or cargo or mixed operation, as well as the 727-100QC (quick change) which cut conversion time to 30 minutes. The early 727's were powered by three Pratt & Whitney JT8D-7B or JT8D-9A turbofans.

In 1984, Evergreen International Airlines established Louisville, Kentucky as its Eastern Regional Operations Headquarters, while on the West Coast, it began to acquire smaller delivery services to help expand its delivery business. These included TRF Delivery Service, Inc. and Pegasus Delivery Co., Inc., which were absorbed into an operation that would be known as Evergreen Express.

In the meantime, the company set up the Evergreen Training Center near its headquarters campus in McMinnville. The center would provide the flight and maintenance, initial and recurrent training that the airline needed to grow and maintain Evergreen's high standards of quality. There was also a desire to streamline the training program, while really concentrating on all the important safety issues. As Tim Wahlberg explains, "When you have a high safety record, you have lower insurance costs."

In the early eighties, Evergreen International Airlines started examining all of its costs in more detail than it had in the seventies. The company had always looked at insurance costs, but now fuel costs were coming under closer scrutiny. The fleet was expanding, but Evergreen International Airlines was looking to the notion of upgrading the fleet as well. Evergreen wanted aircraft with a lower fuel burn rate and lower maintenance costs.

As Tim Wahlberg put it: "When we began to write our own maintenance program, we wrote very difficult specs, so that Evergreen could have the lowest temperatures when the engines came out of overhaul. We were paying the same price, but now we were stretching those engines out to 11,000 hours between shop visits. That meant that our costs went down from $1,000 an hour — while Pan Am overhauled our engines at 2,500 hours between overhauls — to $200 an hour with Evergreen's newly engineered maintenance program. We'd been looking pretty dumb for the money we'd been spending on the engines, but all of a sudden, we were looking pretty smart."

In short, Evergreen measured everything from fuel to human resources — in the context of the Six M's. In every segment, maintenance programs had to achieve better quality, reliability and be more cost effective.

In the mid-eighties, however, the Federal Aviation Administration (FAA) was coming up with new rules that also complicated the maintenance procedures. They became more involved because the big carriers were stretching the maintenance programs so far that reliability and safety were becoming an issue. When the FAA decided to reverse this trend, a great deal of extra pressure was placed on the whole aviation industry for reliability and record keeping.

"They wanted to see the greasy thumbprint on all the maintenance records," Wahlberg recalled. "They wanted to see where the mechanic signed it off. They wanted to see the original compliance sign-off, the original check and the component overhaul. They wanted to see us as leaders in the industry. Evergreen had to go back and re-establish the records on our entire fleet of used aircraft, which involved a work force of about 40 people and probably 10 language interpreters working 12-hour days, seven days a week. This took about six months, from August 1986 to February 1987. We probably expended 100,000 man hours going back and re-establishing, not only our own records, but also those of United Parcel Service on all of their aircraft."

In doing this, Tom Pitzer recalls that "We travelled from South America to Europe recovering documented records from previous owners and operators."

Evergreen International Airlines already had experience in the air courier business because of its previous work with Emery Air Freight, but the United Parcel Service contract really changed the airline. It would also put the airline in a strong position to compete for future air courier contracts. One of the most important of these came in 1987, when Evergreen was awarded the United States Postal Service contract to provide a dedicated fleet of aircraft to operate their Express Mail overnight service.

The Postal Service had started an overnight delivery system called the Moon Light Express, with Consolidated Freightways as the forwarder, Eastern Air Lines as the carrier and Houston as the hub. Late in 1986, when the Postal Service decided to create a network using dedicated freighter aircraft, Evergreen was successful in winning the Express Mail contract. There had been many bidders, but Evergreen's experience with United Parcel Service had given it the advantage.

During the mid-eighties, as Evergreen was establishing itself with United Parcel Service, the company had deliberately avoided competing business. "We were loyal to the point where we didn't chase the other express industry," Del Smith said. "We didn't go to Airborne, didn't fly for Federal Express, didn't fly for Burlington. But when the US Postal Service observed us building that air force for United Parcel Service, they decided to pick Evergreen. They knew that if they picked anybody else, they wouldn't make it, so they chose us. We did a perfect job, and in about eight weeks we had 25 airplanes at work. We really ran that thing on time. I was told that market share had improved from seven to 27 percent."

The US Postal Service contract led to the establishment of a "hub and spoke" delivery operation with the hub located at Hulman Regional Airport in Terre Haute, Indiana. Evergreen had originally proposed to use the same facility that Emery had used earlier in Smyrna, Tennessee, and Evergreen went to work rebuilding it for the new operations. However, just 45 days before the new service was scheduled to start, Evergreen discovered that the community was not going to allow night-time operations of airplanes because of noise. Evergreen had to change the hub location.

When it became apparent that Evergreen was not going to be able to use Smyrna, Del Smith and his team got the charts out and flew back in the Learjet. They visited nearly every airport in the Midwest. Terre Haute welcomed them enthusiastically, but the facilities that were there at Hulman Field had to be reconstructed. They had a large building, but it was smaller than what Evergreen needed. It had to be completely transformed into a new center — and it was. The people in Terre Haute were very responsive. They were welcoming new industry into their community, and they saw the Evergreen operation as a good source of employment for local residents.

During the same year, Evergreen International Airlines acquired Kitty Hawk Aviation's US Postal Service operation, which was centered in Las Vegas, Nevada. This would add eight cities to Evergreen's US Postal Service network.

It was a challenge, not just for Evergreen International Airlines, but for the entire management team. Grouped together, Evergreen had to perform several different tasks. These included building a hub in the central United States, and getting enough aircraft to service the 21 cities originally involved. Evergreen had to muster all of the ground logistics, including facilities for fuel, landing, and handling, at all the airports.

Evergreen put the Terre Haute hub together in record time. Evergreen initially had to subcontract some airplanes to get the original contract going, but soon additional aircraft were purchased and the entire network was operated with an Evergreen fleet, consisting primarily of 727's and DC-9's, plus one DC-8.

In June 1987, a week after the Evergreen operation got underway, Judy Carmine, the general manager of network analysis for the Postal Service, observed, "We're very satisfied with their performance. There were few start-up problems. . . . Any problems there were, were taken care of quickly."

Carmine went on to note that only five of the 110 flights flown the first week were delayed — and those by just a few minutes. She praised Evergreen's work, calling it "outstanding."

By 1988, the Evergreen/Postal Service Express Mail operation was going so well that the Postal Service was running advertising in national publications — including *Newsweek* and *Sports Illustrated* — bragging that the service was "almost perfect."

The original two-year US Postal Service contract was extended to 32 months, but then it was put back out for bid. When they re-solicited, however, Emery Air Freight (Emery Worldwide after 1989) underbid Evergreen to win the contract that Evergreen had been operating.

This included the fleet of aircraft, as well as the operating network and the operation of the hub. The Postal Service contracted for a fleet of 727's, principally 727-200 series, moving to a more uniform fleet under a long-term agreement to permit someone to acquire the fleet.

"The contract renewal was supposed to be automatic and then we got the resolicitation surprise. It was the first bad experience we'd had with our United States government," Del Smith recalled bitterly. "We built that program for them, and it really made them proud. We recovered their market share from the overnight delivery companies, and they were pleased with our performance. Then to lose that job to an outfit that didn't have an airplane, didn't have a pilot, didn't have a mechanic, and didn't have a 121 Authority was unbelievable. They were very inefficient, very costly. But the express industry was growing so well, that growth covered a lot of shortcuts. We did the Postal Service a perfect job and we lost. That was a real setback."

That it was a setback was an understatement, because Evergreen International Airlines had undertaken a major fleet expansion at the height of the US Postal Service contract. These acquisitions, tailored primarily to the needs of the domestic air freight market, included six Boeing 727's and four McDonnell Douglas DC-9's. This fleet expansion was begun in anticipation of the renewal in 1989 of the US Postal Service contract. When this was not forthcoming, Evergreen International Airlines leased much of its 727 fleet to other operators in the United States and abroad, and within a few years, Evergreen retired the last of the 727's.

Meanwhile, since 1982, the US Postal Service has contracted with Evergreen Helicopters to deliver mail between Nome, Alaska and the offshore island of Little Diomede. Little Diomede comprises less than three square miles, and its steep slopes won't accommodate a runway for fixed-wing aircraft.

During the time that Evergreen, and later Emery, operated at Terre Haute under the Postal Service contract, both the aircraft operations and the operation of the hub were part of the same program. However, because of the growth of the Postal Service's Express and

Priority Mail business, operations outgrew the Terre Haute facility, and the Postal Service elected to build a new hub at Indianapolis. The contract for operating this new multi-million dollar Express and Priority Mail center went to Evergreen's EAGLE.

During the latter eighties, the Postal Service delivered Express and Priority Mail in Western United States through buying space on scheduled airlines, and by using dedicated aircraft. The latter operations were leased through such contractors as K. Colmia, Kitty Hawk Aviation, and later, through Evergreen. In 1989, the Postal Service went back to using scheduled carriers, notably America West through Las Vegas, putting the mail into the cargo holds of passenger flights. However, this was abruptly discontinued after the invasion of Kuwait in August 1990. Because of the threat of terrorist letter bombs in the mail, the Postal Service now had to take mail out of the bellies of passenger aircraft. Overnight, Evergreen re-instituted what was then called the W-net, operating through Oakland, California. Evergreen operated this system through August 1999 under a number of different contractual arrangements.

MOVING INTO HEAVY-LIFT

During the mid-eighties, as integrators such as United Parcel Service and Federal Express were building up their own dedicated fleets for the air courier business, Evergreen International Airlines had been making a step in another direction. The step was a big one — into heavy-lift, intercontinental air freight. In 1983, the airline had been awarded a worldwide charter authority, which was initially served by its DC-8-60 fleet. In 1984, Evergreen began upgrading these aircraft to DC-8-70 "Super Seventy" standard, which entailed re-engining them with new technology General Electric/SNECMA (Société National d'Etudes et Construction de Moteurs d'Avion) high-bypass turbofan engines. The DC-8-70 series aircraft retained the DC-8-60 series operating weights, but they had a longer range because of the newer, more fuel-efficient turbofans. The 4,600-

pound CFM56-2 engine used for the DC-8-70 series delivered 22,000 pounds of thrust in a sea level take-off, yet, because of it, the Super Seventy series aircraft were also able to meet the more stringent noise regulations that the United States Federal Aviation Administration began to mandate during the eighties. Tom Pitzer recalls that after the conversions, the engine-on-wing time and reliability improved, immensely reducing line maintenance labor.

In 1986, Evergreen International Airlines began operating its first wide-body jetliner, a Boeing 747-200C. The largest jetliner ever placed into widespread airline service, the 747 (in its 747-100 and 747-200 configurations) had revolutionized passenger air travel in the seventies and set a new global standard for intercontinental travel. The freighter variant provided civilian users with the greatest capacity available. The 747 freighter could easily carry 100 tons across the Atlantic Ocean or across the United States, and its operating cost was 35 percent less per ton mile than earlier jetliners configured as freighters. (Ton miles are weight in tons multiplied by miles flown. A ton mile is an international measure of the capacity for freight carriers.)

In addition to those freighters that were factory-delivered, early passenger 747's were converted into freighters after serving productive years as passenger planes. Meanwhile, there would also be 747C "convertibles" that offered the flexibility of a large airplane that could carry passengers or cargo, or combinations of both.

The first contract for the first Evergreen 747 was an air cargo program for Air India between New York, Bombay and Delhi, by way of Paris and Dubai. The Evergreen 747 fleet would also be an asset to the long-range, international program that Evergreen International Airlines was operating for the Military Airlift Command. A second 747, which operated under contract to Air France, was added in 1987, and by the end of the decade, the Evergreen fleet consisted of 15 of the huge aircraft. The initial 747 deployments would entail Evergreen wet leasing the aircraft on an ACMI (Aircraft, Crew, Maintenance and Insurance) basis.

ADDING 747S TO THE FLEET GREATLY INCREASED EVERGREEN'S CAPABILITIES.

The 747 freighters now symbolized a new direction for Evergreen International Airlines, and an important element of this new direction came in 1989, when the airline won a wet-lease contract with Qantas, Australia's flag airline, for Pacific cargo operations. Discussed in detail in the following chapter, this operation would go on to be one of Evergreen's most important 747 activities in the 1990's.

EVERGREEN HELICOPTERS IN A MATURING MARKET

The boom in seismic activities and other oil exploration projects that had been such an important profit center for Evergreen Helicopters, Inc. in the seventies continued into the early years of the eighties. In 1981, a new facility was completed at Deadhorse on Alaska's North Slope to service the needs of Evergreen's oil company customers in the Arctic.

Evergreen helicopters began support of oil exploration activities in Bangladesh during 1981, and Evergreen Helicopter seismic operations spread into Turkey during 1982. Also during 1982, HeliServices, the Singapore-based subsidiary acquired in 1977 took its operations into the Seychelles. Two years later, new helicopter operations began in such diverse corners of the world as New Guinea, Thailand and Saudi Arabia.

Back in the United States, Instrument Flight Rules (IFR) for helicopters were finally approved by the Federal Aviation Administration for the Gulf of Mexico in 1984, making it possible for Evergreen ships based in the region to begin night flying operations. In 1985, the Evergreen helicopters on the Gulf were retrofitted with the high-technology Motorola Flight Following System. As noted earlier, Galveston, Texas became a satellite base for Evergreen Helicopters, Inc. because of their instrument flight rules (IFR) certificate.

As the older helicopters were sold off, Evergreen was also bringing in newer equipment. As was the case in the Evergreen International Airlines fleet, upgrading the fleet not only involved newer avionics, it would bring lower maintenance costs and higher fuel efficiency. Hughes (McDonnell Douglas after 1985) Model 500 helicopters were added to the Evergreen fleet throughout the decade, and Aérospatiale Puma and Messerschmitt-Bölkow-Blohm helicopters were first added in 1981 and 1984 respectively.

In 1986, Evergreen Helicopters, Inc. purchased a Lear 35 business jet, and the Lear 25 that Evergreen had owned previously went into operation with Evergreen Life Line. Formed in 1979 to provide emergency medical transportation in cooperation with regional hospitals, Evergreen Life Line flourished for much of the decade.

From its original location at Hermann Hospital in Houston, Texas, Evergreen Life Line branched out to over 20 hospitals in eight states, including Methodist Hospital of Indiana in Indianapolis and a pair of hospitals in Phoenix, Arizona: John C. Lincoln and Good Samaritan. Evergreen Life Line also worked with Emanuel Hospital in Portland, Oregon on a service that had originated as a business known as Life Flight.

In 1986, in one of Evergreen Life Line's last expansions, service began at Tyler, Texas, and the operations at University Hospital in San Diego added a third aircraft, a Messerschmitt-Bölkow-Blohm (later Eurocopter) Bo-105CBS. After a decade of service, Evergreen

Life Line was ultimately eliminated because of increasing competition and declining profitability.

Historically, the big era of growth for Evergreen Helicopters, Inc. had been the seventies. The company was successful because it had a good management team and fair pricing. Evergreen had roughly 180 helicopters working worldwide, with operations in Asia, Africa, North America, South America, Europe and Australia. However, as the eighties began, the oil industry fell on bad times. This, and the eventual end of the Evergreen Life Line program, led to a decline in the size of the Evergreen helicopter fleet to around 70 machines. The Evergreen Redding and Roanoke helicopter bases were sold in 1985, and the Prattville, Alabama property followed in 1986.

The reduction in fleet size was because of competition and a reduction in market, but also because the Federal Reserve, under Chairman Paul Volker, raised interest rates from seven percent to 21.5 percent.

Tim Wahlberg recalls, "Evergreen was concentrating more on the airline business and less on the helicopter business because we could see that without the heavy oil industry market, the demand wasn't going to be there as it had been. Evergreen continued to grow and diversify, but we shrunk our helicopter fleet."

Other opportunities were still available, and the Evergreen helicopter fleet kept busy. For example, powerline projects took Evergreen helicopters to El Salvador in 1982 and Sweden in 1983. The Sweden project marked the first deployment to Europe of an Evergreen S-64 Skycrane. Between 1982 and 1986, the Royal Dutch Shell Group contracted with Evergreen for the services of its de Havilland Canada DHC-6 Twin Otter Short Take-Off & Landing (STOL), fixed-wing aircraft for a project in Syria. Shell Oil Company operations in Syria were handled by Evergreen Helicopters.

The River Blindness (onchocerciasis) eradication project, that Evergreen began to support for the United Nations World Health Organization (WHO) in 1975, would continue through the eighties and into the nineties. From its base at Bobo Dioulasso in the West

African nation of Upper Volta, Evergreen continued its assault on the black flies that carried the *Onchocerca volvulus* parasite. These missions were a tribute to both the skill and dedication of the Evergreen pilots, who had to fly beneath the jungle canopy and above narrow, winding rivers that were often a mere five meters in width. The pilots also lived in the jungle, under primitive conditions, for the duration of their missions, which often lasted for a week or more.

Evergreen employees have had some trying moments during the operations in Africa, including moments that have provided anecdotes that are almost amusing in retrospect. "On the first night in my "suite" in Odienne, Ivory Coast, I had several unwelcome visitors," recalled Mary Jo Nichols of Evergreen Helicopters. "My boss was kind enough to run from next door and take his shoe and whack the black snake that was eye-balling me from the corner in my room and toss him outside. My can of Raid was not doing any damage to what I thought was a cockroach that had crawled over my towel that I had blocking the doorway. The eight legs and pinchers above head gave me a good indication that I was not dealing with a cockroach! It ran under my bed (to keep company with the centipede my boss spotted under there earlier after the snake episode) and didn't come out! I had decided that I would not get my boss on this one. . . Needless to say, it was a sleepless night and there were one or two moments that I actually thought I might be returning to the United States in a wooden box in the cargo department!"

"It turned out to be an incredible journey that I will never forget and would do all over again," she says, looking back at being part of the black fly eradication operations. "I feel very honored to be a part of such a valuable and rewarding project."

While over 90 percent of onchocerciasis victims are in Africa, WHO began the eighties by spreading the fight against the disease around the world. In 1981, as WHO went to Nepal to do a pilot study of the onchocerciasis in that Himalayan nation, Evergreen helicopters were tasked with providing logistical support. In the process of

AN EVERGREEN BO-105 ON ALASKA'S LITTLE DIOMEDE ISLAND.

this project, an Evergreen Aérospatiale Alouette III became the first commercial helicopter to cross the entire Indian subcontinent.

The original Onchocerciasis Control Program (OCP) would be expanded to encompass 13 West African countries. In 1986, Evergreen helped launch this third phase of the project by shipping nine Hughes 500 light helicopters to Africa in an Evergreen International Airlines DC-8-73 transport.

In 1987, as Evergreen was marking five years in cataract removal in Nepal on the WHO onchocerciasis project, Evergreen personnel travelled to nearby Calcutta to assist Mother Theresa in beginning the first drug rehabilitation program in India. The Evergreen crews also lent a hand to the diminutive Nobel laureate in support of her vitamin procurement program for lepers.

Evergreen helicopters also continued to be active in spraying and other agricultural work in the Pacific Northwest, as they had been for a quarter of a century. Evergreen's helicopters also teamed up with Evergreen fixed-wing air tankers on forest fire control efforts for the US Forest Service in the Pacific Northwest during fire seasons throughout the decade.

On March 24, 1989, the oil tanker *Exxon Valdez* struck Bligh Reef in Prince William Sound, Alaska, spilling more than 11 million gallons of crude oil. The spill was the largest in United States history, and the resulting slick covered more than 1,000 miles of the Alaska coastline and caused over $3 billion in environmental damage. The spill killed thousands of fish, seabirds and sea otters. Evergreen helicopters responded quickly to the situation, doing what they could to ferry personnel and equipment to the scene of the disaster. Evergreen helicopters were also involved in the long clean-up process that followed.

STOL OPERATIONS

Not all of Evergreen Helicopters, Inc.'s aircraft are helicopters. When Evergreen International Airlines was created in 1975, its mandate was the operation of large, fixed-wing aircraft. The smaller fixed-wing aircraft that Evergreen owned remained with Evergreen Helicopters, Inc. Through the years these have included the Pilatus Porter, Turbothrush, de Havilland Canada DHC-6 Twin Otter, a twin-engine Short Take-Off & Landing (STOL) aircraft, and more recently, the 28-passenger CASA C212-200 and Cessna 206.

STOL aircraft are essential to many of the operations conducted in South and Central America because many of the remote airfields are relatively primitive and have short runways that won't support larger aircraft. Helicopters can operate into these locations, but the STOL fixed-wing aircraft carry more and fly faster and farther. The STOL aircraft are able to deliver shipments closer to their final destination than would be possible with a big aircraft, hence the overall delivery process requires much less trucking.

Evergreen had operated STOL aircraft in Peru as early as the eighties, and had first been contracted by the US Air Force to fly STOL operations from Howard AFB in 1989. In 1992, the Air Force decided to take over these operations themselves with a fleet of 10 C-27A Spartan STOL aircraft that were stationed with the 24th Wing at Howard AFB and flown by aircrews from the 310th Airlift Squadron. After six years, however, the Air Force withdrew the C-

27's from service and Evergreen was again put under contract for STOL operations in the region.

For the operations from Howard AFB, Evergreen Helicopters, Inc. acquired five CASA 212's in the spring of 1989. Manufactured in Spain by Construcciones Aeronauticas SA (CASA), the aircraft are each powered by a pair of Garrett TPE 331-10R-511C turboprop engines. They have a cargo capacity of over 5,500 pounds, a cruising speed of 225 mph and a range of 1,000 miles. A uniquely efficient cargo aircraft, the CASA 212's size and rear-loading capability make it especially versatile for carrying large-sized cargo to small, remote landing fields, such as those which exist throughout rural South America.

EVERGREEN MAINTENANCE CENTER IN THE EIGHTIES

In the early years after Evergreen Maintenance Center (known as Evergreen Air Center until 2007) in Marana, Arizona was acquired in 1975, its maintenance capability had been used mainly to support Evergreen International Airlines' own fleet, especially its DC-8's and DC-9's, but gradually, that had started to change.

Third-party military and civilian work grew steadily in the late seventies, and expanded greatly in the eighties. Evergreen Maintenance Center started doing work on Boeing 727's and 747's. When Evergreen International Airlines bought its fleet of Boeing 727's from Lufthansa, they were sent to Marana to be reconditioned and overhauled. Even this became third-party work, as part of the 727 fleet was sold to United Parcel Service. Evergreen Maintenance Center was also doing a great deal of work for Texas-based Braniff Airlines, and in 1981, the Maintenance Center got some nice publicity when the airplane operated by the then-popular musical group the Bee Gees was brought in to be refurbished.

As Tim Wahlberg, then head of the Maintenance Center, put it, "We'd look into the market for other carriers that had the same type of aircraft that Evergreen International Airlines had, and would offer our services. The big challenge was trying to grow the revenues and grow with new customers. During the eighties, Evergreen Maintenance Center did a lot of work on the United Parcel Service DC-8's and 727's.

"On the management side of the Six M approach," Wahlberg continued, "There was the need to recognize the work opportunities, and adapt the management teams to provide the required service. On the materiel and men and women side, there was the need to develop our tooling and provide training on different components and inspections.

"We looked at the broad authority of the Unlimited FAA repair station, and wanted to employ all the service capabilities," Wahlberg said of the market and machines aspect of the Maintenance Center in the eighties. "Instead of machines, we had the maintenance capabilities. We looked at the marketplace to determine how Evergreen could provide services to the market. We were doing major airframe modifications, but there were customers for maintenance training classrooms, fuel services and aircraft storage. You have to plan ahead, matching the maintenance capabilities Evergreen had internally to the demands of the marketplace."

In the meantime, Evergreen was marketing the Maintenance Center's vast complex of buildings, finding other tenants for the non-aviation facilities on the grounds. For example, in 1983, the Evergreen Maintenance Center became the headquarters of the Federal Law Enforcement Training Corps and for the United States Sky Marshals.

As its business grew, so did Evergreen Maintenance Center's facilities. Evergreen gradually converted the old World War II infrastructure into that of a state-of-the-art center. In 1984, a new million-dollar 6,840-foot runway was rebuilt, and in 1985, the George A. Doole Aviation Center, a wide-body maintenance/office complex, was brought on line. The wide-body capacity came as the Evergreen International Airlines fleet was adding 747's, and it led to more third-party opportunities. In 1989, Evergreen Maintenance Center completed the first wide-body major maintenance and refurbishment D-check ever done in Arizona. Beginning in May 1991, the National

Aeronautics & Space Administration (NASA) would start bringing its pair of 747 Space Shuttle Carrier Aircraft (SCA) to Evergreen Maintenance Center for routine and major maintenance.

"The market was really diversifying," Tim Wahlberg said of the Maintenance Center in the eighties. "We were still trying to focus on 727, DC-9, DC-8, and 747 airframes, but we also got into Boeing 737's and Fokker F-28's."

Meanwhile, the lenders and the leasing companies were still bringing aircraft in for storage. "They liked the high security and the dry storage with no corrosion," Wahlberg said. "And we had the maintenance capabilities available as well. When they were ready to take an aircraft out of storage, we could do everything from upgrade the avionics and change the color of the airplane to providing major maintenance bridge inspections."

THE ORIGIN OF EVERGREEN AIRCRAFT SALES & LEASING

It has always been understood in business that assets that are not performing or are no longer needed should be leased or disposed of, and that if those assets still have value to others, they should be sold. However, Phoebe Hocken, Evergreen's original financial administrator, demonstrated to the company that asset sales could actually be a profit center for the company. Over the years, asset sales have often generated more revenue than operations.

"She would recap on all the year-end closes, and tell us what we would have earned without asset sales, and what our profits were with asset sales," Del Smith recalled. "It turned out that 66 percent of the profit made over the 25 years from 1960 through 1985 was in asset sales, and 33 percent was operating profits."

This was the idea behind Evergreen Aircraft Sales & Leasing (EASL), which was formed in 1983 and incorporated as a subsidiary corporation in 1986. Renamed Evergreen Trade in 2008, the subsidiary is referred to as EASL in this chapter for historical context. EASL evolved from an internal function at Evergreen Helicopters, Inc. and Evergreen International Airlines. There were people within these two operating companies who were paid by the operating companies, but who would also be in charge of selling inventory. Gradually, as this activity expanded, and as there was increasing duplication of effort between the operating companies, it made sense to create a separate subsidiary. In the beginning, EASL's job was simply to dispose of inventory without taking a loss, but gradually, following the prediction of Phoebe Hocken, it evolved into a profit center.

As Evergreen Chairman Tim Wahlberg put it, "EASL was a service that Evergreen had always had internally. If Evergreen required a helicopter we would find one. As our fleet changed, we would have excess materiel that needed to be sold. By doing this, Evergreen generated the in-house capability to buy, sell, and lease."

EASL was originally tasked with purchasing and selling aircraft that Evergreen Helicopters, Inc. and Evergreen International Airlines required or deemed surplus. Soon, however, EASL was being asked to buy and sell parts and components as well. As EASL President Mike Hines notes, by 1988, his organization had surpassed the $500 million mark in aircraft parts trades.

EVERGREEN AVIATION GROUND LOGISTICS ENTERPRISES SPREADS ITS WINGS

On December 6, 1986, Evergreen formally incorporated its ground handling subsidiary corporation. Officially named Evergreen Aviation Ground Logistics Enterprises, Inc., the subsidiary is universally known by its acronym, EAGLE.

The genesis of the ground handling concept occurred when Evergreen was born. Evergreen Helicopters, Inc. was the first customer for the EAGLE concept. That first Evergreen helicopter needed a fuel truck, so in theory, EAGLE can trace its roots to the beginning of Evergreen, to an entity known as the "Truck Shop," that handled logistical support for the helicopter company in the sixties.

Until as late as the mid-eighties, ground handling had been just a function within the two individual operating companies, Evergreen Helicopters, Inc. and Evergreen International Airlines.

Of course, these companies often operated where they had to depend on third-party ground handling. Thus, the idea behind the formal organization of EAGLE came about when the airline was having problems with the service they were receiving at outside stations. The original intent was to support Evergreen International Airlines' own operation, but through that, third-party work developed, and the concept mushroomed.

"They were handling our own airplanes," Michael Spencer, EAGLE's senior vice president of finance and materiel, said of EAGLE in its early days, "because Evergreen couldn't take the risk of somebody else damaging one of our aircraft that had to fly 10 hours a day. So we became as self-sufficient and reliable with the jetliner fleet as we had been with the helicopters."

EAGLE's repertoire includes activities such as baggage handling and freight handling, and basic interior cleaning work within the cabins of the aircraft. EAGLE still does the majority of the ground handling for Evergreen International Airlines within the United States, and it supports Evergreen Helicopters with trucks and drivers, and with logistical support, but at the turn of the century, that had become a very small proportion of EAGLE's business. As Robert Lane, retired executive vice president for EAGLE put it, "EAGLE went to every city in the United States that the airline went, but started serving other airlines."

Now, there was an opportunity to go where other airlines went. In terms of the market for a company like EAGLE, the times were right. During the late seventies, as interest rates went through the ceiling in the United States causing an economic downturn, many international and domestic air carriers were trying to bring their overhead costs down. They started doing more and more out-sourcing with third party companies for various services.

The first major third-party customer for EAGLE was the United Parcel Service at Portland International Airport, but before the end of 1986, EAGLE was doing de-icing, aircraft washing, and turnaround work for United Parcel Service at Portland, and for third-party customers all across the states, including San Francisco International Airport, Los Angeles International Airport and New York City's John F. Kennedy International Airport. By the turn of the century, EAGLE would evolve into the single largest contract handler for United Parcel Service.

In 1987, when Evergreen began operations with the US Postal Service under the A-Net contract, using Terre Haute, Indiana as its operational hub, EAGLE set up operations at 23 cities throughout the United States. As noted earlier in this chapter, Evergreen put the Terre Haute hub into operation in a remarkably short time. Prior to the opening of the Terre Haute hub for US Postal Service operations, EAGLE had acquired other ground handling companies, including E&K Cargo Complex at Portland International Airport, and American World Aviation, Inc. at John F. Kennedy International Airport in New York. Despite the pace of setting up a new center every two weeks, EAGLE ended 1987 having achieved near-perfect performance for the year.

The following year, the growth slowed slightly, as EAGLE purchased SMB Operations of Dallas, Texas, adding six airports to its ground handling activities.

Despite the increase in work for third-party customers — such as United Parcel Service and Emery Air Freight — EAGLE's largest customer during the eighties remained Evergreen International Airlines. After 1989, however, this would change, as EAGLE branched out and became the fastest-growing component of the Evergreen family of companies.

When building these bases, Evergreen was especially attentive to making sure that each one had a good, strong manager. They were responsible for the market and the relationship to the customer, while at the same time keeping costs under control, and monitoring hiring practices and the people who were on board. The managers also made sure that the machines were kept up, that the facilities were clean, and that the staff was uniformed and professional. This did a great deal to inspire confidence in customers and potential customers.

EAGLE has always had a reputation for maintaining its equipment and machines properly, and getting a great deal of use out of them. One of Del Smith's favorite sayings is "If you take care of your equipment, it will take care of you." This is certainly the case with EAGLE. Equipment utilization has always been important to EAGLE's success. Properly maintained equipment can work continuously, and having it lie idle is unproductive.

In the early days of doing third-party work, the customer base was the air express couriers, so the equipment usually worked at night and in the early morning. As EAGLE began to add customers that were passenger airlines in the international gateway cities, the equipment could be utilized all day and all night. There was also a potential for more full-time employment for EAGLE personnel. Getting a day's work out of equipment is a good thing, but having it work day and night is better.

In terms of money, EAGLE started with relatively low overhead and was competitive in the marketplace. After being organized as an independent subsidiary of Evergreen International Aviation, Evergreen International Airlines and Evergreen Helicopters paid EAGLE for its services just as any other commercial customer would.

EAGLE was designed for both site-specific and customer-specific markets, meaning that it might support several customers at one site, while handling a single customer that had operations at multiple sites. For example, with United Parcel Service, EAGLE handled them in nine cities under one general contract. EAGLE was created with the capability to tailor its operations to customers, but it would also establish ground handling operations at various airports that could be marketed to airlines using those airports.

Air couriers such as United Parcel Service, Burlington or DHL obviously wanted multi-city locations, so EAGLE would market

from a regional standpoint and a multi-city standpoint. The major
international passenger carriers, meanwhile, were more concerned
about specific sites. Under the United Parcel Service contract, and
later the postal contract, EAGLE was able to expand into many
cities quickly because the company had a baseline customer at the
airports.

Evergreen marketing personnel were involved in manpower levels, equipment levels and overhead structures. They helped to build
each one of the markets. The backbone of EAGLE's success was its
ability to grow and maintain its profit margin at the same time.

"The program really grew," Tim Wahlberg said of EAGLE in the
late eighties. "During the Gold Rush, everybody had to have a general store, regardless of what they were doing in their mining operations. In the airline business, all the airlines need a ground handling
service, no matter what their fleets are doing. EAGLE was there for
them in the eighties and it has continued to be there."

THE BIRTH OF EVERGREEN AGRICULTURAL ENTERPRISES

In the early sixties, when Evergreen was just a small helicopter
company operating only in the Pacific Northwest, one of the most
important segments of its client base was the agricultural industry.
Evergreen helicopters helped the farmer and the timber industry by
seeding, eradicating pests and spreading fertilizer. With an interest
in the land and in allowing it to fulfill its potential, it is no wonder
that Evergreen itself would become involved in the agricultural
industry.

Evergreen's home is in Yamhill County, in the heart of Oregon's
Willamette Valley, one of the most fertile agricultural regions in the
world. This was the farmland at the end of the rainbow for the thousands of people who came west on the Oregon Trail in the nineteenth
century.

Evergreen acquired its first farmland in Yamhill County in 1979,
and this was managed by a subsidiary known simply as Evergreen

Farms. It was a time of high interest rates. Some of the local farmers were selling and the younger generation had no interest in farming. Evergreen had always believed in Yamhill County and saw that there were investment opportunities to be had.

As Del Smith puts it, "We thought that most of the property, if not all, would appreciate. It was selling for around $400 to $500 an acre and we could see that the value could only increase. We really had two opportunities for earning. One was to farm it efficiently and make a profit operationally, and the second was to, at a later date, sell it and make a capital gain on the investment. The operational profit would be accomplished through making the right selection of crops, and, in turn, through applying good production management and discipline. This would generate the right revenue."

Smith was always on the lookout for farm property that had a potential for something bigger and better than farms, such as the property around the McMinnville Airport where the Evergreen headquarters campus is now located. Today, Evergreen Agricultural Enterprises owns 8,000 acres.

"We knew that as Portland International Airport became 'plugged up,' this airport would be a natural expansion to relieve congestion," he observed. "We've surrounded that airport with 1,800 acres. We were buying that property for $1,500-$3,000 an acre that was worth $20,000-$40,000 two decades later. Weyerhaeuser bought timber land for 25 cents an acre around 1900 that was worth millions per acre by 2000."

Phoebe Hocken, Evergreen's original administrator, had showed the company how important asset sales were. This was especially true with EASL, but it would be true with Evergreen Agricultural Enterprises as well. Land sales had the potential to generate more revenue than operations.

It is also axiomatic that location is the key in real estate. In the case of Yamhill County, Del Smith was certain in the seventies that as Portland grew, its growth was going to come to the south and west, and that is exactly what has happened.

Chapter 6:

PACIFIC EXPANSION AND MIDEAST WAR

(1990-1991)

I N 1989, WHEN EVERGREEN INTERNATIONAL AIRLINES SIGNED
A contract with Qantas to supply cargo service between the
United States and Australia, it was a milestone for Evergreen.
The Qantas contract and the back-haul service that Evergreen
International Airlines was soon able to develop between Hong
Kong and the United States gave the company a significant presence in the Asian marketplace as the nineties began. This positioned Evergreen to be able to respond to the needs and requirements of that market, which were primarily the movement of
freight into North America from what Del Smith characterizes as
"the world's workshop."

The company was no longer simply leasing 747's that others
would operate and maintain, it was now a long-haul airline, and
this paradigm shift would define Evergreen International Airlines
through the decade of the nineties and into the twenty-first century.
With the sudden and unexpected end of US Postal Service operations, the focus of Evergreen International Airlines had changed
overnight from its being a domestic short-haul airline to an international long-haul airline.

The Qantas program began in August 1989 with a DC-8-73F,
but by year end, the service was permanently upgraded to the much
larger, wide-body Boeing 747 to handle the growing cargo require-

ments. The contracts with Qantas were wet-lease, ACMI (Aircraft, Crew, Maintenance and Insurance) packages, in which Evergreen would provide Qantas with freighter capacity from New York to both New Zealand and Australia via Chicago, Los Angeles and Honolulu. This would be Evergreen's first foray into Asia, but it was a one-way market.

Qantas was interested in goods flowing into Australia and New Zealand, but it had no freight returning. The Australian economy had a demand for consumer electronics, automobile parts, pharmaceuticals and cigarettes — the kinds of things that America produces and the Australian economy consumes. Australia consumes high-value-added products, but it does not produce high-value-added products to export back to the United States.

Because flying the 747's back to the United States empty would not have been cost-effective, or even viable, Evergreen International Airlines faced the challenge — and the opportunity — to build a back-haul service out of Asia. The Qantas contract positioned Evergreen aircraft into Asia, which would permit the company to take advantage of the flow of goods coming into the United States from places such as Hong Kong.

In Hong Kong, Evergreen successfully negotiated with the freight forwarding industry to provide a service that they would find attractive and useful. Locations in North America, specifically Columbus, Ohio and New York, were major destination points for cargo moving from Hong Kong and southern China, and these points were easily served by Evergreen International Airlines.

Evergreen's Midwest point of service has always been Columbus, Ohio because major customers were located in Ohio, and because the airline could serve the entire Midwest from Columbus. It has been said that the Chicago area can be served more expeditiously through Columbus than by landing aircraft at Chicago.

By concluding the arrangement with the Hong Kong forwarders, Evergreen International Airlines now had a scenario in place that would fill its 747's on the back-haul as well as the front-haul. This left the middle, and shortest, leg of the route, that from Sydney to Hong Kong. Here, the traffic is primarily in perishable food products originating in Australia. As a United States certificated carrier, Evergreen, like other United States certificated carriers, would face certain restrictions on a route between two non-United States locations. Governments, acting on behalf of their countries' airlines, will place traffic rights restrictions to control competition from foreign carriers. For Evergreen, operations between Sydney and Hong Kong required complex negotiations, but Evergreen prevailed, and was able to set up an operation that would prove to be one of its most successful. With its airplanes filled on all the legs, Evergreen International Airlines had the revenue needed to cover costs, and an appropriate profit margin.

Evergreen International Airlines began with one flight each week serving Qantas, and by 1990, business had doubled. During the nineties, that business would gradually and incrementally grow to a frequency of four flights a week by the end of the decade.

Meanwhile, Air New Zealand had been buying space from Qantas on Evergreen's Qantas service, but by 1991, the traffic had grown substantially, to the point where Air New Zealand could contract with Evergreen International Airlines to buy wet-lease service of its own. With this, Evergreen provided a dedicated 747 freighter to serve only the needs of Air New Zealand. This allowed Evergreen to position more flights into Asia, which, in turn, permitted it to operate more back-hauls into North America from Hong Kong. By 1992, Evergreen could operate as many as five or six flights a week.

The additional 747 flights for Air New Zealand effectively increased service to Evergreen International Airlines' freight forwarding customers in Hong Kong, who desired a growing and higher level of use. From Evergreen's vantage point this was a win for everyone all around. It represented growth in the front-haul which also accommodated the needs of Evergreen customers in Hong Kong, and served everyone extremely well.

MAINTAINING CONTRACTS

Despite Evergreen International Airlines' success in maintaining its wet-lease operations with Qantas for more than a decade, it is worth pointing out that the wet-lease business is a fickle market. Typically, ACMI contracts are for one to two years, and the environment is so competitive that it is difficult to get better terms. The contracts are renewable, but an operator always stands the chance of not having a contract renewed. Despite this, Evergreen International Airlines was typically able to retain its contracts for two important reasons: the first is Evergreen's reliability and service, and the second is that Evergreen can offer customers very competitive rates.

Having been an early pioneer with the concept of wet-leases, Evergreen is also an industry leader in the practice, and has used it very successfully. The company has probably operated more of such contracts than any other carrier in the industry.

DESERT SHIELD/DESERT STORM

The Iraqi invasion of Kuwait on August 2, 1990 resulted in unprecedented international alarm and condemnation. Iraqi leader Saddam Hussein claimed that he was annexing the Kingdom of Kuwait as an Iraqi province, but his actual goal was to seize control of Kuwait's especially rich oil reserves. He also hoped to roll his army south into Saudi Arabia if circumstances permitted.

Evergreen responded by evacuating Boeing technicians from Riyadh, Saudi Arabia, nine days after the invasion of Kuwait. Evergreen also evacuated ARAMCO personnel to Amsterdam, and made ten evacuation flights, carrying foreign workers from Amman, Jordan to Sri Lanka and Bombay, India.

With Iraqi forces threatening to continue their blitzkrieg into the oil fields of Saudi Arabia, President George Bush responded by ordering United States military forces to the region. On August 7, the United States began Operation Desert Shield, the large-scale movement of forces to the Middle East to protect Saudi Arabia. The following day, a US Air Force C-141 carrying an Airlift Control Element landed in Dhahran, becoming the first American military aircraft into the crisis zone. McDonnell Douglas F-15's from the 1st Tactical Fighter Wing, based at Langley AFB, Virginia, and elements of the US Army's 82nd Airborne Division, from Fort Bragg, North Carolina arrived later in the day. United States Airborne Warning & Control (AWACS) aircraft soon began orbiting over Saudi Arabia to monitor Iraqi activities.

The movement of men and materiel to the region soon pushed the capabilities of the US Air Force Military Airlift Command to the limit. On August 17, for the first time in history, the President activated the first stage of the Civil Reserve Air Fleet (CRAF) to increase the availability of airlift to the Middle East.

The Civil Reserve Air Fleet is a program that uses commercial aircraft support capabilities of select United States civil air carriers to rapidly augment military airlift forces during crises and emergency situations. It combines commercial cargo and passenger long-range and short-range airlift capability to meet emergency airlift requirements. Evergreen International Airlines is one of more than two dozen American airlines to have contractually committed resources to CRAF.

The airlines contractually pledge aircraft to the various segments of CRAF, ready for activation when needed. To provide incentives for civil carriers to commit aircraft to the CRAF program and to assure the United States of adequate airlift reserves, the government makes peacetime airlift business available to civilian airlines that offer aircraft to the CRAF. The CRAF has three principal segments, international, national and aeromedical evacuation. The international segment is further divided into the long-range and short-range sections and the national segment into the domestic and Alaskan sections. Assignment of aircraft to a segment depends on the nature of the requirement and the performance characteristics needed.

UNITED STATES TROOPS BOARDING AN EVERGREEN 747.

Three stages of incremental activation allow the United States Transportation Command (USTRANSCOM) commander to tailor an airlift force suitable for the contingency at hand. Stage I is the lowest activation level, Stage II would be used for major regional contingencies, and Stage III would be used for periods of national mobilization. During a crisis, if the Air Mobility Command (Military Airlift Command until 1992), the air component of USTRANSCOM, has a need for additional aircraft, it would request the USTRANSCOM commander take steps to activate the appropriate CRAF stage. Stage II was activated during Operation Desert Shield/Storm. To date, Stage III has not been activated. Each stage of the fleet activation is used only to the extent necessary to provide the amount of commercial augmentation airlift need by the Department of Defense.

Evergreen had been a CRAF carrier before the invasion of Kuwait, and already had planes in the air. Del Smith put three Evergreen DC-8's at the disposal of the Military Airlift Command on August 9, just 48 hours after the President of the United States ordered the troops into the war zone. Soon, the Evergreen 747's would also join the effort.

General H.T. Johnson, who was then the commander-in-chief of
both the Military Airlift Command and the United States Transportation Command, would recall later that "None of the [CRAF] carriers were more responsive in supporting the nation than Evergreen
International Airlines under the leadership of Del Smith."

Evergreen would fly more than 350 cargo missions during the
operation. As General Johnson would remark later, "Given Evergreen's fleet size at the time, that was truly phenomenal."

Prior to the Stage I activation in 1990, however, Evergreen International Airlines 747's had already been working with the Military
Airlift Command under a routine contract, so the transition was
much smoother than for the other CRAF carriers whose fleets were
activated in August 1990. Evergreen International Airlines was a
participant in the incredible airlift that had, by August 21, moved an
unprecedented billion pounds of materiel to Saudi Arabia.

Because Evergreen's contracts under CRAF during the autumn
of 1990 were one-way flights to the Middle East, they actually created a unique business opportunity for Evergreen. The Desert Shield
materiel build-up coincided with the peak season requirement for air
cargo traffic into North America from Hong Kong. Thus, Evergreen
could fly one way trips for the Military Airlift Command into Saudi
Arabia, and then ferry into Hong Kong to pick up loads destined for
North America.

On January 17, 1991, the United States and other international
Coalition forces launched Operation Desert Storm, aimed at liberating Kuwait from the Iraqi occupation.

Many tense moments would occur in the ensuing weeks, especially as Iraq began launching Scud intermediate-range ballistic missiles at Coalition forces with warheads that were feared might contain chemical or biological weapons. To protect the Evergreen crews,
Del Smith purchased chemical protection gear on his own before it
could be supplied for them by United States military sources.

On February 28, Iraq surrendered to the United States-led Coalition, but not before their retreating troops — under orders from

Saddam Hussein himself — set fire to over 700 oil wells and other petroleum facilities. They also opened storage tank valves, releasing 11 million barrels of crude oil into the Persian Gulf. The result was a nearly-catastrophic environmental disaster. The 350-square-mile oil slick in the Gulf was the largest ever, and much larger than that caused by the *Exxon Valdez* spill in Alaska two years before. The toxic smoke from the fires seriously affected air quality in the region and as far away as Turkey and Pakistan.

Sabotage had been expected, albeit not on the scale that actually occurred, so Western damage control experts had been somewhat prepared. Del Smith recognized ahead of time that the crews that would be working to restore the Kuwaiti oil fields after the war would need to work quickly and they would need transportation. With the Kuwaiti infrastructure in a shambles, the most efficient means of getting around would be with helicopters, and Del Smith was determined that they would be Evergreen helicopters.

Even before their retreat, Iraqi forces were known to have destroyed or stolen nearly everything at Kuwait International Airport, except the runways, so it was also clear that crews working in Kuwait after the war — as well as the Kuwaitis themselves — would have an immediate need for ground handling support. It was a requirement that could, and would, be met by EAGLE.

Del Smith and a team that included EAGLE and Evergreen helicopter people met with Kuwaiti officials in London before the war ended to plan strategy. The Evergreen team also met with United States government representatives and with the team from Bechtel, the San Francisco-based engineering firm that had been building oil industry facilities in the Middle East for decades, and who would be a key player in reconstruction.

Evergreen received letters of intent from Kuwait Airways, Kuwait Petroleum Corporation and Bechtel to begin work as soon as the capital city was liberated by Coalition forces. In turn, the firefighting organizations, including Houston-based Boots & Coots and the legendary Red Adair Company, requested Evergreen helicopter support in flying crews in from Dubai when the war was over.

On February 28, the day of the cease fire, John Kiesler, then the Vice President of Operations at Evergreen Helicopters, Inc., received a request for the immediate deployment of two Bell 212's and three Bell 206's. Two days later, Del Smith was in Dubai, meeting with representatives of the firefighting companies. On March 4, Smith arrived in Kuwait City to assess the situation firsthand. His Gulf-stream II was the first non-military aircraft to land at Kuwait International. As one former executive recalled, "Del Smith was the first guy in there when the war ended. He flew in and lined up business with the Kuwaiti corporations and the Kuwaiti government while everybody else was still looking for landing permits."

As Del Smith and the Evergreen personnel soon saw, the situation on the ground in Kuwait in March 1991 was grim. The sooty, toxic smoke from the oil fires hung low over the land and blocked out the sun. Even the most basic of basics were hard to find. Water was at a premium, and even the air was hard to breathe. Helicopter pilots had a difficult task flying through the smoky haze, but landings were often trickier than flying because of all the mines, booby traps and unexploded ordnance that littered the oil field areas. The pilots soon developed the technique of landing in recent vehicle tracks, reasoning that if there had been a mine there, the vehicle would have already detonated it.

In addition to their work transporting the reconstruction crews and their gear, the Evergreen helicopters were pressed into service to evacuate injured and stranded workers. In one instance, Evergreen pilot Ray Anderson rescued the pilot of a downed Kuwait Air Force aircraft before a military medevac helicopter could reach him. An Evergreen helicopter even came to the aid of the crew of a chopper from a rival helicopter company who had run out of fuel.

After the helicopters and the EAGLE crews arrived and went to work, Evergreen brought in a fleet of fixed wing aircraft, including a DHC-6 Twin Otter and two Boeing 727's, one passenger and the

AN EVERGREEN BELL 212 AT WORK IN THE BLAZING OIL FIELDS IN KUWAIT.

other cargo. The latter were used to offer shuttle flights between Dubai and Kuwait through June, when Kuwait Airways was able to re-establish service. Meanwhile, the firefighters and reconstruction crews were also being supported by Evergreen 747 missions being flown from the United States.

Working from bases at Um Al A'ish and Al Ahmedi, the Evergreen helicopters would continue to be the only commercial helicopters aiding the recovery effort for nearly four months, but operations would continue through November 5, 1991, when the last well-head fire was finally extinguished.

Evergreen had been on the scene in Kuwait before the full extent of the damage from Iraqi sabotage was known, and had stayed until the job was done. Evergreen found work opportunities for its helicopters in supporting the oil well firefighting efforts, and the EAGLE staff was instrumental in getting Kuwait International Airport back into working order.

The Evergreen helicopters won praise from many people for flying 843 missions without an accident, an average of 3.5 hours each day, even factoring in the days when the smoke brought visibility to zero. Evergreen could also boast of having had a mission availability rate of 100 percent, despite the primitive, and often hostile, conditions under which the helicopters had to be maintained.

After the war, Evergreen also provided relief flights to Kurds living in the remote regions of northern Iraq, delivering food, water, clothing, and medical supplies.

Evergreen had one of its aircraft on the ground in Kuwait off-loading helicopters the first day after the hostilities ended. Evergreen got up and running by demonstrating that they were *already there.* Del Smith also offered EAGLE's assistance to the Kuwaitis, and gained a commercial advantage over other people in the ground handling and the aircraft operations business. He showed them how Evergreen could help them take advantage of the massive potential revenue stream they had, without having other carriers coming in and taking it away from them. Evergreen provided the aircraft, the personnel and the expertise.

JAPAN AIR LINES OPERATIONS

In early 1991, as Evergreen International Airlines was flying CRAF missions in support of the Military Airlift Command in Operation Desert Shield/Desert Storm, another significant marketing event took place. In addition to service with Qantas and the Hong Kong back-haul operations, Evergreen won another outstanding Asian market contract — an ACMI wet-lease agreement with Japan Air Lines.

This was especially remarkable in that Japan Air Lines had never before hired an outside party to operate aircraft for them on a wet-lease basis. Evergreen had previous relationships with Japan Air Lines in terms of the buying and selling of aircraft and engines, and this relationship led to successful negotiations that started to employ a large number of Evergreen International Airlines aircraft. In fact, the Japan Air Lines business would grow to represent 33 percent of Evergreen International Airlines' total revenue.

The relationship between Japan Air Lines and Evergreen International Airlines began in 1990 at the time of Desert Shield. Each of the nations within the Coalition contributed military forces to help liberate Kuwait from the Iraqi occupation.

Because its constitution forbids Japan from deploying its armed forces abroad, its contribution was carrying non-military air cargo in logistical support of the Coalition forces. Initially, the Japanese government went to Japan Air Lines and Nippon Cargo Airlines, their own country's flag carriers, to request that airlift support. However, both of these carriers denied it on the basis of security and safety for their crewmembers, so the Japanese government approached Evergreen to be its surrogate.

Under the Japan Air Lines contract, the Japanese government contracted directly with Evergreen International Airlines to carry supplies and goods for the United States military from the United States. The cost for these designated flights were paid by the Japanese government. This operation continued through March 1991. At that point, Japan Air Lines issued a three-year contract to Evergreen to wet-lease 747 freighters on commercial routes.

Because of the demographics in Japan, there was a growing crew shortage problem for Japan Air Lines. It became more and more difficult for Japan Air Lines to recruit flight crews, not only to operate their growing passenger fleet, but also for their growing cargo fleet. The solution for them was to allocate their own flight crews to the passenger flights, and to contract out for additional cargo capacity. The Japanese passenger market demanded that the crew flying their aircraft should be Japanese, but cargo flights did not require a Japanese crew. By the end of 1991, Evergreen had six 747's operating under wet-leases for Japan Air Lines.

As Tom Pitzer recalls, "Ground operation and maintenance personnel were selected from within the company in an effort to maintain the highest standard of performance and customer relations within the Japan Air Lines organization. We were an outsider coming into their operation, and had to prove that we were the best choice to be part of their team. It took about six months of hard work, with six arrivals and departures daily, to prove that we were all professionals and could meet their high standards."

This wet-lease contract appeared to represent a milestone for Evergreen International Airlines, because it was Evergreen's largest wet-lease contract to date, and Evergreen was confident that this relationship with Japan Air Lines would be a very long-term arrangement, and one that would allow Japan Air Lines to grow into the North American market.

EVERGREEN 747 FREIGHTERS BEING LOADED.

EVERGREEN INTERNATIONAL AIRLINES EXPANSION

During the 1990 to 1991 period, Evergreen International Airlines enjoyed dramatic growth. Personnel count went from just 2,000 employees to 3,000. The airline went from operating two 747's to as many as eight at the end of 1991. This was principally to serve Qantas, Saudi Arabian Airlines, the Hong Kong back-haul service and Japan Air Lines. Meanwhile, during and after Desert Shield/Desert Storm, Evergreen continued to operate its LogAir DC-9 contract with the Military Airlift Command, which was to become Air Mobility Command in 1992, as well as continuing operations of DC-8's and 727's.

Of course, this build-up required more flight crews to operate the aircraft, more ground personnel to support the aircraft, and more maintenance and engineering technicians to keep the aircraft operating reliably. There was significant growth in the number of individuals hired to perform these tasks with the company, and in the Evergreen management personnel brought in to manage it.

The Japan Air Lines contract also resulted in the opening of an Evergreen sales office in Tokyo and a maintenance operations office at the Japan Air Lines facility in Narita. Under the leadership of Tom Pitzer from the Evergreen International Airlines headquarters in McMinnville, these offices in Japan were staffed by Evergreen experts of the United States, as well as by Evergreen executives who were Asia specialists. This organization meant that Evergreen could provide Japan Air Lines with the personal contact that the contract required.

It seemed at the time that this was certainly a way that Evergreen International Airlines could grow its business and its presence in Asia. However, the Japan Air Lines contract was not as secure as it seemed, and there were other dark clouds gathering on Evergreen's horizon.

Chapter 7:

TRIALS AND TRIUMPH

(1991-1999)

EVEN AS EVERGREEN WAS WORKING LONG HOURS TO SUCCESS-FULLY complete its commitment to Desert Storm, a series of dominoes were being stacked against the company. When those dominoes began to topple, one after another, they would threaten to topple Evergreen itself.

In January 1991, Pan American World Airways, one of the world's oldest and most prestigious airlines, filed for Chapter 11 bankruptcy protection in the Southern District of New York. This would have been of little more than passing interest to Evergreen had it not been for the fact that Pan American was operating seven 747 aircraft that were owned by Evergreen International Airlines. Now bankrupt, Pan American continued to operate the aircraft, but it stopped making its sizable lease payments to Evergreen.

In 1989, Pan American had been short of cash, so it began to borrow. Within a year, the airline had borrowed all that it could, so it needed to sell assets to raise money. Pan American needed its aircraft, but it also needed money, so it was looking for someone who would be willing to buy the airplanes, and then lease them back to Pan American.

Evergreen International Airlines had begun 747 cargo operations in 1985, and these activities were expanding in 1989, so Evergreen saw the Pan American fleet as a good opportunity. Evergreen did not need passenger-configured 747's, but five of the eight Boeing 747 aircraft had already been partially converted to freighter configuration. The manufacturer had cut cargo doors on them when they were designated as part of the original Civil Reserve Air Fleet (CRAF) program. In order to make them useful for carrying troops and/or cargo for the United States military in times of war or national emergency, the cutting of the doors had been financed by the United States government.

Because of these doors, these 747's were very attractive to Evergreen as freighter aircraft. Evergreen didn't need them all right away, but Pan American did, so it looked like a win-win situation for both parties. Pan American could get its cash and airplanes now, and Evergreen borrowed the money to acquire the 747's with a business plan that included a "Freighter Later" program, that called for the aircraft to be converted to freighters as the Pan American lease on each aircraft ended.

The idea was simple. Evergreen borrowed the purchase price from its lender, buy the aircraft, have an orderly lease-back to Pan American, and then take redelivery of the aircraft over time. This brought them into the Evergreen International Airlines fleet gradually, growing the fleet from two 747 aircraft to three and so on. But this plan changed dramatically in January 1991 when Pan American filed bankruptcy.

The Pan American bankruptcy was a shocking turn of events on many levels. Formed in 1927, Pan American World Airways was one of the grandest names in the history of American aviation. For over 60 years it had pioneered transoceanic and intercontinental flying, including the first regularly-scheduled flights between the United States and Europe, and across the Pacific Ocean to Asia. It was the launch platform for aircraft types that set the standard by which all that came later was to be measured. It was the first to offer service across the Atlantic with the Boeing 707 jetliner, and the first with the 747 jumbo jet. It once operated daily flights around the world.

In its prime, which lasted from the late thirties to the early seventies, Pan American World Airways was America's "flag carrier to the world." It was the quasi-official "Chosen Instrument," representing American commercial aviation policy around the world. It has been said that without Pan American the world's air transport would surely be different, and even the destinies of some nations would be changed. By the eighties, however, Pan American's own destiny had changed. Saddled with debt and tired management, and picked at by competitors, the venerable giant began to falter, and finally it failed.

Under Chapter 11, Pan American continued to operate the 747's that Evergreen owned — but they didn't pay the leases. However, Evergreen still needed to pay the banks for the money it had borrowed, but it had no revenue stream. Under Chapter 11, Pan American was supposed to pay their post-bankruptcy bills, but they decided that they didn't want to. Evergreen petitioned the courts, and the courts finally agreed with Evergreen that Pan American needed to pay their post-bankruptcy bills.

In the end, they paid Evergreen the "back rent" through the post-bankruptcy time frame, but Evergreen had to go through the court system and take payment on a much delayed basis. Evergreen International Airlines went through about nine months of having to support the debt service without any revenue stream.

At the same time, Evergreen also petitioned the court to allow it to move on the aircraft to take them back. By May 1991, Evergreen was finally successful in retrieving the airplanes, but the engines were all in unserviceable condition, and all the airframes were in need of extensive maintenance. Pan American had not been maintaining the aircraft to the standard that they needed to be, so when Evergreen took possession of its aircraft, they were essentially not available for service. They were literally unusable. This meant that Evergreen would have to go through a tremendous capital expenditure program, not just to restore the aircraft, but to take them from passenger configuration and put them into full freighter configuration. Five of them had the cargo doors, but

Evergreen needed contracts with Boeing and with Lucas Aerospace to complete the cargo floors in the other two 747's, and to take the passenger interiors out of the aircraft and to install the full cargo loading systems in all seven.

Delta Air Lines was providing Pan American debtor in possession financing, and there was a bankruptcy reorganization plan that allowed Delta to take over certain operations and certain routes and keep Pan American going as an entity. However, Pan American would need to settle with Evergreen prior to the plan being approved by the bankruptcy court. Evergreen would be the stumbling block, so to speak, in that reorganization plan. Evergreen finally negotiated a settlement with Pan American in early December 1991, just before the plan went to court for approval. While it wasn't anywhere close to a full recovery, it was as good as Evergreen could hope for, given the claims on the property.

However, on the day of the plan going to court, Delta pulled out of the reorganization plan, forcing Pan American to file Chapter 7 bankruptcy. Evergreen was left in a very poor position in terms of damage recovery. The Pan American debacle was very costly for Evergreen in the 1989 to 1993 time period. The Evergreen capital expenditure program was about $250 million a year, so Evergreen spent a billion dollars over a four-year period in terms of growth capital, as well as the cost of recovering and restoring capital.

Evergreen had been promised that the aircraft would go through a Structural Durability Upgrade (SDU) at Pan American's expense and they were scheduled for these at Boeing's Wichita, Kansas facility. This was guaranteed in the purchase agreement, and Evergreen had even paid Pan American a premium in order to assure that Pan American would put them through the SDU program and to pay Boeing.

Pan American not only filed bankruptcy, they also defaulted on the SDU contracts, leaving Boeing holding a $22 million lien against two airplanes. In order to get its airplanes, Evergreen had to pay off the lien. In addition to this, there would be the cost of overhauling all the aircraft. For example, the seven airplanes had come with 28 engines on-wing, plus 10 extra engines as part of a collateral package, and every single one of them had to go through an engine overhaul shop. These alone would cost Evergreen between $3 million and $3.5 million apiece.

Under the lease that Evergreen had, Pan American had been obligated to return the engines in mint condition. When Evergreen finally regained possession of the engines, not one was close to mint condition. Indeed, some of the engines were redelivered in boxes, literally in component pieces. Evergreen had to go through all 38 engines and completely restore them. This represented a tremendous amount of cash outflow between 1991 and 1993, without any cash inflow from those aircraft to support it. At the same time, the world economy had gone into a recession, with aviation being especially hard hit.

LOSS AND RETRENCHMENT

Having been hit by the twin blows of the Pan American bankruptcy and global recession during 1991, Evergreen was faced with recovering from a staggering loss at a time when the industry was in a downturn.

One of the ways that Evergreen addressed the cash flow shortfall with the Pan American aircraft was by replacing its short-term bank financing with long-term, high-yield bonds. The investment banking firm of Kidder Peabody helped Evergreen put together a 13.5 percent, 10-year, high yield coupon for $125 million in 1992. That cash went to replace the short-term cash requirements that Evergreen had in terms of some of the recovery and restoration costs.

The next major setback faced by Evergreen International Airlines came with the loss of its most lucrative contracts. Japan Air Lines had been wet-leasing aircraft from Evergreen, but because of the recession, they didn't have enough work for their pilot group. Japan Air Lines found themselves in a difficult situation. The pilot group insisted that the Japan Air Lines pilots be employed before contract pilots, so Japan Air Lines gave Evergreen notice that they were not going to renew their contract.

This abrupt turn of events stunned Evergreen International Airlines, because just a few months earlier, Japan Air Lines had actually been asking Evergreen to add additional aircraft in the renewal period so that they could expand capacity. Now there would be no renewal and no additional work for the Evergreen fleet.

Coming on the heels of the Pan American disaster, the blow of the Japan Air Lines cancellation sent Evergreen International Airlines reeling. Japan Air Lines had represented 33 percent of Evergreen International Airlines' total revenue. All the factors played together.

The Pan American situation was complicated by the recession, and the Kidder Peabody notes had been issued at a time when Evergreen was flying on a higher rate structure. Revenues had been climbing very fast, but suddenly Evergreen was faced with the loss of a vitally important renewal. Evergreen was in a declining yield environment because of the recession, so margins were shrinking very rapidly. In turn, Evergreen was faced with having a payment default on the interest with the Kidder Peabody notes in 1994.

Having suffered the three strikes of the Pan American bankruptcy, the Japan Air Lines cancellation and the recession, Evergreen should logically have been counted out in those dark days of 1993 and 1994. With the last straw of default on the Kidder Peabody notes, the conventional wisdom told Del Smith that it was time that he too, like Pan American, should file for Chapter 11 bankruptcy protection. However, this was not his way of doing business. He decided that Evergreen would fight its way out of the hole into which it had fallen.

His first step was to eliminate any cost inefficiencies from the system. Then he redeployed the airplanes that had been flying for Japan Air Lines, in order to improve the revenue stream as much as possible. Evergreen took this capacity and put much of it to work on a dry-lease to United Parcel Service. Luckily the airplanes never missed a day of work.

Evergreen management cut costs as deeply as they could, going through a reorganization of the cost structure, trying to trim both operating costs and overhead costs, while aggressively selling assets. Evergreen would simply eliminate any unproductive or inefficient assets that could not earn a relative margin. Operations with the Boeing 727 aircraft that had been acquired in the eighties were discontinued, as were DC-8 operations. Evergreen International Airlines would cease to be a 727 operator in 1993, and stopped flying DC-8's in 1996.

These older jetliners had become too cost inefficient in their respective markets. The DC-8's had opened Evergreen International Airlines' international route structure, but they had been replaced by 747 cargo aircraft. The 727's were widely used in the express market, but they were becoming less efficient for Evergreen than newer types. By 1995, Evergreen International Airlines would be redefined as an international carrier using 747 aircraft and a domestic carrier using DC-9 aircraft.

Despite the hard times, the Evergreen marketing group was putting the capacity of the fleet to work at the right rates.

BRIEFLY INTO CHINA

After the Japan Air Lines contract ended abruptly in 1994, Evergreen International Airlines closed its Tokyo office in order to concentrate more resources in its Shanghai, China office. In May 1993, Evergreen had commenced an all-cargo service between the United States and China under the authority granted by the United States Department of Transportation. Because of the bilateral agreement between the United States and China, only one American airline would be permitted to have such an authority. Evergreen had applied for and won the traffic rights in competition with Federal Express, United Parcel Service and Polar Air Cargo.

Both United Parcel Service and Federal Express were especially anxious for this authority because they each offer door-to-door service, and they really pride themselves on taking care of their customers by themselves, exclusively. However, by being door-to-door integrated carriers, they would not be able to provide a "neutrally acceptable service" to the air freight industry at large. In other words, their aircraft would be dedicated to their own ground operations as a first priority. Other freight forwarders would be of a lower priority. By the very nature of the product and the service that they provide, Federal Express and United Parcel Service would effectively exclude other air freight industry participants, such as the freight forwarders. Because it had no ground shipping operations in China, Evergreen would theoretically be "neutral," and treat all customers equally.

The difference between the air courier companies and Evergreen International Airlines is that Evergreen is primarily an air cargo carrier serving the air freight forwarders, the "travel agents" of the freight industry. The air freight forwarding industry is a huge industry that serves all kinds of shippers, great and small, but a specialized, door-to-door service would exclude a very important component of the air freight industry that is organized to serve the entire industry.

Evergreen International Airlines won the authority, but difficulties subsequently experienced in developing the China market led the company to sell its traffic rights to Federal Express in 1995. Through the remainder of the decade, Federal Express would be the only United States carrier permitted to operate all-cargo service into China on a scheduled basis. Of course, other airlines, including Evergreen, were still permitted to operate charter flights in and out of China.

Early in the twenty-first century, however, Evergreen would resume operations into China, and the company now maintains sizable facilities in Beijing.

DARKNESS BEFORE THE DAWN

Throughout the mid-nineties, Evergreen's bond holders were being continuously updated on Evergreen's business recovery plan. In 1996, however, a group of bond holders filed action in court. This was because the expectation was high that Evergreen would pay off those bonds. The lawsuit accelerated expectations, and then the bond holders filed their lawsuit to inflate the price.

Evergreen, now poised for recovery, was about to be tossed another series of difficulties. After the lawsuit, a second blow would be problems lurking in the heart of Evergreen's most valuable working asset, the 747 fleet. Three of Evergreen International Airlines' dozen 747's had been converted as freighters by the General American Transportation Corporation (GATX) Airlog, rather than by the manufacturer, as Evergreen's other freighters were, and suddenly, the Federal Aviation Administration issued an airworthiness directive affecting GATX converted aircraft. Just as Evergreen was putting the recovery together and was about to turn the corner, three of its most essential assets were grounded. With 25 percent of Evergreen's 747 capacity now unavailable for service, hope of recovery was further delayed.

The third, and potentially fatal, strike was a lawsuit from Minneapolis-based Cargill, Inc. One of the world's largest privately-held companies, they were a major holder of the bonds that Evergreen had issued in 1992. Cargill, working with the investment management company TCW (Trust Company of the West), wanted to convert its non-performing bonds into equity, and thus, to take control of Evergreen.

Just as Evergreen was primed and positioned to turn the corner, the company abruptly lost capacity. Because of the aggressive lawsuit over the bonds, and because the expectations of Evergreen being able to pay them off was now dampened by the unanticipated airworthiness directive, Evergreen's revenue and profits were seriously threatened by lack of capacity.

Evergreen needed to take action quickly. Once again, Evergreen was forced to start contemplating seeking bankruptcy protection under Chapter 11. This was not Del Smith's way of doing business. There had to be another way.

"I have learned in life that even adversity can be the launching pad of something bigger and better," Del Smith said. "I came out of an orphanage, but I was blessed with an adoptive mother with a big capacity for love, and who taught me to be honest, to work hard, and that success can be made to follow misfortune."

Faced with the most serious crisis in Evergreen's history, Del Smith was determined that success *would* be made to follow misfortune. He reached for one of his time-tested strategies, that of putting together a "mastermind alliance" of people whose complementary expertise could solve the problem.

THE MASTERMIND ALLIANCE

The Evergreen financial team started looking at alternatives, finally hitting upon the right chemistry when Evergreen matched up with Tom Benninger at Donaldson, Lufkin & Jenrette (DLJ), one of the top investment firms in the United States. DLJ's Banking Group does investment and merchant banking, provides funding for companies via direct investment, and also manages and underwrites securities. In the early autumn of 1996, Chase Manhattan Bank entered the picture as the financier.

At first, in order to protect their interest, Chase Manhattan wanted Evergreen to file Chapter 11. At that time, "pre-packaged" Chapter 11's had become increasing common as a way of working out situations such as those in which Evergreen found itself. Pre-packed Chapter 11's involved putting together a financial plan and working out an agreement with creditors prior to going into court. This could shorten the time frame to about four weeks, compared with Chapter 11's that had occurred in the early nineties, such as that of Pan American, that took nine months and failed.

Del Smith did not like the sound of "Chapter 11," however it was "packaged." Chase Manhattan was very aggressively pushing Evergreen toward that end, but the Evergreen management team did not favor that at all. Evergreen's customers, which are international customers, don't necessarily understand Chapter 11 bankruptcy law, and anything with the word "bankruptcy" in it has negative connotations internationally. Whatever the reasoning or the outcome, bankruptcy of any form would certainly have hurt Evergreen in the marketplace. Evergreen's competitors were already trying to use that against them. Evergreen continued to stretch Chase Manhattan to be creative.

Del Smith reasoned that there certainly had to be a way out that did not involve Chapter 11. He also brought in Jay Goffman of Skadden, Arps, Slate, Meagher & Flom — Evergreen's New York law firm. Goffman is a well-known bankruptcy expert, who had first worked with Evergreen in dealing with the Pan American Chapter 7 bankruptcy situation. Goffman, along with Chase Manhattan and DLJ, became Evergreen's "workout team." This group would ultimately come up with a very aggressive plan.

Del Smith had a group of people around him that could get the job done. He had his Mastermind Alliance. It was comprised of people from both within the company and without. It was the combination of Tom Benninger's negotiation skills and knowledge of the bond holders, Jay Goffman's knowledge of what you can or can't do in a "pre-pack," Chase Manhattan's expertise in syndication, Evergreen's own core management and administrative team, and Del Smith's resolve.

The eventual success of this Mastermind Alliance underscored Del Smith's management philosophy. In the workout team, Evergreen had a group of people, each of whom had expertise in a different area and contributed to the ultimate solution. It is a true testimony to how Del Smith has run his company through all these years. It was yet another illustration of how he accomplishes things that others say are impossible.

"It was a really incredible experience to be a part of Evergreen's internal team," recalls Susie Graves, the Assistant to the Chairman. "All of us took this situation very seriously. It wasn't just the company's livelihood at stake; it was ours too — as it could impact our jobs, not to mention the impact to our customers and vendors. Days, evenings and weekends were spent preparing for the presentation to be given to the syndicated group of financial institution representatives. Mr. Smith truly led by example — as he typically does. It is a leadership quality for which I have always respected him. I recall Mr. Smith having been at almost every session — encouraging, guiding, leading and even orchestrating this presentation effort with our team. The presentation was given in Arizona and it went off without a glitch. The presentation was concise, goal-driven, historical, honest, positive, professional and profit-oriented — ending with — 'the best is yet to come!' It was truly an exciting and memorable experience for me to have played even a tiny part in that successful event — certainly it was a critical moment in Evergreen's history."

IMPLEMENTING THE RECOVERY PLAN

Chase Manhattan put together corporate financing to tender for the bonds, and Evergreen used the proceeds to buy the bonds back at full par, plus accrued interest to the extent that Evergreen could negotiate with the bond holders. Evergreen went into syndication and closed on May 7, 1997.

The business plan that Evergreen put together to restructure the company in terms of its operations, coupled with the restructuring of the company balance sheet, proved to be a very successful strategy. Evergreen would grow from $2 million in profit in fiscal 1996 to $12 million in profit during fiscal 1997 and $26 million in profit in fiscal 1998.

As Del Smith summed up the situation: "The banks recognized that we faced up to a tough situation and that we took the moral high road. We didn't dump "iron" back on the banker's lap, we just said 'let us have more latitude on the amortization.' Nor did we ever ask anybody to take a haircut. Every banker got 100 percent of principal and 100 percent of interest."

By 1996, all of Evergreen's strategies for recovery and future growth that had been implemented earlier in the decade had succeeded. The airline industry had come out of the recession, and the margins, industry-wide, had turned the corner. Evergreen was in a very good position to start growing again. Having weathered the recession of the early nineties and the aviation industry downturn, Evergreen faced the beginning of the twenty-first century in robust health. The business plan forged in the darkest hour of the nineties had been proven. In the final years of the twentieth century, revenues grew and so did profits. Evergreen had been positioned to take the ups, downs and uncertainty that are inevitable in the industry in its stride.

Evergreen was not highly leveraged, and, as such, it was able to provide a high level of service at a low cost for Evergreen's customers.

By the turn of the century Evergreen had developed non-airline service businesses which were almost counter-cyclical. As airlines go through downturns, they out-source more of their non-core businesses, which increases Evergreen's revenue at EAGLE, Evergreen's ground handling company. At the same time, this situation also increases revenue at Evergreen Maintenance Center, Evergreen's maintenance facility, because airlines want to keep their overhead under control, but they still need to have their fleet maintained.

Thus, as the airline industry goes through its cycles, the support businesses, which are growing very rapidly, tend to balance that force. By growing those support services, Evergreen had evolved a very aggressive campaign against the industry cycles.

The support services had been developed initially as support entities for Evergreen International Airlines, but they had been doing third-party business in the early nineties. During the period of turmoil and transition for Evergreen International Airlines, the focus for both EAGLE and Evergreen Maintenance Center had been to grow this third-party business very aggressively and very rapidly. The idea was to turn them into independent profit centers, and this happened almost overnight. The need in the industry was so great for those services that it was very easy to go from 20 percent third-party business to 80 percent in a matter of just a year or two.

Overall, Evergreen had continued to thrive because it never lost sight of its core values and entrepreneurial spirit. It all goes back to the motto that Del Smith coined when he was marketing the services of his first helicopter, and that is simply the notion of delivering "quality without compromise."

"Del Smith still has that same entrepreneurial spirit that he had when he was building the company back in the sixties," Evergreen Chairman Tim Wahlberg said. "He has always had an intuitive sense for recognizing the earning opportunities. The markets were out there, and he always knew what was necessary to respond to the opportunities. I give a lot of credit to Mr. Smith for laying this all out for us, and for showing us the way to come up with a diversified and quality product. This was demonstrated in our early years of growth, and it continues today in the way that Evergreen continues to grow, by being aware of opportunities and understanding the economics to be successful."

John Kiesler, with more than three decades of service with Evergreen Helicopters, added that "Winston Churchill said never to give up, and this is exactly how we have been successful in what we do. It is because of Mr. Smith's vision and leadership."

ORGANIZATIONAL CHANGES

Evergreen International Aviation was created in 1978 as a holding company for Evergreen Helicopters, the original Evergreen company, and the subsidiaries acquired in 1975 — Evergreen International Airlines and Evergreen Air Center (known as Evergreen Maintenance Center after 2007). In 1997, against the backdrop of a growing number of subsidiaries, Evergreen Holdings was formed as an umbrella for all of them. All of the Evergreen operating companies had been contained under the umbrella of Evergreen International Aviation since 1978, but from 1997, Evergreen International Aviation itself became a subsidiary of a new, super holding company known as Evergreen Holdings, Inc.

In August 1998, Evergreen merged another affiliate company called Evergreen Ventures into the Evergreen Holdings group. Evergreen Ventures had been created in 1989, primarily as an asset acquisition company that could secure financing for various aircraft types, and lease them into the operating companies, typically the airline company or the helicopter company. The reason this was necessary was that the Evergreen group of companies had been highly leveraged at the time. Evergreen had grown rapidly and used a high degree of leverage to finance that growth.

Evergreen Ventures provided the capacity to take on additional leverage. The strategy to increase capacity within the fleet was to create a financing vehicle that was affiliated by common ownership, but outside of the Evergreen group of companies. Evergreen Ventures was able to purchase assets, finance them separately, and then lease them to the Evergreen group of companies. Through the nineties, there had been no activity between Evergreen Ventures and the operating companies other than the leasing of aircraft, which was good for the bondholders because that generated operational income.

The change occurred in two phases. In Phase One, begun in August 1998, Evergreen merged Evergreen Ventures into the Evergreen group. The tax advantages to having the accelerated depreciation had run out in Evergreen Ventures, and there were both capital structure and tax advantages to merge the two companies together.

Phase Two of that restructuring was to then obtain a new $73 million facility. This was essentially an amendment to the existing facility, but it allowed Evergreen $40 million of available capital for strategic acquisitions. With a $40 million facility, Evergreen could acquire an asset very quickly and refinance that asset with permanent financing after effecting the acquisition. Evergreen could move more quickly and stay out of a bidding process on acquisitions that tend to occur when a company is trying to arrange financing.

One of the major organizational innovations undertaken at Evergreen in the closing years of the twentieth century was the decentralization of banking and cash management activity. Prior to 1997, the management process within the finance department was such that Evergreen International Aviation, Inc., the holding company, managed all cash and all banking activity for all the individual operating companies. Until the decentralization, these operating companies had no independent banking relationships. Each company had some debt of its own, but the holding company controlled a centralized cash management system. All the cash that was generated by each operating company was upstreamed to Evergreen International Aviation, and the parent company had control over where the cash went.

According to John Irwin, "Del Smith's concept has always been that 'If you can't measure it, you can't manage it,' so what Evergreen attempted to do with this decentralization of financial responsibility was to create more accountability, more motivation, and more independence, and to get away from the finance department at Evergreen International Aviation dictating to the operating companies."

THE AIRLINE REBOUNDS

In the years leading up to the mid-nineties, Evergreen International Airlines had been hard hit by a number of setbacks. The unexpected loss of the United Parcel Service contract in 1987, and the US Postal Service contract in 1989 was followed by the equally unexpected loss in 1994 of the Japan Air Lines contract, which had been accounting for 33 percent of Evergreen's total revenues during the dark days of the Pan American crisis. On top of this came the difficulties in China that compelled Evergreen to sell its operating authority in that market in 1995.

AN EVERGREEN 747 LOADING AT RICKENBACKER AIRPORT IN OHIO.

Despite this, however, Evergreen International Airlines remained strong in the Asian market, with a growing number of flights for Qantas and Air New Zealand, and an increasing presence in Hong Kong. Evergreen's senior management knew that the future of the company depended upon sales.

At about this same time, Evergreen was successful in restarting its business with the Postal Service with a program to support Express Mail and Priority Mail delivery service through a West Coast hub at Oakland, California. Evergreen International Airlines was able to utilize DC-9 freighter aircraft that were on contract with the Air Mobility Command's LogAir program, and put them to work for the US Postal Service. Operations were originally day and night, but had been reduced to service at night only. By the time that the service was discontinued in August 1999, it had gone back to day and night.

The expansion of Evergreen International Airlines' integrator business, which had suffered in the early nineties, continued to rebound in the late nineties. In 1999, Emery Worldwide announced that its new Boeing 747 wide-body service would be provided by Evergreen through a lease arrangement for two aircraft. Operations would serve customers in Southern California through Los Angeles International Airport, as well as customers in the southeastern United States through Raleigh-Durham in North Carolina, and in Puerto Rico by way of San Juan. Also in 1999, Evergreen was operating a DC-9-30 for DHL Worldwide Express into DHL's hub in Cincinnati from Syracuse and Rochester in upstate New York, and from St. Louis.

WORKING WITH FAST AIRWAYS IN AFRICA

In addition to its work with major European flag carriers, Evergreen International Airlines also operates wet-lease operations on behalf of smaller airlines who do not have the expertise for wide-body freighter operations. For example, beginning in September 1997, Evergreen International Airlines wet-leased a 747 to Kenya-based Fast Airways, an affiliate of the Merhav Group. This aircraft was earmarked for operations between Luxembourg and Johannesburg, South Africa, returning via Harare, Zimbabwe, and Nairobi, Kenya. Luxembourg was chosen for the northern terminus because the majority of the southbound freight that was being carried by Fast Airways originated with Cargolux.

The Fast Airways southbound freight included industrial tools and precision machinery, as well as parts and components for vehicles, primarily for vehicle interiors. These automotive parts were incorporated into cars and trucks manufactured in South Africa by both Volkswagen and Mercedes Benz for the African market, as well as for export back into the European market.

Among the northbound freight that was carried back to Luxembourg by the Fast Airways service were animal hides that were being taken to Europe for preparation as leather and then returned to South Africa to be incorporated into the interiors of automobiles manufactured in South Africa.

However, Fast Airways picked up the majority of its northbound cargo from Harare and Nairobi, rather than from Johannesburg. Though it's a further distance, there was not as much revenue freight from Johannesburg as from Harare and Nairobi. This freight consisted primarily of flowers, fruit, vegetables and other perishables.

Flying freshly cut flowers can present some unique challenges. Most of the time when you push a box on an airplane you don't have to worry about whether its hot or cold, but flying flowers is one of the toughest things to do because of climate. They're very temperature sensitive, so there is a temperature monitoring system in each pallet that tracks and records the temperature continuously, from the flower farm in Africa to the market in Europe.

From 1997 through 1999, Fast Airways operated on a frequency of three rotations each week, with refuelling stops in Cairo. The refuelling stops were necessary because of the weight of the loads, often including as much as 100 tons of flowers, and because of the fuel requirements for operating through Nairobi, which is situated at an elevation of 5,580 feet above sea level.

Under its lease with Evergreen, Fast Airways was actually the first indigenous Kenyan carrier to operate main deck 747 cargo aircraft. By providing that aircraft and service, Evergreen International Airlines was assisting a Kenyan company with Evergreen expertise, crews, and experience to get into the large main deck cargo market. The cargo picked up on the northbound leg of the Fast Airways route allowed the Kenyan economy to benefit from the export of those goods.

Evergreen has been singled out for congratulations from the United States State Department for the work being done in Africa, for what has been described as helping to "build the bridge from Nairobi to Western Europe," and for helping the Kenyan people to build a better economy. Fast Airways could not have done it without the Evergreen lease, because they could not have purchased their own 747 with their own capital resources. Evergreen International Airlines operated the flights, but they also trained local people for operational and managerial work.

Other interesting service to Africa provided by Evergreen International Airlines included carrying electoral documents for the South African elections and currency which has been produced in Europe. Evergreen International Airlines also carries cargo into Africa on a commercial basis for groups such as the United Nations High Commission for Refugees (UNHCR), the International Committee of the Red Cross, and the World Food Program, which is a logistical arm of the United Nations.

During the Rwanda emergency in 1994-1995, Evergreen International Airlines carried humanitarian relief supplies for the World Food Program that included food, tents, blankets, ground sheets, and even four-wheel-drive vehicles. Within the space of 14 days, Evergreen International Airlines completed 10 rotations with two 747 freighters through the airport at Bujumbura in neighboring Burundi. The final destination of the goods was Kigali, Rwanda, but the Kigali airfield wasn't suitable for 747s, so the materiel had to be trucked into the emergency areas. Still, the supplies delivered by Evergreen were there two weeks before overland distribution of additional relief supplies caught up.

THE KOSOVO CRISIS

During the closing years of the twentieth century, one of the world's most serious humanitarian crises was Yugoslavia's ethnic cleansing rampage in the formerly autonomous Yugoslav province of Kosovo that reached its horrible climax in 1999. In Kosovo, which was then an autonomous province within Yugoslavia, 90 percent of the people were Albanian-speaking Muslims. The Yugoslav government had traditionally allowed them to observe Islamic holy days, as well as to have schools in which the classes were taught in their language. In 1989, however, Yugoslav President Slobodan Milosevic stripped Kosovo of its autonomous status and declared the Albanian language unofficial. Two years later, a referendum showed that most Kosovo Albanians favored forming an independent republic. Yugoslavia refused to accept such an idea and a decade of violence ensued.

In March 1999, an agreement was finally reached that called for a return of autonomy to Kosovo, but Yugoslav forces invaded Kosovo and began burning entire villages and murdering Kosovar people by the hundreds. As the air forces of the North Atlantic Treaty Organization (NATO) began air strikes against Yugoslavia, tens of thousands of people began to flee Kosovo, spilling across the borders into neighboring countries, especially Macedonia and Albania.

The enormous influx of refugees escaping Kosovo overtaxed the resources of the nations in which they sought refuge, and an international humanitarian relief effort was launched. This is where Evergreen stepped in to help. Evergreen Chairman Del Smith responded to the Kosovo refugee crisis by donating a 747 cargo aircraft to carry relief supplies collected by the Feed The Children organization. Smith, his wife Maria and Feed The Children executive vice president Frances Jones were on hand at John F. Kennedy International Airport in New York City to help launch the big 747 freighter, which had been christened as the "Feed The Children Express."

On its first mercy mission, Evergreen's "Feed The Children Express" was loaded with over 200,000 pounds of emergency supplies for children and adults, including baby food, non-perishable milk, flour, pasta, canned goods, diapers, coats, blankets, and over-the-counter medicines. The relief flight landed in Athens, Greece. From there, supplies were transferred to trucks for transport to Tirana, Albania's capital city.

Meanwhile, in Oregon, an estimated 100,000 people were mobilized by a disparate group of organizations — including the Archdiocese of Portland, Portland-based Northwest Medical Teams International and Providence Health System — to donate money and supplies for Kosovo refugees. For the second time, Evergreen International Aviation donated a 747 freighter to carry relief aid destined for Albania. The flight, loaded with 100 tons of contributed items, including medicine and medical equipment, departed from Portland

Airport after receiving a blessing from Father Michael Maslowsky, director of pastoral services for the archdiocese. The value of Evergreen's gift of this second 747 and related expenses was estimated to be $500,000. Including these two donated flights, Evergreen International Airlines would make five relief trips into Athens with tents, blankets and food.

EVERYDAY OPERATIONAL CHALLENGES

If it can be transported by a 747 aircraft, the odds are good that Evergreen International Airlines has transported it. The company's fleet has carried everything from racing boats to herds of goats. Its repertoire has ranged from delicate communications satellites to the biggest electrical generator ever moved by air.

Beginning in 1999, Evergreen International Airlines carried modules and components for the International Space Station (ISS) from the US to the Baikonur Cosmodrome in Russia. Baikonur is in an area not commonly traversed by carriers from outside Russia, so the Evergreen flight had to stop and pick up a "navigator," a person who speaks Russian and who could translate between the flight crew and ground control.

In 1998, Evergreen International Airlines had an especially unusual Transatlantic charter that provides a good example of the high level of support that is delivered to its customers. An Evergreen 747 carried a load of large aquatic animals from Miami, Florida to a new oceanarium in Lisbon, Portugal. There were 14 large sharks and rays in an arrangement of pools on board the aircraft, with a large number of attendants. The pools were modified hot tubs provided by Jacuzzi in Florida that were strapped to pallets and distributed around the main deck of the aircraft.

The 747 was specifically modified by the addition of electrical power to the main deck to supply power to the air pumps, because the animals are very sensitive. They cannot go without their air for much longer than an hour or two, so Evergreen had battery back-ups with the pumps. That was something that Evergreen's crew just did on their own. The engineering department took the lead, and the customers greatly appreciated it. One of the great strengths of Evergreen as an airline is going the extra mile for the customer.

The tops of the hot tubs were not sealed because the attendants accompanying the animals had to have access, so they just had lift-off covers on them. It is normal in operations like that for the Evergreen flight crew to carry out a very low angle of attack ascent and descent as well, but to avoid upsetting the animals, the take-off and landing required an extremely skilled flight crew and a great deal of runway.

The marine biologist that was on board accompanying the animals commented on what a smooth ride it had been. "Sharks are incredibly sensitive animals," he said. "They navigate by way of the Earth's magnetic pulls in the ocean. When you get them out of that, they become very confused and stressed."

Also in 1998, Evergreen International Airlines was called on to transport the national equestrian teams from Italy, France, Spain, Portugal, the Netherlands, and the United Kingdom. Evergreen carried 58 priceless show horses, plus 12 attendants, from Amsterdam to Calgary in western Canada for the Spruce Meadows Nations Cup event. The animals were loaded on the main deck in double and triple horse stalls supplied by Lufthansa Cargo. Evergreen already had experience carrying race horses for Qantas, usually between Melbourne, Australia and other points such as Hong Kong and the United States.

The airline has also carried exotic animals from giraffes and ostriches to a pair of Bengal tigers that were transported from Nairobi to Frankfurt. "It's a little bit strange to look back through the cargo access door and the restraining net into the cage with a Bengal tiger when you're flying at 33,000 feet," the pilot laughed. "You just hope he's well fed."

In June 1999, Evergreen International Airlines airlifted the McClaren and Benetton Formula One racing teams and their cars from Montreal in Canada to London Stansted Airport in the United Kingdom on behalf of Lufthansa Cargo. It was a very high profile operation for Lufthansa, but they had been declined the necessary route authority, so they went to Evergreen because there is no other carrier that can do what Evergreen can on such short notice.

In March 2000, Evergreen International Airlines donated a 747 flight to carry 10,000 apple trees from Oregon to North Korea. Called "Operation Appleseed," the flight was made on behalf of Mercy Corps International, a non-profit relief agency, in response to severe famine that was gripping the communist-managed northern part of the Korean peninsula. Mercy Corps intended to use the Oregon-grown seedlings to start a 480-acre orchard in South Pyongan province. The trees, which included five apple varieties, would potentially produce more than a thousand tons of fruit annually at maturity.

Flying the 10,000 trees required special systems in the 747's cargo hold, because the trees had to be kept within a moderate range of 70 degrees Fahrenheit. There was no temperature monitoring gear for the compartment, so Evergreen installed a remote sensing thermometer and 200 feet of line to give the crew an indication of the status of their cargo. It worked very nicely. They left the heat off in the cargo hold in the beginning of the flight, and switched it on as the temperature started to drop.

In addition to the demands of unique cargo, Evergreen International Airlines also faces the challenge of airports where operational conditions are especially extreme. This includes landing and taking off at cites that are located in the thin air of very high elevations, such as Bogota, Colombia (9,200 feet); and Quito, Ecuador (9,850 feet).

Some of the most challenging airports that Evergreen International Airlines has encountered are those within Russia and the former Soviet Union, which the airline started to serve in the nineties after the collapse of the Soviet government. They did not have the money to maintain their runways, and it gets so cold there that the ground freezes, and it buckles when it thaws.

Evergreen helicopters have also gone to the ends of the earth in support of various customers. For example, in 1992, Evergreen Helicopters — supported by Evergreen 747's and EAGLE logistical personnel — flew in support of the National Science Foundation in the first American commercially funded scientific study of Antarctica.

Later in the 1990s, Evergreen Helicopters, Inc. worked with the Columbia River Bar Pilots' Association to provide transportation services in the vicinity of the Columbia River Bar. Located where the mighty Columbia River empties into the Pacific Ocean, the vicinity of the Bar is one of the most treacherous waterways in the world. The shifting sands of the bar are hazard enough, but the unpredictable winds that howl off the North Pacific multiply the risk. In the early years of navigation across the Columbia River Bar, hundreds of ships were lost. For many years, however, the Columbia River Bar pilots have made their services available to help guide ships across.

The Bar Pilots Association will come aboard merchant vessels to guide them on the 90 minute trip between the Port of Astoria, Oregon, on the south shore of the Columbia, or the Port of Knappton, Washington, on the north shore, into the safer waters of the Pacific beyond a depth of 30 fathoms.

For most of their history, the Columbia River Bar pilots were rowed out to the ships in sturdy whaleboats, and it was not until the 1960s that the use of motorboats became common. Even with motorboats, the life of the Columbia River Bar pilot was a hard one. As one Bar pilot remarked, the Evergreen helicopters "changed our lives."

THE SPACE AGENCY PARTNERSHIP

Evergreen aircraft have never flown into outer space — although if there was a customer on the moon that needed cargo service, Evergreen would find a way — but the company *has* worked with America's space agency. Since 1991, Evergreen Maintenance Center had maintained NASA's 747 Space Shuttle Carrier Aircraft (SCA),

EVERGREEN MAINTAINS NASA'S SPACE SHUTTLE CARRIER, PART OF ITS
ONGOING COMMITMENT TO NASA. (PHOTO COURTESY OF NASA)

and in 1999, the agency asked Evergreen International Airlines to
place a small instrument on board one of their 747 aircraft to map
radiation levels at various altitudes around the world.

Evergreen volunteered to become a partner in this project — in
cooperation with the NASA/Goddard Space Flight Center in Mary-

land — to aid the scientific community in understanding more about radiation levels and their long-term effects on crewmembers and instrumentation in aircraft. The device, known as the LIULIN-3M spectrometer, was placed on an Evergreen International Airlines 747 out of New York's John F. Kennedy International Airport, and was left on board for several months to collect data. A similar device accompanied John Glenn and the crew of Space Shuttle Mission STS-95 in October 1998.

The LIULIN-3M evolved from an international cooperative project by a team of Bulgarian, Russian, German, and American scientists. The results of the data gathered on Evergreen flights was shared at several international radiation conferences, including the 36th Annual International Nuclear and Space Radiation Effects Conference, held in Norfolk, Virginia in July 1999. Because Evergreen 747's traverse the world — from New York to Australia, to Asia, and to Central Europe — its participating aircraft generated a significant amount of information for the project.

Evergreen International Aviation President Tim Wahlberg's summarized the history of Evergreen's relationship with the space agency: "Evergreen is proud to continue its long standing history of supporting NASA's important missions with our quality maintenance and operations expertise."

ANGELS OF MERCY

Back in April 1961, an Evergreen helicopter made an emergency flight from McMinnville to Portland, Oregon to carry 29 pints of blood that were needed for a patient undergoing open heart surgery. Over the course of the next four decades, Evergreen helicopter and fixed-wing aircraft crews stepped in to help in countless medical emergencies. In 1999, Evergreen's humanitarian story came full circle when the American Red Cross in Portland called on Evergreen for help. A man who was scheduled for surgery in Juneau, Alaska, had donated his own blood for the operation, but the blood had been sent to Portland for tests. It now had to be returned to Juneau, but no commercial airline would agree to transport the blood.

According to registered nurse Julie Anne Borman, normal blood delivery became a problem when it was learned that the two pints of blood "were infected with a virus." Ms. Borman, assistant director at the Red Cross Pacific Northwest Regional Blood Services in Portland, said that "The commercial carriers refused to carry the units, though we assured them of the safety measures that we take in packing blood for transport."

The Red Cross contacted Life Alaska, which, in turn, referred them to the fire chief in Ketchikan, who told the Red Cross to call Evergreen, who answered the challenge. Evergreen pilots delivered the blood from Portland and handed it off to a Red Cross staff nurse at the Juneau Airport. From there, it was on its way to the hospital where it was needed.

Also during 1999, Evergreen put together another mercy flight in a situation where limitation on their operations prevented the airline from doing the actual flying. In Accra, Ghana, a five-year-old boy named Samuel Neeplo had a severe infection in his legs, and gangrene was setting in. The boy was in danger of losing not only his legs, but his life.

In Charlotte, North Carolina, the Carolinas Medical Center could save young Samuel, but a way had to be found to get him across the Atlantic quickly, so they contacted Del Smith at Evergreen. Evergreen itself did not have an aircraft available for such a flight, but Smith knew that EAGLE had a ground handling relationship with Ghana Airways at John F. Kennedy International Airport in New York. After a few phone calls from Evergreen, Samuel Neeplo was on his way to the United States via Ghana Airways. Thanks to the fast thinking of Del Smith and the Evergreen team, a little boy's life was saved.

Throughout the 1990's, there would be many instances of Evergreen personnel and machines operating as "angels of mercy." One outstanding example came on August 13, 1993, when an Evergreen helicopter responded quickly to the crash of an aircraft carrying seven missionaries in the Bering Sea off Alaska. Evergreen's Eric Pentilla received the American Eurocopter Golden Hour Award for "outstanding heroism in a specific emergency," the world's most renowned peacetime civilian helicopter award.

In Africa, the company's support for the World Health Organization effort to eradicate River Blindness earned recognition from that agency as their most successful relief program. Elsewhere on that continent, Evergreen supported United Nations peacekeeping efforts and other programs in Angola, Liberia, Mozambique, and the Western Sahara regions during the 1990's. Evergreen evacuated United States government employees and other American citizens from the Republic of the Congo during the period of civil unrest in 1991. In Somalia, Evergreen supported United Nations peacekeeping operations, using Boeing 747 aircraft to deliver supplies. Between August 1998 and January 1999, Evergreen Helicopters provided freight and passenger transportation and evacuation services for the International Committee of Red Cross in Sierra Leone.

At home, Evergreen responded to numerous natural disasters during the 1990's, including Hurricane Andrew in 1992, the costliest natural disaster to strike the United States in the twentieth century. The following year, Evergreen DC-9 aircraft carried sandbags to the American Midwest to support the US Army Corps of Engineers' critical flood containment efforts.

In 1995, when the Great Hashin Earthquake slammed Kobe, Japan, Evergreen International Airlines assisted in the US Agency for International Development response by transporting supplies to Japan that were necessary for rebuilding.

SETTING RECORDS WHILE SAVING LIVES

For many years, Anchorage-based Evergreen Helicopters of Alaska, Inc. — a subsidiary of Evergreen Helicopters, Inc. — has been on 24-hour notice to the US National Park Service to fly search and rescue missions on Mount McKinley. Evergreen pilots have over four decades of mountain flight experience, from the Himalayas to the Arctic, so they are a good choice for the National Park Service.

Helicopter operations are especially challenging at higher altitudes because the atmosphere is thinner. The capability of helicopters to operate diminishes as the operating altitude increases. The higher that a helicopter climbs, the less air there is for the rotors to "grab" to achieve lift.

The commitment to quality and excellence of performance by Evergreen Helicopters of Alaska is demonstrated nearly every day, but usually not as dramatically as it was in the summer of 1999, when Evergreen pilot Jim Hood saved three injured climbers from the icy slopes of North America's highest mountain, 20,320-foot Mount McKinley.

Each year over 1,200 climbers register to climb Mount McKinley, which is located in Alaska's Denali National Park and Preserve. Most of those who actually climb on the mountain during the climbing season, which officially lasts from April 14 through July 12, do so without incident. However, the mountain can be treacherous and unforgiving, and the weather on its slopes is notoriously unpredictable. Such was the case for three experienced British climbers, Nigel Vardy, Antony Hollinshead, and Steve Ball. They were climbing the peak, fighting stiff winds and nighttime temperatures of minus 40 degrees, and just below the 20,320-foot summit, the frostbitten men decided to head down. In the process, Vardy and Hollinshead, who were roped together, lost their footing and fell onto a virtually inaccessible ice plateau at 19,500 feet on the mountain's "West Rib" route. They were trapped in a dangerous situation, but they were able to radio the Kahiltna Glacier base camp for help.

EVERGREEN'S "DENALI LAMA," THE ANGEL OF MERCY ON MT. MCKINLEY.

Evergreen's Jim Hood — then a six-year veteran of the Mount McKinley operations — got a break in the weather and managed to fly his Aérospatiale Lama up to 20,000 feet to assess the situation. He also dropped a radio, warm drinks, cold weather gear, and a "screamer suit" (a body bag with arm holes and reinforced with webbing). Hood could see that the situation called for the "short-haul" rescue technique, which involves attaching the person to a rope. This method is used to extract injured parties, as well as rescuers, from locations where the helicopter itself is unable to land.

Hood returned an hour later to rescue Vardy, who was suffering from frostbite on both his hands and his face. Taking his Lama in close enough for the man to clip his climbing harness to the end of the helicopter's 100-foot lift rope, Hood plucked him off the ice shelf and flew him to the 7,200 foot Kahiltna Glacier base camp. Hood returned to 19,500 feet and successfully delivered Hollinshead, also dangling from the rescue rope, to the base camp. These two rescues were the highest elevation short-haul rescues ever made.

Meanwhile, however, the third climber, Steve Ball, was still on the mountain and suffering from severe exposure. He had begun his descent alone when the others fell, and he was later found by some other climbers at 17,500 feet. With the help of the other climbers, Ball was secured in a stretcher-like Bowman Bag. Meanwhile, Hood flew Denali National Park Ranger Billy Shott up to 17,500 feet outside the Lama on a 100-foot short-haul line. While Hood hovered over Ball, Shott and the team on the ground attached the stretcher to the line. Hood then flew Shott and Ball to base camp. Hood's rescue at 17,500 feet set another record for the highest Bowman Bag lift ever made.

The three injured climbers were transported to Talkeetna, Alaska, and from there, the men were taken to an Anchorage hospital by an Alaskan Air National Guard helicopter.

Jim Hood, who set his rescue records that day, became a two-time winner of the Helicopter Association International's "Salute to Excellence" Robert E. Trimble Award.

John Clark, the director of the federal Office of Aircraft Services observed that both Jim Hood and helicopter crew chief Raymond Touzeau "Exemplify true aviation professionalism, coupled with a keen eye for safety while operating in one of the world's most challenging environments."

Chapter 8:

EVERGREEN IN THE TWENTY-FIRST CENTURY

E vergreen International Aviation entered the twenty-first century as one of the world's most diversified aviation service
companies, and is clearly one of the world's most respected.
In celebrating the company's 45th anniversary in 2005, founder Del
Smith observed that while he and the people of Evergreen could take
great pride in their accomplishments, "We always have a healthy
discontent for the present. We know we must focus on the future.
Evergreen will continue to play a pivotal role in the economic stability and development of aviation and commerce throughout this
century. We are determined that our role will be one of leadership,
safety, quality standards, and commitment to our customers, business
associates, and employees."

Looking forward to the new millennium, he added that "We
will continue to share our purpose and dedication with our many
worldwide alliances that we appreciate and value. The evolution
of these alliances created jobs, changed the direction of commerce,
and brought constructive solutions to the needs of mankind. I
believe the best is yet to come. Every job we perform and every
mission we undertake impacts the lives of many individuals and the
success of numerous business endeavors. Our responsibility is to
assure that our customers, lenders, vendors and employees receive
positive results."

Responding to Global Challenges

It is well understood that permanent changes were imposed upon the world by the events of September 11, 2001. "I agree with the general belief in the world that it was an atrocity," Del Smith said of the terrible events of that day. "I compare it to the attack on Pearl Harbor."

Like the 1941 Pearl Harbor attack that brought the United States into World War II, September 11 wrought many changes, especially in the aviation world. For Evergreen International Airlines, the immediate changes were manifested in a dramatic shift in the relative proportion of military versus commercial work. As commercial work entered a recession, contract work for the US Air Force's Air Mobility Command increased. For six months, Evergreen's Hong Kong work was curtailed entirely. The international air freight business would not recover until early 2004.

In response to the terrorist attacks, the United States Treasury Department created the Air Transportation Stabilization Board (ATSB) to evaluate each of the American air carriers that were negatively impacted by the events of September 11 to ascertain whether they were candidates for special government programs. The first step for the ATSB was to consider cash disbursements to stabilize the airlines that were shut down by the Department of Transportation immediately after the attacks. Meanwhile, because of the instability caused by the events of September 11, the financial markets were restricting loans to the aviation industry. The ATSB would offer Government guaranteed loans after evaluating each company's performance and future stability. This was an opportunity for Evergreen to potentially secure good financing in a poor financial market for aviation companies.

Del Smith, along with a group that included David Rath, a board member and president of Evergreen Helicopters, Inc., spent four to six months in Washington, DC over the coming year to ensure proper execution.

"He brought me along, though he could have done this by himself with some high paid attorney and lobbyists," Rath recalls. "The process to execute these programs took much longer than anyone originally expected. Mr. Smith and I were together for breakfast, lunch and dinner seven days a week. One Saturday morning we walked into a restaurant for breakfast. A waitress waived to Mr. Smith and motioned him to a nearby table. When we were seated, she said, 'Good morning, Mr. Smith. It is great to see you again! This must be your son.'"

"No, I'm sorry, this isn't my son, but I would be very proud if he were," Del Smith replied as Rath sat by slightly embarrassed.

"To be honest, I am not sure how I reacted," Rath recalled. "I was so struck by Mr. Smith's statement, that I said nothing and just smiled. From that moment on, I wanted to excel in everything I did at Evergreen. Not only for my family and my co-workers but most of all, for Mr. Smith for having so much faith in me and for everything he has done for me."

Even in the face of one of the worst crises to confront the United States since Evergreen was founded, Del Smith had the power to inspire his team to excel.

During the period from September 2001 until the air freight business returned to its earlier levels, Evergreen International Airlines operated more than 1,500 Boeing 747 missions, which exceeded 45,000 hours of flight time, for the Air Mobility Command. The majority of these were in direct support of Operation Enduring Freedom and Operation Iraqi Freedom.

Throughout its history, Evergreen International Airlines has supported the United States armed services. The airline has worked with Air Mobility Command — and its predecessor, the Military Airlift Command — continuously since 1975. Evergreen's aircraft, training facilities, crew qualifications, maintenance procedures, quality control practices and financial status all meet Department of Defense inspection criteria.

The Evergreen campus in McMinnville. The corporate offices are
below, with the Museum and IMAX Theater at the top.

Just as Evergreen International Airlines had operated the first
commercial flight into Kuwait after Gulf War I in 1991, the airline
was the first commercial carrier to fly into Kabul, Afghanistan after
the end of the air combat campaign of Operation Enduring Freedom.
Landing on February 12, 2002, Evergreen's Boeing 747 was the first
747 to reach Kabul since 1974. Originating in Portland, Oregon,
the aircraft carried relief supplies, including clothes, shoes, blankets,
hygiene products, and medical supplies — as well as feed for animals
in the Kabul zoo. A 500-pound shipment of Oregon smoked salmon
was also transported on the flight as a gift for United States soldiers
deployed to Afghanistan.

The flight was a cooperative effort between Evergreen Humanitarian and Relief Services Inc., the company's nonprofit relief organization, and other relief organizations, as well as corporate sponsors in Oregon, California, and Ohio. Until Evergreen arrived on the scene, most humanitarian relief supplies had reached Afghanistan by truck, traveling over damaged roads that crossed snowbound mountain passes. Evergreen successfully added commercial airlift to the mix.

During Operation Iraqi Freedom a year later, Evergreen International Airlines supported the Air Mobility Command by flying more than 200 missions and 7,500 hours between February 8, 2003 and June 18, 2003. On October 15, 2004, Major General Mark Volcheff, Director of Operations at Air Mobility Command Headquarters presented approximately 200 Evergreen pilots and 20 loadmasters with awards for their part in this heroic effort.

Regarding Operation Iraqi Freedom, Del Smith said: "I probably had a different understanding than a lot of people in America. We had been involved in Desert Storm and Desert Shield. We went into Kuwait right after the war and teamed with [legendary oil fire expert Paul] "Red" Adair to put out the oil well fires. We saw the atrocities committed by Saddam Hussein's people in Kuwait. We saw the children hanging from powerlines. I was supportive when President Bush went into Iraq. It had to be corrected, and I think he did the right thing. We're proud to have helped with the reconstruction."

EVERGREEN INTERNATIONAL AIRLINES IN THE TWENTY-FIRST CENTURY

Evergreen International Airlines, the airline component of the world's most diversified aviation services company, has become one of the world's largest contract cargo carriers. With nearly a half-million hours of Boeing 747 experience, the company has established a reputation as a leading full-service cargo operator with a performance record second to none.

"I've watched the company grow from two 747's flying Air France and Air India contracts out of New York to a fleet of thirteen 747's that continuously keeps humming along all around the world," said Tammy Lewers, Manager of Inventory and Tech Data at Evergreen Trade Fixed Wing. "Mr. Smith is a remarkable businessman that has forever been in pursuit of the ultimate and sometimes unbelievable. We all, as the Evergreen team, put our heads together to make the unbelievable a reality. It's what we love to do — set and reach goals. The ability to apply our knowledge and resources to achieve what is conceived was instilled in all of us under the direction of this truly great man."

The airline provides significant lift capacity with its fleet of Boeing 747 freighter aircraft with both side-door and nose-door configurations. Evergreen International Airlines offers customers both long experience and a wide variety of transportation solutions. These include operating the aircraft on an ACMI (Aircraft, Crew, Maintenance and Insurance) basis, as well as on an ad-hoc, long-term, or less-than-planeload basis to support any special project needs.

"Insurance can be a critical part of the costing model, and if not monitored properly will be very costly to your company," John Irwin, chief financial officer for Evergreen International Aviation points out. "It is important to remember that the hull and liability composite rate is not the only cost that must be considered when bidding any type of job. There are two other ingredients to factor in when costing insurance: hull deductible costs, and brokerage fees. The best way to factor in brokerage fees is to take all fees associated with obtaining your policy, and divide that by the total cost of the insurance. This will give you a percentage to add to the initial composite rate. The best way to factor in deductible costs is to look at your loss history and how many times the deductible has come into play compared to total dollars paid to the insurance company. Add this percentage as well to your composite rate. Tracking these costs is an important method in assuring maximum profitability."

AN EVERGREEN 747 LANDS AT HONG KONG.

As for fuel costs, Ryan Smith, vice president of finance at Evergreen International Airlines explains that the company "historically has been very successful by not putting very volatile costs on their back. A prime example of that is fuel. Evergreen traditionally either has the customer pay for fuel for the jobs, or in the case of our airline work fuel is set at a certain rate and anything above that we would charge more and anything below that we would rebate to the client. This concept allows Evergreen to not be at the risk of the volatile fuel markets."

Known as "the airlines' airline," Evergreen has a long history of operating under ACMI contracts for some of the world's leading airlines, including Air France, Air India, Japan Air Lines, Lufthansa, and Saudi Arabian Airlines. Evergreen's experience with safe, reliable and cost-effective airport-to-airport operations also makes it a leading service provider for freight forwarders, direct shippers and charter brokers.

"The air cargo market is strong because people want their goods quicker than ever," Ranjit Seth of Evergreen International Airlines in

Hong Kong points out. "As customers grow more accustomed to fast delivery, the air cargo market will continue to grow. People want to order things and get them the next day. They don't want to wait. If you quote somebody eight weeks for a delivery, they'll go somewhere else. Manufacturers now subscribe to the 'Just In Time' concept. They don't keep inventory anymore. Often, they don't even own the goods, they just 'sell them through.' The quicker you can get them to the market, the more advantage you have. In this day and age, things go out of style very quickly, so even fashion garments are perishable. If you don't get into the market when people are buying, you're left with goods on your hands, which you haven't been able to sell. They've gone out of fashion and they'll wind up on the sale rack."

AIR FORCE CONTRACTS

Even before September 2001, Evergreen's efforts on behalf of the US Air Force had been increasing as the Air Mobility Command was reducing the amount of routine cargo that they carried in their own aircraft. The Air Force airlift fleet had become increasingly over-extended. After half a century of service, the US Air Force's Lockheed C-141 Starlifters were being retired. The Lockheed C-5 Galaxies were relatively few and were used for "out-sized" combat cargo that wouldn't fit in a 747. The Air Force prefers to use 747 commercial lift for "normal" cargo which saves the C-5's for large objects that only they can carry.

The Air Force's relatively new Boeing C-17 Globemaster IIIs, meanwhile, are capable of hauling large-size cargo and operating from short, unimproved runways in forward operating areas. Hence, the Air Force has earmarked them for use in missions in such areas. They also have sophisticated defensive systems to protect them in high-threat environments. All of these features mean that the Globemasters are in high demand when it comes to mission planning.

Meanwhile, the US Air Force has long resisted buying its own fleet of off-the-shelf 747 freighters to augment their fleet of military airlifters. The service chose instead to contract with 747 freight operators, such as Evergreen International Airlines, which has had long-standing regular contracts with the Air Mobility Command for multiple, weekly Transatlantic flights into Europe and the Middle East.

As noted earlier, Evergreen International Airlines was flying approximately 55 percent of the Air Mobility Command cargo between the continental United States and American overseas bases in Germany, Italy and the United Kingdom prior to September 2001. In the years that followed, this increased dramatically. Meanwhile, Evergreen had always done a great deal of work for Air Mobility Command on its routes in the Pacific as well.

BACK TO THE FAR EAST

By June 2005, Evergreen International Airlines had served the Transpacific commercial air freight market for more than three decades when it announced that it would begin twice weekly 747 freighter service between Nagoya, Japan, and the United States. Evergreen already had Far East sales offices in Hong Kong and Beijing, and would now establish a new office in Nagoya, and reestablish a Tokyo office.

As Brian Bauer, President of the airline, pointed out, "We have a customer base in Asia that has been supporting us since the 1980's and they are the driving force behind Evergreen's expansion into Japan."

Prior to the initiation of the Nagoya service, three quarters of the airline's revenues were still derived from Air Mobility Command work, according to John Palo, Vice President of Planning, Military & Government Contracts at the airline. Another 20 percent was coming from Hong Kong back-hauls, freight business originating in Hong Kong and the Pearl River Delta area, and coming eastward to the United States.

As Blair Berselli, Director of Sales in Hong Kong for Evergreen International Airlines explains, the eastbound Air Mobility Command flights originating in the United States terminate in the Middle East, so the Evergreen aircraft continue eastward to Asia to pick up cargo destined for the United States. This way, an Evergreen aircraft is able to serve the needs of two separate customers in a single round-the-world flight.

The Nagoya service offers customers, including major freight forwarders, the advantages of central locations at both ends. Opened less than four months prior to Evergreen's first flights from the region, Nagoya's new Chubu International Airport is located halfway between Tokyo and Osaka in the Chubu region, which is the center of automobile and electronic manufacturing in Japan. On the opposite end of the route, Evergreen has long been an operator at Rickenbacker International Airport near Columbus, Ohio, which is recognized as the "Gateway to the Midwest." Columbus is also within a day's drive of more of the United States population than any other major city in the United States or Canada.

EVERGREEN HELICOPTERS IN THE TWENTY-FIRST CENTURY

Evergreen was created in 1960 as a helicopter services company, and in the twenty-first century, the Evergreen Helicopters, Inc. component of Evergreen International Aviation is stronger than ever. Through more than four decades of service, Evergreen helicopters have flown far beyond their roots in the agricultural and timber industries of the Pacific Northwest to serve customers in more than 170 countries around the world. Nevertheless, the green and white helicopters are still a familiar sight in the Pacific Northwest and Alaska, where the company is still a leader in the forest industry. In Alaska, Evergreen helicopters, and Evergreen managers such as Sabrina Ford, have made a significant contribution to the petroleum, energy, and aeromedical industries, flying daily to save lives and provide essential services across a vast state.

When Evergreen was involved in emergency electrical support work in Alaska during 2001, Thomas A. Lovas of the Chugach

Electric Association wrote that the mission "was carried out most expeditiously, professionally, and efficiently. I appreciated the care given in the scheduling to assure an understanding of expectations. And, the emphasis placed on the performance review is evidence of Evergreen's focus on customer service."

Evergreen continues to be active in logging, herbicide and insecticide spraying, seeding, fertilizer application, and straw mulching. As the new century began, Evergreen helicopters were flying in support of agricultural projects, not only in the United States, but also across the world.

Since the first summer that the company began operations, Evergreen has continued to supply aircraft to support firefighting efforts in Alaska, the Pacific Northwest and elsewhere. Evergreen Helicopters, Inc. now provides the service on an exclusive use, standby and call-when-needed basis for the US Forest Service, the Bureau of Land Management, and the Canadian Interagency Forest Fire Center,

IN JULY 2000, AN EVERGREEN S-64 SKYCRANE PRECISELY PLACED A 75-FOOT DIGITAL ANTENNA ATOP THE SEARS TOWER IN CHICAGO. (PHOTO BY RON MAY)

AN EVERGREEN B212 IN ALASKA.

as well as to the state governments of Alaska, California, Florida, Oregon, and Washington.

Another area of operations with a long history for Evergreen Helicopters, Inc. is emergency medical service. Having pioneered dedicated air medical industry programs in the United States with Evergreen Life Line and the Alaska Medevac System, the company's medical aircraft have also worked in the Afghanistan, Africa, Europe, the Persian Gulf, the Philippines, the South Pacific, and in Sudan as well as in Central and South America.

Melissa Bucknall, a Mobile Intensive Care Paramedic and regional EMS Trainer with Alaska's Maniilaq Association, wrote the Evergreen office in Alaska to say "I am very thankful that Evergreen has such safety conscious and awesome pilots. . . . I am proud to have pilots who are very skilled and professional. I would not hesitate for one second to climb into the cabin of a plane piloted by any one of these guys here in Kotzebue. . . . Please let the people at your headquarters know that they did a great job when they selected the crew here. . . . It is refreshing to have a team like Evergreen to work with."

Maniilaq is a tribally-operated, non-profit organization that has been providing extensive health, tribal, and social services to residents of rural Northwest Alaska for more than three decades.

Hand in hand with emergency medical services are search and rescue operations. Evergreen has saved the lives of many climbers stranded in the high mountains of Alaska, especially in six-million-acre Denali National Park. For example, Evergreen's Aérospatiale SA-315B Lama, known as the "Denali Lama," has rescued numerous stranded climbers from above 19,000 feet. As noted in Chapter 7, Evergreen pilots hold world records for the highest helicopter rescues. Prior to the introduction of the Lama, Evergreen had used Bell 205's and an Alouette III in Denali.

District Ranger Daryl R. Miller of the National Park Service has called the Evergreen crews working at Denali "extremely experienced and understanding." This sentiment is seconded by Dean Seibold of the Alaska Division of Forestry, who said that "The safety and professionalism that [Evergreen flight crews] bring to our operations is a chief factor that keeps our employees striving to maintain their own effort to provide for safety and a professional climate."

Evergreen is also a leading cargo and personnel shuttle service provider for industrial, scientific and community support customers. The company's helicopters annually fly in support of the National Science Foundation and international polar research efforts across the North Slope and on the ice floes of the Polar ice cap.

Evergreen is the only operator to deliver mail via helicopter in the United States, serving the island of Little Diomede in the Bering Straight between Alaska and Siberia. The steep terrain of the island has precluded the construction of a runway, and until recently, there was not even a helipad — Evergreen pilots had to land on an old, grounded barge. The Evergreen helicopter offering this unique airmail service has occasionally been called upon to do medical evacuation and search and rescue work in the vicinity of the island.

Other Evergreen Helicopters transport activities also include marine services such as crew transfer, parts and equipment delivery, and oil spill response. To facilitate operations involving ocean-going cargo vessels, Evergreen Helicopters became the first company in the United States to obtain full FAA certification for single-engine

AN EVERGREEN SKYCRANE TAKES ON WATER FOR FIREFIGHTING.

Category A, Class D external hoist operations ashore and at sea. This permits much faster pilot transfer than traditional ship-to-ship transfers, which is especially important under adverse weather conditions. Evergreen has conducted over 2,500 marine pilot transfers.

More than four decades after Del Smith took the first Bell 205 to the "oil patch" in Alaska, Evergreen helicopters continue to support oil exploration and drilling work from the Arctic to the jungles of Peru. Evergreen has worked in nearly every oil patch in the world, supporting offshore drilling rigs, moving personnel and survey parties, and using the company's heavy-lift capability to deliver major construction supplies.

In the twenty-first century as before, Evergreen helicopters have also been involved in humanitarian operations around the world — most recently in Afghanistan, Angola, Cambodia, Kenya, Kuwait, Liberia, Mozambique, Sierra Leone, Somalia, Sudan, Western Sahara and the new nations of the former Yugoslavia. This includes continuing more than three decades of supporting the United Nations World

Health Organization in its efforts to eradicate the black flies that have caused River Blindness (onchocerciasis) in millions of people in Africa.

Today, Helicopter Services, Inc., a division of Evergreen Helicopters, offers extensive helicopter maintenance repair and overhaul services from its base at T.F. Green Airport in Warwick, Rhode Island. This pproved Part 145 Repair Station offers maintenance for the Bell Helicopter products and a general mix of all helicopters, including component and structural overhaul and repair.

Through the decades, Evergreen has operated more than two dozen helicopter types. As the new century began, the king of Evergreen's heavy-lift operations was still the Sikorsky S-64 Skycrane, with its 20,000-pound lift capacity. The company also operates the Sikorsky S-61's with an 8,000-pound lift capacity. Other craft in the fleet capable of lifting over 5,000 pounds, or carrying more than 15 passengers, include the Agusta/Westland AW139 and the Eurocopter SA 330J Puma.

In the 2,500 to 4,999-pound class and carrying up to 18 passengers, are Evergreen's Bell 205, Bell 212, Bell 214ST and Eurocopter BK-117. The third group of helicopters operated by Evergreen include the Aérospatiale SA-315B Lama; AStar AS 350 B2 and B3; the Eurocopter Bo-105; and the Bell 206 B-III, L-III and L-IV; as well as the Hughes 500D and 500E. These helicopters lift between 1,200 and 2,499 pounds or carry five to eight passengers.

Evergreen Helicopters, Inc. also operates fixed wing aircraft, including the Cessna 206 and CASA C212-200's that are operated in Panama under contract with the Department of Defense. The Panama operations have earned Evergreen high praise. Colonel Edward F. Martin, the aviation commander of US Contingent Forces to the Military Observer Mission to Ecuador and Peru (MOMEP), and Joint Task Force Safe Border said that Evergreen's "operations management and flight crews responded, often on less than 24 hours notice, to changes in the air flow schedule. The management and flight crews of Evergreen Helicopters [of Alaska] performed

EVERGREEN WAS THE FIRST OWNER OF THE AW139 HELICOPTER.

in a superb manner while providing CASA 212 air bridge support. . . . Weather conditions at Patuca [Honduras] are often under Instrument Flight Rules (IFR). Because there being no instrument approach to this site or nearby Macas, the successful completion of daily flights in the mountainous terrain is commendable. In my opinion, other operations, to include those of the US Air Force and Brazil, do not have the mission success rate of Evergreen Helicopters. They handled difficult and physically demanding situations that changed with the weather and suitability of the airfield for landing. The flexibility of the Evergreen operations provided MOMEP the needed support nearly 100 percent of the time. . . . They adapted to mission requirements and completed the flights."

Richard Silva, the Air Operations Officer for the United States Southern Command (USSOUTHCOM), and Elaine Hayes, the Air Force Contracting Officer, jointly lauded the service that they received, stating that "Evergreen's management has been outstanding. Whenever an issue arises, Evergreen has gone out of its way to meet our mission requirements. . . . Their flexibility and willingness to work with USSOUTHCOM's users has been the key in their success. USSOUTHCOM would highly recommend Evergreen for future contract considerations, to include this contract."

Silva added that "Evergreen has provided outstanding coordination of all activities necessary to execute this contract. . . .The Evergreen staff has demonstrated outstanding initiative and foresight in achieving USSOUTHCOM's logistical support requirements." He then went on to praise Evergreen's station manager and aircrew, observing that they "have been extremely flexible and cooperative in allowing USSOUTHCOM to meet its many missions throughout the AOR [Area Of Responsibility]. This has largely been achievable by the flexibility demonstrated by Evergreen as a whole. The contractor's scheduling and operational flexibility has been instrumental in meeting USSOUTHCOM's logistical requirements. Evergreen has been very proactive in suggesting alternative scheduling solutions to meet USSOUTHCOM's logistical requirements."

Lieutenant Colonel John T. McNamara, the commander of the 1st Battalion, 7th Special Forces Group (Airborne) at Fort Bragg agreed, sent a commendation letter regarding the Chief Pilot for the Evergreen USSOUTHCOM team in which he cited "superb performance, technical assets, can-do attitude and a degree of positive thinking and problem-solving that is truly refreshing."

For its service in Central America, Evergreen received the Joint Task Force Bravo Certificate of Appreciation "For outstanding professionalism, expertise, and flexibility in support of JTF-Bravo's firefighting efforts in Guatemala. . . . The can-do attitudes and enthusiasm of all the employees of Evergreen Helicopters of Alaska who supported and expedited. . . were crucial to mission completion and contributed greatly to its success."

The Evergreen Helicopters, Inc. safety record is one of the best in the industry because Del Smith insists on keeping his machines operating in the most impeccable condition. One is again reminded of the phrase "Quality Without Compromise."

"He's extremely interested in safety," one former executive observed. "I once saw him almost shut down an operation that was running 17 helicopters because the company that was providing the fuel couldn't guarantee good fuel quality. This was a multi-million dollar, long-term contract, and I saw him personally tell them, 'If you can't get the quality of your fuel better than this, we'll shut this operation down.' Almost overnight, they got the fuel situation straightened out."

VERTREP SHIPBOARD REPLENISHMENT

Another example of the support that Evergreen Helicopters, Inc. provides for the United States armed forces are Vertical Replenishment (Vertrep) operations for the US Navy. As explained by Evergreen Helicopters President David Rath, "Vertrep essentially involves the use of helicopters to bring supplies aboard ships while they're at sea."

Under a contract that began on December 1, 2004, Evergreen provides support of ships based in the Mediterranean Sea and operating in the Middle East. This service uses Eurocopter SA330J Puma aircraft that are uniquely equipped for the tight confines aboard a floating ship.

In one operation, Evergreen's "Puma Detachment" moved 113 pallets of high priority fleet freight, mail, frozen food and other goods. Commander Sidney J. Kim, Officer in Charge of the USNS *Spica*, called Evergreen's effort "By far the largest and best executed internal/external Vertrep conducted. . . . [Puma Detachment] participation throughout the planning phase, as well as

A VERTREP PUMA IN ACTION.

A PUMA SA330J CONDUCTS VERTREP OPERATIONS ABOARD A NAVY SHIP.

performance in the air/ground helped set the new benchmark of excellence for this evolution."

Commander Kim went on to say that the Evergreen Engineering Team led by Mark Allen, "Performed superbly the last two days, under the most arduous conditions, to get the rotor swash plate replaced. To a non-maintenance person such as myself, it appeared to be a monumental achievement. I watched as they worked together as a tight team. . . all eight persons [engineers and pilots] pitched in during the maintenance. It was 'beautiful scenery' watching them work like a happy 'family.' Thus far, it's been a great pleasure working with the new Evergreen Team. They got the job done within an extremely tight space and timeline, while the flight deck was being clobbered in preparation for an upcoming major UNREP [Underway Replenishment], 650 pallets, with the USS *Harry S Truman*.

Previously, Evergreen had provided vertical replenishment support to the US Navy during 1997, flying a Bell 212 and a Bell 214ST aboard the USS *Saturn*. Evergreen maintained a 100 percent operational readiness rate while on this contract, flying night and day missions with 92 percent mission completion, which was in contrast to the Navy's prior 35 percent mission success rate. At one time, while moving supplies to the USS *John F. Kennedy,* Evergreen transported 40,000 dozen eggs without any of them arriving cracked.

CORPORATE CHARTERS

Under the umbrella of Evergreen Helicopters, Inc., Evergreen Corporate Charters offer the services of Evergreen's Lear 35A and Gulfstream IV for secure and confidential private charter opportunities. Evergreen Corporate Charters is capable of supporting a customer's aircraft needs with 24-hour schedule flexibility. Using its global operating authority, Evergreen can help support a customer's business requirements virtually anywhere in the world.

The Lear 35A seats seven, and the Gulfstream IV has seating for up to 14 passengers in a large cabin with comfortable amenities. There is also a private meeting room, dual lavatories and two couches that fold down into beds. The customized interior also boasts an Airshow DVD, VCR and stereo system, with individual screens for inflight entertainment.

EVERGREEN MAINTENANCE CENTER IN THE TWENTY-FIRST CENTURY

As the new century began, Evergreen Maintenance Center (known as Evergreen Air Center until 2007) celebrated its silver anniversary as an Evergreen facility. Located at Marana, Arizona, near Tucson, the Maintenance Center was acquired in 1975 and was greatly expanded during the eighties to provide maintenance, repair and storage services for the Evergreen International Airlines fleet, as well as for third-party customers, which continue to include commercial, government and private operators.

In the Maintenance Center's early years, men such as Tom Pitzer, Tim Wahlberg, and Murry Vinson did an excellent job of making the

Maintenance Center the success that it is today. They implemented positive policies and practices, while instilling a sense of discipline in the way business was meant to be conducted.

One of the Maintenance Center's prominent strengths is how it fits in with the rest of the company through successful capitalization on the synergies that exist within the Evergreen sister companies.

While Evergreen International Airlines has always been one of the Maintenance Center's biggest customers, combinations of third-party customers have often constituted a majority of the Maintenance Center's workload through the years. The proportions have shifted several times between majority third-party work and majority Evergreen work, and these cycles coincide with the cycles of the aviation industry. The early years of majority in-house work shifted to majority third-party work in the eighties and the early nineties.

By the turn of the century, the pendulum had shifted again, and Evergreen International Airlines represented about 70 percent of the Maintenance Center business. However, five years later, the figure was around 40 percent. As Tim Wahlberg pointed out, "The Maintenance Center grew its third-party business so significantly [in the early twenty-first century] that our airline is just one of our major customers."

According to Wahlberg, the airlines in the United States have been more inclined to consider outsourcing their maintenance since the turn of the century. "We're having more and more discussions with major US airlines on outsourcing of heavy maintenance to our facility, and I believe very clearly that the issue there is cost. As for the outsourcing strategies of airlines in Europe and Asia. . . we expect to do some work for European airlines, again based on lower cost. Asian airlines tend to do their own maintenance or outsource to companies that they have a financial interest in. . . For example, Singapore Airlines has Singapore Airlines Engineering, an in-house service, doing all its work. Ameco in China does a lot of work for Chinese airlines."

INSIDE THE EVERGREEN MAINTENANCE CENTER.

About 75 percent of the Maintenance Center's business is domestic. The lower dollar exchange rate has had some positive impact, but against that a factor to consider is the ferry cost: where it might make good business sense to ferry a large aircraft for a big project to Arizona from Europe or Asia, likewise it would not make sense to ferry a small aircraft, or an aircraft which requires just a few man-hours of work.

Evergreen has observed airlines pursuing third-party business for their own maintenance shops, but because their costs are so high, there has yet to be a strong competitor to Evergreen among the other MRO (Maintenance, Repair & Overhaul) facilities. The rule of thumb has been that their costs are double Evergreen's costs.

Evergreen Maintenance Center is one of very few companies in the United States with several Federal Aviation Administration Certificated Repair Station ratings, as well as European Joint Aviation Authorities (European Equivalent of FAA), JAR-145 (Joint Aviation

EVERGREEN MAINTENANCE CENTER SERVICES INCLUDE INTRICATE PAINTING.

Requirements 145) ratings and those of other international agencies, such as the International Organization for Standardization (ISO), European Aviation Safety Agency (EASA) and the Chinese Civil Aviation Authority (CAAC).

Evergreen Maintenance Center is one of a handful of major MRO facilities in the United States that has unlimited Class IV ratings from the Federal Aviation Administration. Evergreen Maintenance Center has the facilities, equipment, and trained personnel to work on fixed-wing aircraft of every size.

Evergreen Maintenance Center has had an on-site engineering department since its early days. This department supports both routine maintenance and project-type work. All the engineering documentation is electronically generated and can be easily tailored to fit customer and Federal Aviation Administration requirements. In terms of its machines, the department has full computer-aided drafting capability and a library of over 60,000 design and engineering drawings, including a complete installation drawing for the Boeing 747 aircraft. The department has a plotter for generating drawings up to 20 feet in length, and also has complete drawing duplication capabilities.

Among the repair station services performed are aging aircraft inspection, aircraft painting, avionics modifications, composite repair, and interior reconfigurations, as well as aircraft A, B, C, and D Checks. The C and D Checks on an aircraft involve a general overhaul, performed at intervals of roughly six to nine years, depending on flight hours. It usually involves stripping the paint back to natural metal in order to inspect for corrosion or material fatigue. The instruments are removed, checked and, as necessary, repaired or replaced. Any manufacturer upgrades to the aircraft type that have been introduced since the aircraft was built are also incorporated during a D Check. This might include structural modifications, system improvements, and having the engine mounts modified. The engines are routinely removed and sent to the engine shop for overhaul during a D Check.

Evergreen Maintenance Center is highly experienced in aircraft modifications. The Evergreen Maintenance Center team is also well-versed in all the activities, including major modifications, that are required for reconfiguration of passenger aircraft. Evergreen Maintenance Center is also capable of complete aircraft interior installation or modification, and specializes in the installation of carpeting, soundproofing, and cargo net repair, as well as seat, floor, and wall coverings, including the fabrication of seat covers.

While conducting maintenance on numerous Boeing aircraft for various customers, one of Evergreen Maintenance Center's most important customers has been the Boeing Company itself. They originally came to Evergreen for flight line storage of non-deliverable aircraft — planes which were ordered, but for which the customers did not have the cash to "live up to their commitments." Boeing would park these orphaned aircraft in Marana while they looked for another customer. In essence, they used the Evergreen Maintenance Center like a "showroom" for these new aircraft.

When another customer materializes, the old customer's paint scheme comes off, and the new customer's paint scheme will be put on. The interior will also need to be redone in the colors and upholstery of the new airline, and Evergreen is in a position to do this work as well.

Everything from the storage to the maintenance to the painting and reconfiguration can be done on-site. Clients will know that every aspect of this process will be done accurately and professionally.

The mild Arizona climate permits most line maintenance operations to be performed outside on the flight line, while the heavy maintenance hangars form the heart of the Evergreen Maintenance Center. At any given time, there are usually about a dozen aircraft undergoing flight line maintenance and others in the hangars. The flight line maintenance might include engine changes or reconfiguration of interior seating.

Evergreen Maintenance Center is also known for long-term storage of aircraft. Not only is it a full-service MRO, it is one of the largest commercial aircraft storage facilities in the world.

The storage business is very counter-cyclical to the heavy maintenance business, and plays to the advantage of the Maintenance Center. When aircraft are being used, they need to be maintained. When they're not, they need to be in storage.

Aircraft can be stored outdoors for the short term almost anywhere, but for long-term storage, the Pinal County, Arizona climate is ideal. Annual precipitation is less than 12 inches, temperatures average between 54 and 82 degrees, and the air is clean and dry. With a total capacity of over 300 aircraft, the Maintenance Center is the world's largest storage and preservation facility for non-military — both private and commercial — aircraft. The storage department has the expertise to offer complete storage programs that can be specifically tailored to meet the exact requirements of the aircraft or engine manufacturer's specifications, or airline procedures.

While aircraft can be parked in any dry climate location, the Maintenance Center offers the unique advantage of a co-located storage and heavy maintenance facility. If a customer parks an aircraft at a storage site that is not near a source of maintenance, they will have a much harder time getting the aircraft into flying condition after it has been sitting for a long time — not to mention a limited capacity for reconfiguring or repainting the aircraft.

The marketing point people for the Evergreen Maintenance Center are the field sales teams, who are, in turn, supported by customer service teams who provide in-house services for customer inquiries, proposals and presentations and become the liaison for customers with the maintenance organization. When a sales representative obtains a potential maintenance opportunity from a customer, the customer service team will work with the planning, maintenance, quality assurance, engineering and materiel departments to formulate a bid proposal for the work. The customer service team is an integral part of the sales and marketing department. Each representative on the team is trained to handle a myriad of details associated with heavy maintenance on commercial aircraft.

When the customer's aircraft arrives at the Maintenance Center, the customer service team will work with the customer's on-site representative to ensure that the work proceeds efficiently and in accordance with the production flow through the maintenance process. This is done primarily through daily customer meetings with the operations staff, in which past work is reviewed and planned work is explained. When the maintenance process is completed and the aircraft departs, the customer service team, along with the sales representative, follows up with the customer to make certain that the aircraft is operating correctly and that the customer is satisfied with the work that has been done.

Evergreen Maintenance Center essentially offers "cradle to grave" service, with the "cradle" being the brand new aircraft off the manufacturer's production line, and the "grave" being the disassembly market. Evergreen Maintenance Center personnel conduct the

MATCHING MACHINES TO MISSIONS SINCE 1960:
THE EVERGREEN FLIGHTLINE IN MCMINNVILLE, OREGON.

disassembly process with an orderly removal of parts, components
and systems according to a predetermined sequence. Care is taken
during the removal to ensure the integrity of the parts. After each
part is tagged for identification and listed on a master inventory, it
is carefully packed and crated for shipping. In many instances, after
removal from the aircraft, the part is sent to Evergreen Maintenance
Center's component repair and overhaul shops for reconditioning
and certification. The customer then has a part ready for immediate
use, or for resale to the market.

As Tim Wahlberg once said of the Maintenance Center's future
strategy, "We're growing the company. We're looking at expansion.
. . we're improving our facilities, and from a strategic point of view
we're looking at more of a 'home-base' strategy by which we can
provide airlines, leasing companies or banks with a home for their
aircraft and meet all their needs for maintenance, storage, records

review, analysis, and help with the sale of aircraft. We're in a situation where we have our own facility, we're at our own airport, we
have a well-established work force and so have full control over all
those services we offer to our customers."

EVERGREEN TRADE IN THE TWENTY-FIRST CENTURY

In the beginning, the idea had been simply to have a component
within the corporation that would trade excess aircraft inventory as
quickly as possible at the right price. However, by the 1980s, it was
apparent that asset sales and trades had the potential for being a
profit center. Evergreen Aircraft Sales & Leasing (EASL) was formed
to serve the market, and continue to meet Evergreen's in-house
requirements. With this, the philosophy of "Matching Machines to
Missions" within the company was applied to the global aviation
industry. In 2008, EASL was renamed Evergreen Trade.

As the twenty-first century began, the aviation surplus sales
market worldwide was about $3 billion annually and growing. EASL,
now Evergreen Trade, was aggressively interested in being a bigger
and bigger part of that market. Through a global network of field
representatives, Evergreen Trade buys, sells, leases, consigns, and
brokers fixed-wing aircraft, helicopters, and parts. In the first five
years of the twenty-first century, more than $40 million worth of
aircraft were purchased.

"We are basically a trading group," Evergreen Trade President
Mike Hines explains. "That's what we do. Anytime anyone in Evergreen wants to buy a large inventory of anything, we provide the
service and get the right price. Evergreen Trade is integrated within
the helicopter company and the airline, so they're part of a purchasing organization. Every time there's a buy, we hope that there's a sale.
Evergreen Trade has the knowledge and the data necessary to offer
the operating companies the very best price."

Del Smith prides Evergreen Trade on its ability to barter. "Those guys
are extraordinary traders," he has said. "Start them with a jack knife, and

EAGLE GROUND HANDLERS LOAD AN EVERGREEN 747.

they can turn it into a Schwinn bicycle. People with that degree of creativity will be in the catbird seat in the twenty-first century."

As the new century began, Evergreen Trade had access to the
company's $180 million spare parts inventory, which was supported
by a superior maintenance records system that helped guarantee
quality. Meanwhile, this inventory is well organized and tracked to
such a degree that Evergreen Trade can offer its customers immediate responsiveness to critical operational deficiencies. In other words,
Evergreen Trade can instantly determine whether a particular part is
in stock and get it on the way to the customer just as quickly.

Recently, United Parcel Service had an aircraft grounded in
Chicago with a blown engine. They needed two engine side cowls.
They contacted Evergreen Trade, who had two available in New
York. A deal was struck and the side cowls were on the way to Chi-
cago by the end of the day.

Evergreen Trade is continually replenishing its inventory, not only for its worldwide customer base, but also to keep Evergreen International Airlines and Evergreen Helicopters up to date.

Each year, Evergreen Trade receives consignments of inventory from Evergreen International Airlines and Evergreen Helicopters, Inc. These operating companies, in turn, pay Evergreen Trade a sales commission to sell the property. Evergreen Trade also procures inventories on the open market that have no direct connection with the operating companies. For example, Evergreen Trade recently bought an entire 747 aircraft from United Technologies that was never intended to be used by Evergreen International Airlines. Evergreen Trade "parted it out," selling the components individually. Evergreen Trade funds all of its projects through its own working capital. The United Technologies 747 was purchased for cash.

On the management side, Evergreen Trade was originally staffed by people who held positions in the operating companies. They were paid by the operating companies, but they would also be in charge of selling inventory. In the early years, the company didn't even have its own accounting system. Today, Evergreen Trade is managed through its own fixed wing department, rotor wing department and aircraft sales department. In turn, there are sales and procurement representatives in eight domestic and four international regions.

As the new century began, the fixed wing department had been given a goal of selling a million dollars worth of inventory each month, while the rotor wing department had a target of a quarter of a million. This inventory was tracked through an integrated, web-based software system that kept tabs on the assets, from availability through price quotation, through shipping and finally with invoicing.

"We can pull up a part on the computer, and know exactly where it's been," Evergreen Trade President Mike Hines said of the system. "We know how much it cost to repair and how long it's been sitting there. We can look at another screen, and see the list price and the market price. It gives the salesperson the ability to serve the customer quickly. Good customer service is providing information immediately.

Saying that we'll call back in two hours or the next day doesn't cut it anymore. Nobody has the patience for that. We have the systems in place so that customers don't have to wait."

Though one of the smallest of the Evergreen family of companies, Evergreen Trade was one of the fastest growing at the turn of the century. As Evergreen Trade grows, many of its people are doing jobs that had not existed when the company then known as EASL was dominated by the operating companies. As Mike Hines explains, "We have people who just buy parts and sell them. That's all they do, all day long. Ten years ago, we didn't have people who did only that. We have some sales people that are just constant purchase-order-getters who write purchase orders for $100 or $1,000. Then we have some other people that swing for the home runs. They don't do a lot of purchase orders, but when they do them, it's for $200,000, $500,000, or even $750,000."

Evergreen Trade maintains three major inventory locations within the United States — including one at the corporate headquarters in McMinnville for helicopter parts — plus an overseas site in Beijing, China. A 30,000-square-foot warehouse at New York's John F. Kennedy International Airport houses airframes and engines, as well as other parts. At the Evergreen Maintenance Center in Arizona, Evergreen Trade has four warehouses comprising 34,000 square feet that stock more than 48,000 line items in inventory. The Beijing site is the 10,000-square foot Aerospace Logistics Support Center, a warehouse and distribution facility located near the central business district of the Chinese capital.

Evergreen Trade markets its inventory through the databases — such as those on the Internet — that the industry uses, and the company is a member of a number of associations. Evergreen Trade also advertises in all the important trade publications to maintain a high level of name recognition.

Another important part of marketing for Evergreen Trade, as it is for the operating companies, is maintaining a presence at the major aviation trade shows. The two biggest are the Farnborough

Air Show in England and the Paris Air Show in France, which are held every other year in alternating years, but Evergreen Trade also attends all of the major regional shows, such as the Singapore Air Show, as well as industry events such as the Air Carriers Purchasing Conference, where operators, trade vendors, and repair vendors visit and exchange ideas and make deals.

According to Mike Hines, the Paris and Farnborough events are the key industry events. "This is where the most powerful people in aviation come. It's a very good air show to visit with the heads of all the billion dollar companies. I would never be able to take a purchase order for a starter generator from the president of General Electric, but I will see him, and I will have the opportunity to mention that our General Electric account rep is doing a good job — and that he needs to be buying more parts from Evergreen Trade. And when the account rep comes in, I can tell him, 'I visited with the president of your company.'"

By the twenty-first century, Evergreen Trade had established itself as a globally recognized source for quality aircraft components. "We can go to the Middle East, we can go to Russia, we can go to Asia, to South America and to Africa," Mike Hines said of the Evergreen name recognition factor, "and they know Evergreen because Mr. Smith has been involved in so many different things, in so many different countries, and for so many different missions."

EVERGREEN AVIATION GROUND LOGISTICS ENTERPRISES IN THE TWENTY-FIRST CENTURY

By the beginning of the twenty-first century, Evergreen Aviation Ground Logistics Enterprises (EAGLE) had established itself as a dependable service provider at major airports throughout the United States, including the international gateway airports such as Anchorage, Atlanta, Chicago, Dallas, Los Angeles, Miami, New York, San Francisco, and Seattle. In addition to cargo and baggage handling, EAGLE was applying its expertise to aviation hub management, aircraft ramp services, passenger services, warehousing and security, as well as to aircraft ground equipment maintenance, sales and service.

Through contracts with the US Postal Service dating back to the 1980's, EAGLE continues to be active in mail handling, sorting and distribution. Among the more specialized services offered to customers in EAGLE's portfolio of total capabilities are airport property management and leasing.

As the century began, EAGLE had evolved, in less than two decades, from being a small organization serving the ground handling needs of Evergreen International Airlines and Evergreen Helicopters to being one of the fastest-growing entities within the Evergreen family of companies, with $54 million in assets. Second only to Evergreen International Airlines in revenue, EAGLE is actually the largest Evergreen company in terms of personnel. These 3,400-plus employees are active at 37 locations from Anchorage to Miami, serving more than 200 customers. Within five years of the turn of the century, EAGLE's annual contracted revenue approached $126 million.

Express package handling and mail services account for roughly half of EAGLE's total work. This includes EAGLE's long history with the US Postal Service. About a quarter of EAGLE's work involves both loading and unloading of air cargo, as well as passenger baggage handling. EAGLE also has the capability to build-up and break down cargo shipments and arrange for warehousing and security, though this is usually done by warehouse agents.

Other routine services performed on the aircraft themselves range from de-icing to interior cleaning. EAGLE crews provide ramp services and offer maintenance support for both aircraft and ground handling equipment. When the plane lands, regardless of whether it's passenger or cargo, EAGLE can do all the coordination for everything that's required.

As EAGLE's Robert Lane put it, "At a basic level, ground handling is taking off whatever is on the aircraft, whether it be people, cargo, or baggage, and replacing it with the correlating outbound load. Our staff also provides the ticket counter services, handling of cargo and warehousing, baggage delivery and cleaning of the airplane as required. This highly choreographed service appears effortless when performed by EAGLE's well-trained employees and quality ground support equipment."

"The more you look at EAGLE, the more impressed you're going to be," Del Smith has said. "It's got an excellent management team and they bid sensible numbers. They don't gouge anybody, but they don't work cheap. It's a quality company that provides quality service, and they grow with their customers.

In terms of its market, EAGLE has a very diverse mix of customers, with the largest customer base being the air express couriers. In 2001, the Postal Service awarded EAGLE the S-Net contract for three of its seven regions, Great Lakes/Midwest, Pacific and Southeast. The Postal Service also awarded EAGLE the Atlanta Hub-and-Spoke Trucking Network.

Other important express customers are Kitty Hawk, Menlo Logistics (formerly Emery Worldwide) and DHL, all of whom have had a long history with EAGLE. The EAGLE customer base has also included scheduled airlines, such as Air France, Air New Zealand, British Airways, China Airlines, El Al Israel Airlines, Taiwan's EVA Airlines, Korean Air Lines, Lan Chile, Lufthansa, Mexicana, Nippon Cargo Airlines, Singapore Airlines, Virgin Atlantic, and Westjet.

In 2004, EAGLE expanded its operations at John F. Kennedy International Airport in New York as it began handling 22 daily flights at British Airways' Terminal Seven. These flights included British Airways, as well as All-Nippon Airways, America West, Cathay Pacific, Icelandair and Qantas. Said British Airways executive Steve Clark, "The start-up plan was handled in a very team-oriented manner. . . we are pleased with the service and how everyone contributed to a successful transition, effecting seamless change, without impacting ongoing operations." In 2005, Iberia Airlines operations were added into the Terminal Seven operations, adding two additional daily flights.

EAGLE does not operate big capital assets, such as Evergreen International Airlines and the Evergreen Maintenance Center, but it is the most labor intensive of all the Evergreen companies. EAGLE provides varied aviation services requiring specific training of its employees. EAGLE's growth in the market has matched its growth in employee head count. As the customer base and the needs of customers have grown, EAGLE expanded.

In terms of staffing, 20 percent of EAGLE's personnel are full-time employees, and 80 percent work part-time with EAGLE. The express couriers launch their flights between 7:00 pm and 10:00 pm, depending on the location, and they return between 5:00 am and 6:00 am. Personnel often work three or four hours of each day increasing their work schedule as EAGLE's customer base expands.

EAGLE enjoys an excellent reputation for quality and safety, and is also well known for its agile responsiveness. It maintains the ability to mobilize immediately to establish operations and aviation support worldwide for customers who need things done quickly.

In the last half of the nineties, EAGLE nearly doubled its annual revenue. Even with the airline recession, EAGLE did not stop growing. The fortunate thing is that ground handling is always required at an airport. Catering can be trimmed back, aircraft types will be changed to fit the passenger need, but there is always a need for the ground handling services.

EAGLE has found that in times of airline recession, the carriers turn to increased outsourcing. The airlines tend to take a hard look at their costs and the service that they get for those costs. EAGLE is able to give them not only competitive costing, but also a high level of service and reliability, which are increasingly more important than cost.

As EAGLE has grown and has captured an increasing share of the marketplace, there has been a steady growth of personnel and a constant focus on training. Within the Evergreen family of companies, EAGLE is the largest employer of minorities, and has the largest number of women in supervisory and managerial jobs.

AN EAGLE CREW HANDLES A BRITISH AIRWAYS FLIGHT.

In terms of money, EAGLE is highly profitable, highly growth-oriented, and is in the top one percent in the industry in terms of yield and money returned for investment. EAGLE is also one of the fastest growing ground handling companies in the United States.

The EAGLE sales staff is taught to be aggressive and innovative. As Brian Bauer, EAGLE's Chairman puts it, "We tell our team to go after anything that has potential. We're always eager to meet our customers' needs, and will continue to diversify ourselves through innovative and streamlined processes allowing for greater efficiencies at responsible rates."

In terms of machines and materiel to perform its tasks, EAGLE has expanded with the needs of its customers, although the level of technological sophistication of equipment within the ground handling industry has not and does not increase on the same curve as it does with aircraft, engines and avionics. Cargo loaders, conveyor belts and vacuum cleaners have evolved only slightly since 1984.

"There has been no revolution in ground handling equipment to the point where there is a straight forward need for hard-core upgrading like you see with avionics packages or engine stages as mandated by the government," Michael Spencer explains. "Our equipment acquisitions have matched our needs and our growth. EAGLE has every type of ground service equipment, from the big $450,000 heavy-lift loaders for the aircraft to floor deck loaders, push-backs, airstart units for the engines, lavatory service units, vacuum cleaners for the aircraft, and a lot of hands."

"One key to EAGLE management, is our young, aggressive managers," says EAGLE's Chairman Brian Bauer. "We're heavily into management succession. All the Evergreen companies are, but since EAGLE experiences the most personnel growth and turnover, management succession is a mainstay of our success. EAGLE is constantly recruiting, both internally from our operational staff and externally from colleges. We like getting management trainees into our program. These trainees actually start on the ramp, doing physical labor, to get an idea from the ground up of what EAGLE does. From there, they move on to a supervisory category, which is one of the hardest things for people to learn. Since we are a labor business, proper supervision is everything."

Management trainees move from the ramp into administration, where they learn skills from managing costs to processing paperwork to taking care of employee relations. Moving to the maintenance side, they learn how the equipment works, how to manage the equipment, what equipment is required, when to order it, how parts flow, and how to keep the inventory to a minimum. From there, the management trainees move into an assistant manager role, and eventually into a management role. They may stay at their initial location, or they may move to a new base to replace a manager who is moving to a larger one.

"As management succession is definitely a key to our success, so is consensus management," Bauer added. "Since EAGLE does grow so fast, that is one of our accomplishments. We firmly believe that no one is smarter than everyone. By managing consensually, we ensure that all major decisions are made not by one person but by the participants of our group, each with their own unique understanding and perspective. Our executive group includes the vice presidents of operations, finance, sales, administration, maintenance and materiel. Everything is discussed in the group."

Regarding EAGLE management, Del Smith points out that the company goes the extra mile in training. "Several times a year, they marshal all their managers and key people to a central meeting place," he explains. "It might be Denver, it might be Dallas, it might be McMinnville. It's costly, but there's a fast payback. They are very successful at teaching each manager to be a better manager. Then they teach finance for the non-financial — the people who came up by moving freight and who probably never had one accounting course. They train the managers to measure their revenue and their expenses. They become sensitive to controlling costs and being efficient. They teach each station manager to be a General Schwarzkopf, because leadership is the rarest talent on earth. Each guy gets a leadership course and they get a sales manager course."

EVERGREEN SYSTEMS LOGISTICS

Recognizing the customer's need for a one-stop solution to freight forwarding, consolidation and air charter service, Evergreen formed Evergreen Systems Logistics, Inc. early in the twenty-first century. This subsidiary company functions as a fully integrated third-party logistics provider, with the operational

EVERGREEN SYSTEMS LOGISTICS DELIVERING CARGO.

flexibility to react promptly to the urgent transportation requirements of customers worldwide.

In addition to domestic and international air freight, the subsidiary's specific services include customs clearance, international ocean
freight for both imports and exports, long- and short-haul trucking,
military shipments, and special handling for perishables, as well as
access to third-party logistics services such as build-and-break, distribution and warehousing.

Evergreen Systems Logistics has access to the resources provided
by Evergreen's own extensive fleet and ground handling services, but
it has also partnered with others. These include more than 166 other
FAA-certified operators, as well as more than 350 national surface
transportation providers, and a vast network of the world's most
reputable ocean shipping lines.

These relationships enable Evergreen Systems Logistics to
supply both full-load and less-than-full-load service for all modes

of transportation. Evergreen Systems Logistics is a Transportation Security Administration certified Indirect Air Carrier, and a participant with United States Customs Service in the Customs-Trade Partnership Against Terrorism.

The Evergreen Systems Logistics website offers real-time tracking and up-to-the-minute information on all shipments, providing both a seamless and consistent level of inter-modal logistics services and helping to provide each client with the best possible air or surface transportation service. The youngest of the Evergreen family of companies, Evergreen Systems Logistics has a promising future in the twenty-first century.

EVERGREEN AGRICULTURAL ENTERPRISES IN THE TWENTY-FIRST CENTURY

Based in Oregon's Willamette Valley, where a near-perfect combination of mild weather conditions and fertile soil produce some of the world's most abundant crops, Evergreen Agricultural Enterprises was formally created on October 14, 1986 to manage the agricultural land that Evergreen began to acquire in 1979. Through the years, the Evergreen land holdings have doubled and redoubled, and by the early years of the twenty-first century, more than 8,000 acres of prime Willamette Valley farmland were managed by Evergreen. This included over 2,000 acres of land — primarily vineyards and hazelnut orchards — owned by the Smith family.

Evergreen Agricultural Enterprises is comprised of Evergreen Farms, Evergreen Orchards and the Evergreen Nursery division, as well as Evergreen Agricultural Products, LLC. The crops include nursery stock, walnuts, hazelnuts, and wine grapes, as well as premium Christmas trees. Recently, organic blueberries, blackberries and raspberries have joined the roster of Evergreen crops.

Evergreen has 1,350 acres devoted to hazelnuts and 850 acres of Christmas trees. The nursery business is the largest in terms of Evergreen Agricultural dollar volume followed by hazelnuts. Meanwhile, a great deal of growth potential is inherent in the Evergreen Vineyards.

Started in 1988 with just 25 acres, Evergreen Nursery has expanded its acreage and capacity to about 200 acres, producing over 200 different varieties of landscape ornamental plants including a line of specialized topiary. Among these plants are rhododendrons, bushes and landscape material, mostly for customers on the East Coast. According to Evergreen Nursery General Manager Kevin Klupenger, "the nursery is also one of the fastest growing activities within Evergreen Agricultural Enterprises, having experienced a 25 percent growth in the last three years of the twentieth century. It is also an area into which Evergreen was putting a great deal of marketing muscle. There isn't one agricultural crop in Oregon that matches the nursery business."

The Evergreen Nursery division is a wholesale nursery that includes quality, container grown nursery stock and a wide variety of different plant species which are propagated and grown under the supervision of the Evergreen Agricultural Enterprises Quality Control Program staff. The plants benefit from the exceptionally moderate climate and long growing season provided by the Willamette Valley. The Nursery's location is a key ingredient in the finishing time and the quality of the plants.

"The exciting thing about the nursery business, and that which is a big contrast from aviation," Del Smith has said, "is that you take a cutting from a plant, put it in a propagation house and grow a new plant. You can't take a sliver off the side of an engine and put it in a pot. I wish we could grow engines that way."

Though there are indeed differences between aircraft engines and nursery stock, Evergreen has brought the same level of quality and precision practiced with engine maintenance to the agricultural side of the business. For example, the greenhouses at the nursery facilities were constructed using lasers to assure precision in the construction. "There might be 60 ribs in the frames of the hot houses,"

Del Smith said, "but none of them have a sixteenth of an inch variation. They're very accurate. Everything is in line, and everything is on cardinal headings, north, south, east, and west. Everything is properly tiled underground as well."

The nursery is specially engineered so that water is recaptured in the tiling system and pumped back into holding ponds.

"We have the jump on most farm operations because we have a market and we do know how to sell," Del Smith said. "We work toward building better management skills and better management capability. We supervise people pretty well and we have developed our leadership skills and our management skills. We believe in being orderly. We're good quartermasters."

Oregon is the largest producer of hazelnuts (aka filberts) in the United States, and within Oregon, Evergreen Agricultural Enterprises operates one of the largest hazelnut orchards in the state.

Mike Wilhoit, vice president for hazelnut production and sales, explained that "Evergreen Orchards has discovered that we can grow a higher quality hazelnut tree of which the production is in high demand around the world. The Oregon hazelnut industry's traditional market has been Germany where the per capita consumption of hazelnuts is the highest in the world. However, in the past five years the Hong Kong/China market for Oregon hazelnuts has greatly surpassed the demand from Germany."

He went on to say that "with an Evergreen International Aviation office located within the heart of Hong Kong commodity market, Evergreen hazelnut production has been sold smoothly and profitably into China. In addition, Evergreen Orchards hazelnuts have been in demand in other countries such as Spain, Egypt, Israel, Argentina, Tunisia, and Mexico. Of course, the United States is an important market for Evergreen Orchards hazelnuts as well."

Evergreen Orchards not only harvests hazelnuts, but processes them at the company's facilities near Dundee, Oregon. Among the consumer products marketed under the Evergreen Orchards and Sweet Nana labels are hazelnut biscotti, dry-roasted hazelnuts, dry-

AN AERIAL VIEW OF THE EVERGREEN NURSERIES.

EVERGREEN CONSUMER PRODUCTS RANGE FROM WINE TO HAZELNUTS.

roasted hazelnuts with dried fruit and hazelnuts in a variety of flavors, such as hickory-smoked, jalapeno, and chocolate-dipped. Evergreen also processes the nuts as both hazelnut paste and hazelnut butter.

Another more recent high-value crop from Evergreen Agricultural Enterprises is organic berries. With organic blueberries selling at a premium compared to conventionally grown blueberries, especially in the Far East, the decision was made to enter that business. In 2005, 200 acres of Evergreen land were set aside for blueberry, blackberry and raspberry production.

An important part of the Evergreen business model has always been keeping assets from sitting idle, and the same is true within Evergreen Agricultural Enterprises as it is within Evergreen Aviation. While most crops are harvested in the spring and summer, another important Evergreen crop — the evergreen tree itself — is harvested at the beginning of the winter. For the Christmas tree business, Evergreen manages the cultivation of over a million Douglas fir, grand fir and noble fir trees. The annual harvest ranges from 50,000 to 100,000 trees

EVERGREEN VINEYARDS.

that vary in size from tabletop to 20-foot display trees. Evergreen is able to consistently deliver the highest quality trees thanks to a skilled and experienced sales and field operations team. The sales team markets these trees to schools, churches and civic organizations, as well as through major retailers and retail garden centers.

Evergreen Farms operations include Evergreen Vineyards, located in Yamhill County just outside the Oregon wine country town of Dundee, in an area recognized for producing some of the finest wine grapes in the world.

"Geographically, Oregon is very much like many of the important wine regions of France." Del Smith added. "We're on the forty-fifth latitude, and the Willamette Valley has the right soil and the right climate."

The Evergreen Vineyards expanded quickly, from just 33 acres in 1995 to 200 acres of pinot noir and pinot gris grapes a decade later. Early in the twenty-first century, Evergreen began producing its private-label Spruce Goose Pinot Noir, Pinot Gris, Oregon Rosé, and DelMar Reserve Pinot Noir wines, as well as semi-sparkling Pinot Noir Grape Juice. In 2006, in its first year of being bottled, the Evergreen Vineyards Spruce Goose 2004 Oregon Pinot Gris won a silver medal in the *Dallas Morning News* Wine Competition, one of the wine industry's most prestigious awards.

YOU ARE IN BUSINESS FOR TWO REASONS – FUN AND PROFIT.

IF THERE IS NO PROFIT – IT IS NOT FUN.

Evergreen Agricultural Products, LLC markets the private label pinot noir products, as well as the various consumer-packaged hazelnut products and gourmet gift baskets that also include salmon and dried fruits.

Evergreen Agricultural Enterprises has also moved into livestock production, and has formed a marketing partnership with Mountain States/Rosen LLC. This major vertically-integrated lamb supplier was formed in 2003 as a joint venture of Wyoming's Mountain States Lamb & Wool Cooperative and New York-based B. Rosen & Sons Inc., a leading supplier of quality veal and lamb products. The Cooperative represents lamb producers in ten states including Wyoming, Idaho, Colorado, Montana, Utah, California, Arizona, Nevada, Oregon and South Dakota.

Under the terms of the 2003 agreement, the cooperative would supply its highest quality lambs to existing Rosen processing and distribution facilities in New York and Greeley, Colorado. Evergreen lambs are processed at Greeley, and Evergreen provides transportation expertise.

"This is one of the most significant partnerships formed in the history of the American lamb industry," said Bruce Rosen, President of B. Rosen & Sons. "We are thrilled that our vision for creating a vertically-integrated lamb supplier has come to fruition."

Del Smith has likened the business model of Evergreen's cooperation with Mountain States Rosen to "having four aces — the property, the livestock management, the processing capability and the retail expertise."

He thinks of Evergreen Agricultural Enterprises as both "fun and profitable," but he often adds that "If you're not making a profit, it isn't very fun."

He always stresses the management aspect as well, commenting that "We want to create a culture and a discipline where we make an operating profit."

Del Smith has always looked at Evergreen's agricultural land as a two-part investment with, as he puts it, "two opportunities for earning." One of these is the operational profit, and the other is the real estate value of the land itself. "Evergreen Agricultural Enterprises invested $12 million worth of capital in land and it has appreciated to $75 million," Smith has said. "We are going to continue to do it. It hasn't topped out. Today's high price is still tomorrow's bargain."

SUPERTANKER SERVICES, INC.

When Del Smith put his first Hiller helicopters to work in 1960, one of the first tasks was supporting the timber industry. This continued to be a part of Evergreen's ongoing work activity. With this in mind, it should come as little surprise that one of Evergreen's most imaginative twenty-first century innovations has its roots in some of the earliest projects ever undertaken by the company.

Through the years, forest fires have been one of the most serious challenges to forest management, and the use of aircraft to fight them is an integral part of Evergreen's heritage. In 1975, Evergreen acquired Johnson Flying Service, which had been awarded the first US Forest Service Prime Contract for aerial firefighting work in 1931.

The use of aircraft to drop retardant on fires had been ongoing for more than half a century when Evergreen completely revolutionized the strategy. In 2004, Del Smith and Evergreen International Aviation proudly announced the Evergreen Supertanker, the most innovative development since the aerial suppression of fires began.

Evergreen proposed the use of a Boeing 747 freighter to attack fires. A Boeing 747 can carry over 20,000 gallons of fire retardant. This is more than *seven times* the drop capability of the largest aerial firefighting aircraft in use prior to 2004, which was the Lockheed P-3 Orion. The Evergreen Supertanker also has the capability of performing multiple segmented drops, each of them in quantities greater than or equal to the total capacity of the P-3.

The upper deck of the 747 provides over 200 square feet of space that can be assigned as a command and control center, where personnel involved in mapping, incident monitoring and video/communications via a downlink relay could be stationed. Evergreen International Airlines possesses an FAA exemption permitting its flights to carry up to five persons who are essential to the flight operation in this area.

THE EVERGREEN SUPERTANKER IN ACTION.

To illustrate the concept, Evergreen modified one of the 747 freighters in its airline fleet at the Evergreen Maintenance Center in Marana, Arizona and conducted a series of demonstration flights between March 21 and April 24, 2004. The Evergreen Supertanker made 82 actual drops and more than 100 "dry runs" over the course of nearly 50 flights, many of which were conducted in the steep terrain of Black Mountain near the Maintenance Center. During the series of flights, the aircraft released a total of 536,000 gallons. Even with more than 20,000 gallons of retardant, the 747 is 150,000 pounds below maximum takeoff weight limits, providing an enhanced safety margin. By comparison, current aerial tankers take off at their maximum certified takeoff weight, leaving no margin for error.

As an added margin of safety, the Supertanker is equipped with a pressurized drop system to permit release of retardant from higher altitudes. Other fire suppression aircraft use a gravity drop system, requiring flying at a release altitude of approximately 200 feet. The Supertanker can operate effectively at 400 to 800 feet, well within the 747's normal operating parameters. The drop speed of approximately 140 knots provides a 30 percent cushion over the aircraft's stall speed. Additionally, the Evergreen Supertanker is outfitted with a sophisticated flight data recorder able to monitor airframe loads.

On August 24, 2006 Supertanker Services, Inc. was incorporated as a company under the Evergreen umbrella of companies. Sam White, Senior Vice President of Evergreen International Aviation in the Washington, DC office, announced that "the Supertanker received its FAA Supplemental Type Certificate (STC) on October 27, 2006 and received its Operating Part 137 Certificate on November 6, 2006."

During the development of the Supertanker, Evergreen had worked with Boeing on preliminary engineering studies. Based on preliminary studies, Boeing supported the concept and confirmed the capability of the 747 to perform aerial applications. Evergreen is also working to assure that the Supertanker is maintained under the strictest Federal Aviation Administration airline regulations, with standards of safety, maintenance and training much higher than in the rest of the aerial firefighting industry.

The Supertanker demonstration came as the National Interagency Fire Center (NIFC) confirmed that 61 million acres of American forest and range land had been burned over the course of the previous 15 fire seasons, and that $6.9 billion had been spent to suppress these fires over the previous decade. This figure did not include losses in terms of timber and other property. In 2005 alone, 8.7 million acres were burned, with cumulative fire suppression costs for the preceding decade exceeding $9 billion.

The capabilities of the Supertanker are not limited to fighting fires. The aircraft's exceptional drop capabilities, loiter time, and size make it an ideal tool to help control large, environmentally-disastrous oil spills. Important homeland security missions are also within the capabilities of the Supertanker. For example, it could be used to neutralize chemical attacks on military installations or major population centers, or as a spray platform for insect control.

The Evergreen Supertanker is modestly seen by the company as "just another tool in the aerial firefighting toolbox." This is clearly an understatement. While it cannot replace helicopters, or all of the aerial tankers currently in service, it certainly has the potential to be the *biggest* and most effective tool in the aerial firefighting toolbox.

In addition to the Supertanker being used as an aerial fire fighter, it can and will do much more including: nuclear-biological-chemical knock down, weather modification, oil spill dissipation, pollution dissipation and soil stabilization. With these additional capabilities this revolutionary tool will become vital to foreign countries and local authorities.

Thinking of the Supertanker as a tool in a toolbox is also an example of how the Evergreen people think *outside* the box. As Jim Dineen of Evergreen International Aviation puts it, "Someone asked me at the Farnborough International Air Show 'what do you like about working at Evergreen?' The answer is easy — nowhere else in the aviation industry could you be allowed to think outside the box, present your idea, and bring a vision to fruition all under one roof. Throughout Evergreen's management, the doors are open to innovation and creativity. You don't battle a bureaucracy to get a project done, and you get unequivocal answers fast when you need a decision. You can team any element found in aviation right here, get some of the most experienced minds together, and go. As those of us on the Supertanker program would say when trying to solve engineering challenges: 'it's Monster Garage meets Boeing!'"

DREAMLIFTER

The Supertanker is just one example of Evergreen thinking outside the box when it comes to very large aircraft. In December 2005, The Boeing Company picked Evergreen to operate and maintain the fleet of unique 747 aircraft the company is using to transport major components of its all-new family of 787 Dreamliners. Boeing's newest family of jetliners, the 787s are super-efficient airplanes designed to provide passengers with a better flying experience though significant improvements including cleaner air, bigger windows, a lower cabin altitude and higher humidity.

To efficiently carry very large Dreamliner subassemblies to its Everett, Washington assembly plant, Boeing created the Dreamlifter fleet, comprised of modified 747-400-passenger airplanes with enlarged upper fuselages, and aft sections that swing open for loading and unloading. Evergreen International Airlines operates the Dreamlifters, each of which is equipped with Electronic Flight Instrument Systems (EFIS). Meanwhile Evergreen Maintenance Center conducts maintenance, and Evergreen Aviation Ground Logistics Enterprises provides ground handling.

"The aircraft will be monitored from Evergreen International Airlines' McMinnville headquarters during their worldwide operations, which will include bringing components from four global points into the Boeing assembly at Everett, Washington for final assembly," said Raymond "Buzz" Wright, Executive Vice President of Evergreen Airlines. "This very complex operation is supported out of Charleston, South Carolina; Wichita, Kansas; Grottaglie, Italy; and Nagoya, Japan. It offers additional opportunities for Evergreen."

"Evergreen International Airlines is an expert in its field, with over a half million hours of 747 experience," Scott Strode, Boeing's Vice President of 787 Airplane Definition and Production, said when announcing Evergreen's selection. "We have complete confidence that EIA will meet the aggressive schedule required to transport Dreamliner components around the world."

BOEING PICKED EVERGREEN AS OPERATOR OF THE DREAMLIFTER. (© BOEING)

Evergreen International Airlines President Brian Bauer added, "Evergreen is thrilled to be such a key player in the production of the Dreamliner. Evergreen has operated Boeing 747 aircraft since the 1980's, and purpose-built aircraft since its inception in 1960. The Dreamlifter program will play well on these capabilities."

THE UAE SEARCH AND RESCUE CONTRACT

On July 20, 2006, Evergreen Helicopters, Inc. was awarded a United Arab Emirates Armed Forces Search and Rescue Helicopter Contract. Evergreen took what was merely a concept in the minds of UAE Armed Forces planners and turned it into a full-blown search and rescue contract in just 42 days.

The contract officially started on September 1, 2006. The scope of the contract is to provide year-round Search and Rescue (SAR) services to the UAE Armed Forces on a 24/7 basis. The aim of the SAR team is to minimize the loss of life and injury by rendering aid to distressed Defense Force crew members in the UAE operating theater. Evergreen's main operational base is strategically located at Al Bateen Airfield, with two satellite bases at Minhad and Al Ain which allow Evergreen to respond to any emergency within the UAE in minutes, day or night.

Evergreen partnered with a local aviation company called Falcon Aviation Services (FAS) who assist in this contract on a day-to-day basis. A strategic local partner to all of the Evergreen's companies in the UAE, FAS was formed in 2005 under the initiative of His Highness Dr. Sheikh Sultan bin Khalifa bin Zayed Al-Nahyan to fill a significant gap in the Aviation Services Market in the UAE and the Gulf Region. FAS provides helicopter and fixed wing charter and maintenance services.

"We were drawn to Evergreen's reputation for safety and extensive experience in Search and Rescue. They were a great fit; they have the agility and resources to respond within the tight time frame of the contract," said Captain Salem Al Kayoumi, FAS Chairman of the Board.

EVERGREEN AT WORK IN THE UAE.

Having been able to propose any type of aircraft fleet mix to fulfill the mission requirements, Evergreen picked two new Bell 412EP helicopters, because of their tested reliability, and a pair of new state-of-the-art Agusta Westland 139 helicopters. Able to harness the latest in technology to assist the pilots in every condition that they may face, the AW139 is one the most powerful helicopters in the industry when considering the power-to-weight ratio. This power allows the helicopter to perform missions at high altitudes and or in hot climates without reducing aircraft performance or compromising safety.

Having been awarded the contract, the real work began for Evergreen as the company had to negotiate the end to other contracts that these aircraft were servicing, order the special parts and configuration equipment to equip the aircraft for the SAR role, and find, hire and train all 45 personnel that were required to perform this contract. With this, Evergreen flew the aircraft to the appropriate facilities for modifications on all four aircraft, provided currency checks for all the new crews, and provided maintenance training on new aircraft types and systems. Evergreen Engineers had to design many of the applications as they were not yet available on the open market. Equipment installed on the aircraft included the Forward Looking Infra Red (FLIR) cameras, rescue hoists, Night Sun Spot Lights, and the latest four-axis autopilot with auto- hover to ensure operations in severe conditions.

Evergreen then prepared all the aircraft, special tools, administrative supplies, inventory, and crew uniforms for shipment and chartered a large Russian Antonov An-124 cargo carrier to transport the aircraft and equipment. Having delivered everything to the appropriate operations bases, Evergreen reassembled and flight tested the helicopters, and presented the operation to the UAE Armed Forces for inspection.

EVERGREEN UNMANNED SYSTEMS

Since the turn of the century, Unmanned Aerial Vehicles (UAVs), such as the RQ-1 Predator and RQ-4 Global Hawk have received a great deal of attention for their contributions to American military operations. The great strides that have been made in UAV technology have turned these remotely-piloted aircraft into a useful component in the American aerial reconnaissance arsenal. Steps have also been made toward turning these versatile aircraft into weapons platforms. UAVs perform tasks that are considered too dangerous for a pilot or which exceed the endurance or altitude limits of manned aircraft.

One of the most promising areas for commercial usage of UAVs is by petroleum companies. These range from seismic testing to drilling as well as pipeline and pumping operations monitoring. An autonomous UAV can accomplish many tasks at much farther range and greater safety than deploying manned aircraft in this unforgiving part of the world

These remarkable aircraft are now making their way to the commercial market as a safe and reliable solution for missions and applications previously not thought possible. With this in mind, Evergreen Helicopters, Inc. has formed Evergreen Unmanned Systems (EUS), a division dedicated to offering UAV services. EUS will provide remotely operated aircraft for nearly any dull, dirty, or dangerous aviation job keeping pilots safe and reducing long term operating costs. Unmanned systems have already proven their ability to operate day or night with extended loiter times, and these systems provide small logistical and operating footprints. Commercial unmanned systems are especially well suited for long duration missions such as Intelligence / Surveillance / Reconnaissance (ISR), Fire Mapping, communication hubs, pipeline security, search and rescue, hostile environments and a host of others.

"Our clients find civil missions that could not be performed in the past due to the associated risk and prohibitive cost are now easily performed by unmanned systems," explained Chris Rushing of Evergreen Aviation UAV/UAS Sales. "Because Evergreen is not a manufacturer, Evergreen Unmanned Systems (EUS) is able to seek out and provide the best possible machine for the mission. As more and more missions require aircraft operations in dull, dirty or dangerous locations, the UAS will stand ready to fill those requirements."

Evergreen Unmanned Systems has been approached by numerous UAV producers, but chose Insitu with its A-20 Insight UAV as the partner with which to begin commercial operations. Insitu, based in Bingen, Washington, developed the A-20 Sea Scan originally for ocean fishing surveillance. However, following the attack

AN EVERGREEN UNMANNED AERIAL VEHICLE

of September 11, 2001 it was converted into the Scan Eagle UAV system, which is flown in military operations by Boeing. Seeking a civilian, commercial counterpart to the defense related business, Insitu and EUS have quickly moved toward a strategic alliance in this arena. The civilian variant has been dubbed "Insight."

"We do not need to invest in a number of different UAV systems at this point when we have the world's best system and the world's best partner," said Bob Smith, EUS Executive Vice President. This relationship promises to be beneficial for both companies.

Chapter 9:

GIVING BACK

D EL SMITH HAS ALWAYS BELIEVED IN THE IDEA OF GIVING back to the community, whether that community is the city of McMinnville, Oregon, where Evergreen is headquartered, or the global community in which Evergreen has operated for many decades.

As Lacey Summers, Del Smith's executive assistant, has observed, "I have watched his fierce business wheeling and dealing, his brainstorming of solutions to challenges, his hiring of bright new talent. I have also witnessed countless acts of compassionate generosity for the downtrodden, the hard working, and the needy. Mr. Smith never seeks recognition or acclaim for these deeds."

Through the years, he has supported both local and state organizations and activities, from baseball teams and the Boy Scouts of America to theater and symphony, to conservation and humane society associations. Oregon citizens and employees know of many thoughtful gestures and contributions he has made without recognition. He has taken the time to serve the McMinnville community on the city council, the Yamhill County Fair Board and as a trustee of Linfield College. In November 2005, Del Smith was inducted into the Linfield College Athletics Hall of Fame, after having supported the school's athletic department for more than three decades. His acceptance speech at his induction provided a memorable quote. "We believe that the Linfield athletic program is one of the best classrooms on campus," he said. "Linfield athletics teach young students principles to be successful. Success is defined by integrity, Christian values, virtuous behavior and achievement — not fame and fortune, which are false values."

Internationally, Evergreen has worked with the World Health Organization in West Africa since the seventies to combat onchocerciasis, a formidable disease that causes blindness. In 2001, building on this 30-year commitment and other charitable projects, Del Smith founded Evergreen Humanitarian & Relief Services, Inc. (EHRSI). This non-profit organization was created to expand Evergreen International Aviation's ongoing legacy of support to both local and international humanitarian and relief projects, while advancing these efforts in the twenty-first century.

The goals of EHRSI include assisting developing countries in order to improve and deliver health care, to eradicate disease, and to promote economic development, while supporting self-sustaining communities to care for orphans and children at risk. EHRSI promotes the health and well being of children worldwide by supporting medical research. The organization often partners with other non-profit groups, corporations and governmental agencies, combining resources to assist those in need.

Because of its association with Evergreen International Aviation, Evergreen Humanitarian & Relief Services is in a unique position to provide fixed-wing and rotor-wing airlift support for relief projects.

A Legacy of Humanitarian Activities

As described throughout this book, Evergreen has had an admirable record of being in the right place at the right time that long predates the formal creation of Evergreen Humanitarian & Relief Services. Whether it has involved helicopter rescues on the highest peaks in North America and the Himalayas, or transported relief supplies into remote corners of the globe, Evergreen has a long record

AN EVERGREEN MD500 AT WORK IN AFRICA FOR THE WORLD HEALTH
ORGANIZATION'S ONCHOCERCIASIS (ONCHO) PROGRAM.

of being on the spot when the unique capabilities of its machines and
personnel were desperately needed.

Since it was formed, Evergreen Humanitarian & Relief Services has taken the lead in a number of important relief efforts. For
example, Evergreen partnered with Northwest Medical Teams, Mercy
Corps, and Save the Children in the "Winter Relief Flight," by providing the cargo plane that transported more than 15,000 pounds
of blankets, tents, and medical supplies to Afghanistan. Evergreen
donated the estimated value of the 20-hour flight and raised about
$200,000 to cover the cost of fuel and landing fees.

In December 2004, Evergreen International Airlines transported
more than 3,000 pounds of clothing from the United States to Ger-

many, where it was distributed to injured American soldiers in United States military hospitals. Officially designated as "Operation Warm and Fuzzy," this project was initiated by Oregon Air National Guard Chaplain Lieutenant Colonel Richard Sirianni and the 142nd Fighter Wing Community Foundation. Troops at the Landstuhl Regional Medical Center who had been injured in Iraq and Afghanistan were in need of clothing, so Oregon corporate and community partners collected the donations. Among those involved in the collection were the Woodburn Company Stores, G3 Corporation, Portland Police Association, Portland Employee's Credit Union, and St. Henry's Church in Gresham. At its John F. Kennedy International Airport base in New York, Evergreen loaded five pallets of clothing valued at approximately $75,000, and flew them to Ramstein Air Base, from which they were then trucked to the medical facility.

"Oregon has a large heart so the major challenge of the operation is not just collecting donations, but actually getting the donations

SPRAYING BIODEGRADABLE CHEMICALS AS PART OF THE ONCHO MISSION.

to the hospital in Germany," said Blythe Berselli, the Evergreen Humanitarian and Relief Services president. "Evergreen will help assure that 100 percent of what is donated will arrive to help our brave military personnel," she emphasized.

In January 2005, in the wake of the terrible Indian Ocean tsunami, Evergreen Humanitarian and Relief Services donated the services of an Evergreen Boeing 747 freighter to the American Red Cross International Response Team. The aircraft transported relief supplies to Colombo International Airport in Sri Lanka, a nation hard hit during the tsunami disaster. This delivery included approximately 200,000 pounds of mobile kitchen sets and other relief supplies procured by the American Red Cross.

"The donation of transport services from Evergreen International Airlines is helping the American Red Cross rush aid to the victims of this devastating disaster," said Skip Seitz, senior vice president of growth and integrated development for the American Red Cross. "We are grateful to Evergreen for their support in getting these relief supplies to those who need them most. Evergreen's contribution allows the Red Cross to stretch our donated dollars further and provide additional services to disaster victims."

In February 2005, Evergreen International Airlines followed up on the earlier mercy mission by delivering nine living water treatment systems to Sri Lanka. Delivered in partnership with Water Missions International, the treatment systems provide a continuous supply of clean and safe drinking water for communities of up to 3,000 people and help reduce disease by removing waterborne pathogens.

In July 2005, Evergreen Helicopters, Inc. donated the use of its Lear 35 to airlift a severely burned two-year-old child from San José, Costa Rica to the Shriners Burn Center in Galveston, Texas. The arrangements were made by Evergreen, working with the Center for International Medicine (CIMA) in San José, the Costa Rican Government, the Baylor Health Care System, and many charitable organizations and businesses that donated resources. Configured for aeromedical transport by Houston Aviation technical services, the Evergreen Lear flew into San José on July 8, with a doctor from Baylor, and a flight nurse and respiratory therapist from the Shriners Burn Center aboard.

RESPONDING TO HURRICANE KATRINA

Hurricane Katrina made landfall on the Gulf Coast near New Orleans, Louisiana as a Category Four storm August 29, 2005. The damage done to the coastal regions of Louisiana, Mississippi, and Alabama, as well as the subsequent flooding of the city of New Orleans, led Homeland Security Secretary Michael Chertoff to describe Katrina as "probably the worst catastrophe, or set of catastrophes" in American history. The official death toll exceeded 1,200 persons and the cost of the damage was higher than $200 billion. Federal disaster declarations blanketed 90,000 square miles, and an estimated five million people were left without power. More than a million people were rendered homeless.

As it has done in the face of past natural disasters, Evergreen quickly moved into action. A large fleet of Evergreen Helicopters' aircraft were dispatched to the Gulf Coast from as far away as Alaska, flying over 49,000 miles to aid in the rescue and relief efforts. Using Galveston, Texas as their operations center Evergreen helicopters were at work within 48 hours, rescuing people from levees, and transporting such necessities as water, food, and fuel, and bringing support crews in and out of the area.

On September 3, Evergreen donated the use of a Kenworth freightliner truck used in EAGLE operations, a 48-foot refrigerated trailer used for shipping the products of Evergreen Agricultural Enterprises, and a driving team to transport relief supplies. The refrigerated trailer reached the stricken area filled with 30,000 bottles of donated water, diapers, formula, and baby food.

"We are glad to be providing our aircraft to act as angels of mercy in these efforts," Evergreen Helicopters President David Rath said, paraphrasing Del Smith. "We plan to have our fleet there helping with everything from rescues to reconstruction."

Four months after Hurricane Katrina, Del Smith donated a truck load of Christmas Trees to the residents of New Orleans, and Evergreen's Jim Porter was on hand to distribute them.

It had been more than four decades since Del Smith had first coined the phrase describing helicopters as "angels of mercy," and to the desperate people of the Gulf Coast, the green and white choppers were still that.

THE KID BANK

Of all his achievements as an industry leader, Del Smith is especially proud of a project through which he promotes entrepreneurship among the youngest of budding business owners. When he was starting on his own business career during the Great Depression — at the age of seven — Smith had borrowed money from a bank to buy a lawn mower. He quickly mowed enough lawns, at 15 cents each, to repay his loan. As he grew, so did his entrepreneurial spirit. He worked various jobs in fields such as newspaper delivery, forestry, and agriculture. By the time he was 11 years old, he had saved $50 — enough to use as a down payment on a $1,200 house for himself and his adoptive mother.

That initial loan of $2.50 was all that Del Smith needed to start his amazing career as an entrepreneur, but gradually the door closed to others who would follow in his footsteps.

Over time, banks have adopted policies that restrict loans to those over the age of 18. Feeling that this practice is unfair and stifling to the entrepreneurial spirit, Del Smith moved to establish his "Kid Bank" through the Valley Community Bank in McMinnville which enabled children to borrow interest-free money in order to start their own businesses.

Now officially known as the Michael King Smith Kid's Fund, the Kid Bank began in 1983, helping children with entrepreneurial

EVERGREEN CREWS AT WORK DURING POST-KATRINA OPERATIONS.

dreams start or expand businesses by providing them with resources unavailable from a traditional bank.

The non-profit mandate of the Kid Bank is to help enterprising children establish a business or expand an already existing business. Through its operation they can gain maturity, develop standards of ethics and fair play, and learn about the free enterprise system first hand. The fund is open to children 18 years of age and younger, and requires applicants to formulate a business plan.

Del Smith never forgets his early childhood, where he learned about the rewards of hard work and the self-confidence it brings to those living in a free enterprise country. Mark Victor Hansen, the motivational seminar leader and best-selling author of such books as *Chicken Soup For The Soul* and *Dare To Win*, visited Smith in his McMinnville office in 1983. In discussing his early childhood, Smith explained to Hansen that borrowing money from a bank was no longer an option available to kids because of restrictive banking regulations. Hansen suggested to Smith that he ought to start a "kids' bank." When Hansen returned from a one-hour tour of the Evergreen facility, he was told that Del Smith had just earmarked $25,000 to start such a non-profit lending institution.

When bank commissioners later closed down the institution because it was illegal for children to sign a contract, Del Smith called in his lawyers and directed them to "figure out a way to make the bank work." They did. By granting, rather than lending, the money.

"What a marvelous philanthropic act," said Mark Victor Hansen. "For making this possible, and for all his other unselfish and innovative acts of philanthropy, I consider Del Smith to be the Andrew Carnegie of our time."

Applicants for Kid Bank grants are guided through the process of organizing a business and writing a business plan. In turn, they are asked a variety of probing questions, including "How much do I know about what I want to do?" "How much money do I need," and "How will I make a profit?" "Do I need another person to help get the job done? If so, how much money do I need to pay them?"

In the application process, children are given a basic outline to follow in order to reach their goal of becoming an entrepreneur. They are counseled to:

(1) Develop the idea;

(2) Determine what supplies and materials are needed to get the job done;

(3) Determine how much the supplies will cost;

(4) Estimate how much money they will make;

(5) Determine, after they cover costs and loan repayments, how much of this money is profit;

(6) Determine a timeline to pay back their loan; and

(7) Create a Giving Plan to share their success with their community.

Over the years, several young entrepreneurs have borrowed funds to raise rabbits and other livestock, and to grow crops for market at the end of the summer. One entrepreneur secured a grant to buy the materials to start a window-washing business and another to buy a riding lawn mower. One teenage girl who wrote poetry borrowed $1,200 to publish her work. She sold out the first edition and published a second at her own expense.

During the Cold War, a six-year-old borrowed money to print bumper stickers in his own handwriting that read "Peace: Please Do It For Us Kids." It was signed "Tommy." He sold them for a dollar apiece and had to order a second printing. It is said that Mikhail Gorbachev had the sticker placed on the bumper of his official limousine.

In 2006 The Kid Bank loaned $1,200 to 17-year old Michael Wight to expand his vending machine business. The high school student's venture began with six machines, selling gumballs, espresso beans, and various other types of candy, and grew to eighteen machines with the assistance of The Kid Bank loan. Wight manages his business by tracking finances, maintaining relationships with clients, and seeking expansion opportunities. Along with repaying the loan, Wight donates a monthly percentage of his profits to his church and ChildSearch.org, an organization that searches for lost children.

All of these young business owners made a profit, and all repaid their grants. Through the Kid Bank organization, they were able to learn valuable business lessons that would benefit them in future careers.

The primary goal of The Kid Bank, funded by Mr. Smith, is to encourage entrepreneurialism, responsibility, success, and hard work in children, benefiting the future of mankind. He said, "I know from my own experience that success is partly due to finding the right support at the right time." He wants to provide that source of support for young entrepreneurs. His own experience taught him that, "what the mind can conceive and believe, it can achieve," and he desires to instill this faith in America's future entrepreneurs by giving them the means to reach their dreams.

THE EVERGREEN AVIATION MUSEUM AND THE CAPTAIN MICHAEL KING SMITH EDUCATIONAL INSTITUTE

Evergreen International Aviation is the most diversified aviation company in the world. Not only does it operate 747's and other fixed-wing aircraft throughout the world, it has had helicopter operations on every continent and an unlimited aircraft repair station. None of Evergreen's competitors in any of these businesses are also a major player in both the ground handling and aircraft leasing industries — and certainly none are the proprietor of a world-class aviation museum campus.

Located in McMinnville on 35 acres, the Evergreen Aviation Museum's award-winning, 121,000-square-foot main hangar facility formally opened on June 6, 2001, the 57th Anniversary of the D-Day invasion of Normandy in World War II. An additional facility, which opened in April 2007, is one of the largest IMAX® 3D movie theaters in the Pacific Northwest. This addition will enhance the educational mission, and create a major entertainment destination.

The United States is home to many world class aviation museums, but Evergreen's Museum has, as its centerpiece, one of the three most famous one-of-a-kind aircraft in aviation history. The Wright Brothers' *Flyer I* and Charles Lindbergh's *Spirit of St. Louis* are both in the Smithsonian Institution's National Air & Space Museum in Washington, DC. Across the continent in McMinnville, Evergreen displays Howard Hughes' legendary HK-1 Hercules Flying Boat, best known by the name "Spruce Goose."

While Evergreen International Aviation and its family of subsidiary companies stem from the pioneering vision of Delford M. Smith, the Museum was the vision of his eldest son, the late Captain

THE EVERGREEN AVIATION MUSEUM, HOME OF THE "SPRUCE GOOSE."

Michael King Smith. Born on January 20, 1966, Mike Smith graduated from McMinnville High School in 1984, having been an honor
student, varsity athlete, and Eagle Scout. He went on to the University of Washington and graduated in 1989. Like his father, he had
enrolled in Air Force ROTC, and he was commissioned as a second
lieutenant in the US Air Force. After earning his wings, Smith qualified as a fighter pilot and a flight leader. He was promoted to Captain
and went on to fly the F-15 Eagle air superiority fighter with the US
Air Force and with the Oregon Air National Guard 123rd Fighter
Squadron, the "Redhawks."

It was Captain Smith's idea to create a learning environment that would provide the opportunity for people to experience a complete encounter with the evolution of flight. He wanted to build a Museum that would bring guests into contact with the events, people, and technologies associated with aviation. He also wanted visitors to be able to touch real aircraft, the tangible artifacts of the history of flight.

In 1992, Michael Smith wrote about this vision of a place dedicated to preserving, commemorating, and communicating the great story of aviation.

"This facility will embody all of the components involved in this particular story of flight," Smith said of the Museum that he was developing for Evergreen. He went on to say that "elements including aviation, adventure, challenge, technology, risk, enterprise, courage, spirit, vitality, speed, performance, service, and global influence, are to be present. The story will be told through the Museum's unique complex of facilities, priceless collection, dynamic exhibits, extensive visitor amenities, educational programs, and the Museum's unique location near a working airport."

"He loved to fly," Del Smith said of his son. "When he was little and I was flying somewhere, he'd sit in my lap all the time. That kid was with me all over the world. He became a very accomplished pilot. When he joined the Air Force, he was number one in his class. When the Aero Club of Southern California was looking for a suitable home for the Hughes Flying Boat, he said, 'Dad, why don't we go for it?' I thought this was impressive. He prepared the presentation that won us the Hughes Flying Boat."

The original Evergreen Aviation Museum first opened on November 15, 1991 in a 12,000 square foot hangar located at the Evergreen Aviation headquarters campus in McMinnville. A year later, thanks to Mike Smith's efforts, the Aero Club of Southern California named the Evergreen Museum as the new custodian of Howard Hughes' famous wooden Flying Boat.

Departing from the Port of Long Beach on October 13, 1992, the Flying Boat sailed north, traveling 20 miles off the coasts of California and Oregon at an average speed of eight knots. The Sause Brothers barge *Nehalem* and tug *Natoma* completed the 980 nautical mile journey to Portland, arriving at sundown on October 18. With an official proclamation of October 22, 1992 as "Spruce Goose Day in Portland," thousands of people came to Waterfront Park to welcome the Flying Boat to Oregon.

The barge was then pulled to an industrial park in Vancouver, Washington and off-loaded. Throughout the next several months, weather and river levels wrought havoc on the schedule. A recurring obstacle was the Willamette River, which was then at levels that were too high for huge components of the disassembled aircraft to pass under bridges. Finally, in February 1993, the river reached the proper level and the Hughes Flying Boat was moved up the Willamette to Western Bar, where it was off-loaded seven miles from the future Museum site.

The final trek over the narrow backroads saw a caravan of disassembled sections and heavy moving equipment that stretched more than a quarter mile. The 181-foot fuselage was pulled by three 475-horsepower prime movers, each with 104 forward gears. On its cradle and transport dollies, the fuselage reached a height of 35 feet. Each 158-foot wing was seated in a steel cradle and tipped in vertical position on its trailing edge, towering 62 feet above the equipment moving them. The tail section, also encased in a steel cradle and resting on its trailing edge, measured 39 feet high and 62 feet in length. Joining the convoy on the final mile of its 1,055 mile trip from Long Beach were classic automobiles, antique fire and farm equipment, equestrian groups, school bands and scout troops.

The Hughes Flying Boat reached McMinnville on February 27, 1993, as charter memberships were offered in the Museum. By now, plans were underway for a new and much larger building with adequate room to properly display the Hughes Flying Boat and other significant historical and modern aircraft.

Sadly, Michael Smith would not live to see his vision come to full fruition. He passed away on March 22, 1995, from injuries sustained in an automobile accident. The Museum, and the educational Institute that bears his name would form his legacy and serve as a fitting tribute to his vision.

To commemorate that legacy, the first aircraft visible to visitors approaching the Museum and Institute is a McDonnell Douglas F-15A Eagle, the type flown by Captain Smith during his service career. Located on the Evergreen International Aviation campus across the highway from the Museum, the aircraft serves as a memorial to Captain Smith and to Major Rhory Roger Draeger, a fellow 123rd Fighter Squadron pilot who was killed in the same 1995 accident.

The F-15 Eagle was designed as the world's ultimate air superiority fighter and, to date, it has never been beaten in aerial combat. The Eagle went to war with the US Air Force in 1991, after a dozen years in service and chalked up a record of 31 aerial victories against Iraqi fighter jets without defeat. On January 17, 1991, the first night of Gulf War I, US Air Force F-15C's shot down six Iraqi interceptors in air-to-air combat, and two days later, a Saudi F-15 pilot downed two Iraqi aircraft. Subsequent action was sporadic because Iraq's air force chose to run or hide, but at war's end, F-15C's accounted for 31 of the 34 Iraqi fixed-wing aircraft shot down during the war. Two of these enemy aircraft, a MiG-23 and a MiG-29, were downed by Major Rhory Roger Draeger.

After the loss of Captain Smith and Major Draeger, Evergreen International Aviation submitted a request for an F-15 for use in a memorial, and this request was granted by the Museum of the United States Air Force. It is a testament to Evergreen's reputation and to that of Captain Smith and Major Draeger that this was for many years the only F-15 Eagle in civilian hands.

After the request was formally approved, Evergreen personnel were invited to Davis-Monthan Air Force Base to select a specific aircraft. After a detailed physical review of the aircraft and records, they determined that the most complete aircraft was

CAPTAIN MICHAEL KING SMITH IS SEEN HERE WITH A T-38 AIRCRAFT
DURING HIS US AIR FORCE FLIGHT TRAINING.

serial number 76-0014, an F-15A that had been delivered to the
US Air Force on April 12, 1977.

Over the next several months, the activity accelerated at a
rapid pace. The Evergreen Properties Department selected an
architect, engineer, lead contractor and surveyor, as well as obtaining permits and geotechnical analysis. The aircraft re-assembly was
undertaken with help from the Oregon Air National Guard, with
Chief Master Sergeant John Rasmussen as lead. The guidance and
assistance from the Oregon Air National Guard assured that the
F-15 display would exist.

The Museum received the Eagle in May 1996, and reassembly took several weeks. This involved reattachment of the wings, horizontal stabilizers and afterburner assemblies. Finally, the aircraft was painted in the colors of the 123rd Fighter Group of the Oregon Air National Guard. The names Captain Smith and Major Draeger are stenciled on the side of the aircraft next to the canopy.

On the rainy, blustery morning of September 19, 1996, the Oregon Air National Guard crash recovery team worked with Evergreen crews to hoist the aircraft atop its pedestal and weld it into position. Over the next several weeks, the platform was completed, stainless steel sheeting was placed at the pedestal, three flag poles were installed around the seat wall, and lights were placed around the back perimeter of the memorial. The flags of the United States, Oregon, and the 123rd Fighter Squadron, as well as the POW/MIA flag, continue to fly alongside the F-15.

The F-15 is not only a permanent fixture at the Evergreen campus and a valuable artifact in the Museum collection, it is also recognized as the gateway to the City of McMinnville.

In 1997, the citizens of McMinnville gave their vote of approval for the construction of the new main Museum building, and in August 1999, ground was broken. On September 16, 2000, the Hughes Flying Boat was moved across Highway 18 from its temporary hangar, and construction crews proceeded to complete the building around it.

When the new Evergreen Aviation Museum building formally opened on June 6, 2001, the Hughes Flying Boat and 25 other historic aircraft from the Evergreen Collection were on exhibit together for the first time. Many of the aircraft are part of the Evergreen collection, while others, including the F-15, an F-102, a T-33 and a T-38, are on loan from the Museum of the United States Air Force.

Assembly of the Hughes Flying Boat would continue through the year, culminating with the tail cone installation on December 7, 2001, the 60th Anniversary of Pearl Harbor. In July of the following year, the American Society of Mechanical Engineers designated the Hughes Flying Boat as an Historic Mechanical Engineering Landmark. Within two years, the collection would double in size, and include the famous Lockheed SR-71 Blackbird, as well as a Titan I missile.

In addition to Mike Smith, another man who was instrumental in facilitating the transfer of the Hughes Flying Boat to the Evergreen Museum was Jack Garrett Real, a man who had served as one of Howard Hughes's closest and trusted personal advisors for nearly two decades.

Having joined Lockheed in 1937, Real became the company's chief of engineering flight test in 1960, and two years later, he was promoted to chief engineer of research, development and testing. During his tenure at Lockheed, Real was intimately involved in a wide variety of aircraft projects from the R6V Constitution to the SR-71 Blackbird, and he headed the AH-56 Cheyenne helicopter project. In the meantime, Real had been one of Howard Hughes's only close personal friends since 1957, and in 1971, Hughes appointed him as the senior vice president of aviation for the Howard Hughes Corporation. After Hughes died in 1976, Real became president of Hughes Helicopters (McDonnell Douglas Helicopters after 1984), where he earned a Collier Trophy for his work as head of the AH-64 Apache attack helicopter program.

In 1993, Real joined Evergreen as chairman of the museum, a post that he held until 2001 when he became chairman emeritus. Jack Real passed away in September 2005 after a long illness.

While Evergreen employs people from around the world, occasionally coming to work in McMinnville means coming home. Such is the case for Katherine Huit, a former Director of Collections for the Evergreen Aviation Museum, who grew up here. A few years after completing her education, with history as a major, she learned that Evergreen was planning an aviation museum. She applied for a position and was hired in 1999. Soon after, Del Smith

SCOUT GROUPS ARE AMONG THOSE THAT REGULARLY VISIT THE
EVERGREEN AVIATION MUSEUM.

called Katherine into his office and asked if she would like to be
the company historian.

"I first learned of Evergreen during a visit to the McMinnville
Municipal Airport around 1962," Katherine remembers. "I observed
several small Hiller 12 E helicopters scattered about a hangar at the
airport, which belonged to a fledgling company known as Evergreen
Helicopters. Who knew that forty years later, Evergreen would
become the most diversified global aviation provider in the world?
Thinking back to that visit, I'm amazed to realize what a major role
Evergreen has played in my personal life. It was great to have found
a job in my hometown."

Katherine Huit began work on several projects celebrating the company's 40th anniversary. "I was then given the awesome yet challenging assignment of documenting the construction of the new museum facility and the restoration and reassembly of the Hughes Flying Boat," she said. "That assignment led to my writing and producing the documentary *Dream to Fly: Howard Hughes and the Flying Boat,* with Walter Cronkite as the narrator — the highlight of my career so far! Now, I believe I truly have the best job at the Evergreen Aviation Museum. I work with history every day in a very real and personal way. Caring for the artifacts and aircraft; listening to the veteran's stories — and preserving them for future generations; relating those stories in exhibits connecting the machines to missions — that's what it's all about here."

Today, the Evergreen Aviation Museum is open every day, except Thanksgiving, Christmas, New Year's Day, and Easter. The expansive and elegant steel and glass facility, with its floor-to-ceiling windows hosts numerous events, and can accommodate up to 3,000 people amidst one of the most unique aviation collections in the world.

"The Evergreen Aviation Museum and the Captain Michael King Smith Educational Institute fulfills Michael's vision of creating a place that inspires people to be the best they can be." Del Smith has said. "The Institute is a continuously renewed gift from Evergreen to the community, celebrating many years of learning and growing together."

The Institute's Educational Program

The role of the Institute is to support and enrich existing education and trade programs, while creating new opportunities to meet the challenges of the future. The Institute operates within an alliance of interests and resources that make Oregon a model for a changing work force through education and training.

The education department at the Institute provides extensive support to Oregon's public elementary and high school programs, colleges, universities, and vocational and technical schools in an effort to prepare Oregon's young people for careers with a technology focus.

Students of all ages can experience the four-part personally-guided educational tour at the Captain Michael King Smith Educational Institute. The first part of this educational tour consists of the oldest, biggest, and fastest airplanes in the world. Here, the students also learn about the four forces of flight, the three axes of flight, the center of gravity and stability problems inherent with flight, and the materials utilized in man's first attempt to achieve sustained, controlled, and man-powered flight. Bernoulli's principle, and the development of the aircraft power plant are also explained and explored.

The second part of the educational tour involves the students participating in the computer flight simulation lab. Here students apply the three axes of flight to navigate a Piper J-3 Cub through the skies over Portland International Airport. Once students have mastered this simple primary trainer, they can then upgrade to more complex and challenging aircraft. Also in the simulator lab are four RealFlight G-3 radio-controlled airplane and helicopter simulators with transmitters for those students wishing to try their hand at the challenging world of radio-controlled flight.

The movie theater, a third component of the educational tour, has age-appropriate aviation and aerospace films. Here, students sit in the comfort of first-class airline seats complete with folding tables and seat belts. The audience takes in films that cover the historical perspectives of flight, as well as Space Shuttle flight training at the Johnson and Kennedy Space Centers. These include an actual Space Shuttle launch. There are also aviation cartoon films for the younger crowd. The theater incorporates the electronic systems necessary for special presentations, including computer access to digital projection equipment for teachers with specific curricula.

The fourth and final part of the tour has the students building and test-flying their own experimental model gliders. Here students use basic building techniques to construct and fly a variety of models, depending upon the group's age and dexterity. At the end of the session, the students are allowed to take their flying models home, in the hope that the experience will inspire a lifelong passion for the world of flight.

In addition to group Museum tours, the Institute also offers Merit Badge Training in partnership with the Boy Scouts of America; the Girl Scouts of America; the Ninety-Nines, the Organization of Women Pilots; the Civil Air Patrol; Evergreen International Aviation; and local pilot groups. Merit Badge training is currently offered for badges including Aviation and Space Exploration. Merit Badge classes are offered periodically and are open to Boy and Girl Scouts and students throughout the region. The Captain Michael King Smith Educational Institute is approved by the Cascade Pacific Council to provide authorized training for all Boy Scouts.

STUDENTS OBSERVE A MODEL ROCKET LAUNCH AT THE MUSEUM.

The Institute is highly involved with the Cadet program of the McMinnville Composite Squadron of the Civil Air Patrol which has served Yamhill County and Oregon for almost 20 years. The Captain Michael King Smith Educational Institute plays a vital role in the aviation education component of this program. The aerospace training officer holds all training and educational programs at the Institute. Topics covered include history of space flight, radio-controlled flight training, meteorology, history of aviation, career paths in aviation and aerospace, and general aviation topics, discussions, and video presentations.

The Institute also offers scholarship opportunities in memory of Captain Michael King Smith, to local high school students, which support youth interest in achieving pilots' licenses and careers in aviation.

A recent addition to the Institute is the extension campus of Embry-Riddle Aeronautical University, the world's largest independent aeronautical university, which boasts a student body of 30,000 from all 50 states and more than 100 nations. Embry-Riddle Aeronautical University and The Captain Michael King Smith Educational Institute have an agreement with Embry-Riddle to offer undergraduate and graduate degrees on-site at the Museum and online courses for those students unable to attend classes at the Museum. This new partnership is a giant step for the educational department and the vision of Captain Smith.

A NEW MUSEUM FOR A NEW CENTURY

As the new century began, the Evergreen Aviation Museum and the Captain Michael King Smith Educational Institute were far more than the sum of the artifacts in its collection. Certainly it is important to exhibit the aircraft and artifacts, but the educational component is also vital to the Institute's mission. The Institute is a place for scholarly research, as well as training in astronautical history, technology, trades, and careers.

VOLUNTEERS ARE THE CORNERSTONE OF THE MUSEUM.

In addition to the educational opportunities discussed in the preceding section, the Museum also offers internships in artifact preservation and museology, and supports an oral history program to preserve the stories told by those who lived the experience. The Museum's Library and Archive are a repository for primary source material on Oregon aviation, as well as materials related to the Hughes Flying Boat and other Hughes aircraft.

In terms of its aviation preservation and restoration mission, the Institute engages in training staff and volunteers to select and restore technological artifacts essential to advancing the nation's efforts in preserving precious artifacts from its significant aviation heritage.

The aircraft restoration facility is not only a primary support component, but also operates as an active educational and exhibit area. The public is afforded the opportunity to discover the secrets of the trade while learning how the aircraft take shape. The facilities also provide a continuous expansion of aircraft inventory and revenues from external restoration contracts.

Students obtain hands-on experience, with hourly credits toward their A&P (Airframe & Powerplant) certificates. Training programs at the Institute will be a valuable component in the nation's collection of historical aviation artifacts, including military, commercial, and general aviation.

In September 2006, Evergreen began construction of the Space Museum, a 121,000-square-foot facility reflecting the same design as the home of the famous "Spruce Goose." The new museum will feature artifacts the museum has already acquired, including the Titan II SLV missile, the Titan IV SLV missile, the Willamette Meteorite, the replica Lunar Module, the replica Lunar Rover, and the Rus-

sian Photon Space Capsule. The facility also plans to feature a mission launch room with interactive opportunities. The components of

HOWARD HUGHES'S "SPRUCE GOOSE," CENTERPIECE OF THE EVERGREEN
AVIATION MUSEUM COLLECTION. (© PHOTOGRAPHER CHARLIE VAN PELT)

the Space Museum will start with the beginning of the space age, and include the space race, destination moon, living in space, unmanned spacecraft, and space tourism. These facilities will establish the Evergreen campus as one of the premier education and entertainment destinations in the world.

Since 2003, the Evergreen Aviation Museum has been designated by the State of Oregon as the official location for the Oregon Aviation Hall of Honor, which was established by the Oregon State Department of Aviation to recognize outstanding men and women in Oregon aviation.

Through its exhibits and programs, the mission of the Evergreen Aviation Museum and the Captain Michael King Smith Educational Institute is to "inspire and educate, to promote and preserve aviation history, and to honor the patriotic service of our veterans." Through the exhibits, as well as the educational components of the Institute, this is the legacy passed along to future generations.

In recalling his son's vision, Del Smith said, "He wanted a living institute. He didn't like the word 'museum,' because what he wanted to do was teach kids how to fly, and teach them meteorology and the principles of flying. In his name, I want it to be more than just a museum. I want it to be a place for growing young people. That's what he wanted, so I want to do that for him."

"YOU ARE UNIVERSALLY ADMIRED"

There is no more fitting tribute to Delford Smith, and to the spirit of unselfish dedication that he has inspired at Evergreen, than that which came from former President George Herbert Walker Bush in May 2005. The circumstances of the tribute are especially telling because they involve Del Smith's wanting to pay tribute to someone else!

The story begins with the Horatio Alger Association Annual Awards Dinner on April 8, 2005. Horatio Alger was the nineteenth-century American author who championed entrepreneurship and the American dream of wealth and success through hard work, courage, determination, and concern for others — principles that have also been embraced by Del Smith. Since 1947, the Horatio Alger Association has bestowed an annual award on outstanding individuals who have succeeded in the face of adversity. Del Smith received his Horatio Alger Award in 2002. The Association also awards scholarships "to encourage young people to pursue their dreams through higher education."

Each year, past honorees are invited to be present at the Annual Awards Dinner, which is held in Washington, DC to recognize ten distinguished Americans for their outstanding contributions in their chosen fields. Over a thousand members and guests attend the prestigious event and they often invite dignitaries and important individuals to join them at their tables. Typically, those invited include politicians and celebrities, but in 2005, Del Smith decided to invite wounded soldiers from the Walter Reed Army Medical Center in Washington, DC.

Two of these special guests were Specialist Jereme Coker of Clarendon, Arkansas and Specialist Tom Wiggins, an Airborne Ranger from Hawthorne, Florida. Specialist Coker was injured in Iraq when an armor-piercing, rocket-propelled grenade penetrated the door of his armed Humvee and exploded. He was hit a second time with two AK-47 rounds to the right thigh as he ran to the rear of the Humvee. He called medevac for himself and nine other wounded soldiers. While holding his intestines inside his stomach, Specialist Coker continued to fight for an hour until medevac arrived.

Specialist Wiggins had his hearing shattered in a firefight while on a classified Special Operations mission in Afghanistan during his fifth overseas tour of duty. A ranger from the 1st Ranger Battalion of the 75th Ranger Regiment, he received several rounds in the back and two in the head in Afghanistan causing permanent

DEL SMITH WITH HIS SONS, MIKE (LEFT) AND MARK (RIGHT)
IN FRONT OF A NEWLY PURCHASED S-64 SKYCRANE IN 1975.

deafness. At Walter Reed, he was treated for closed head wounds, skull fractures and neurological complications. When he woke up one morning on Walter Reed's traumatic brain injury ward to absolute silence, he became a candidate for a cochlear implant to restore his hearing. His surgery was performed by Navy Commander Brian McKinnon, an inner ear and cochlear specialist at Walter Reed. According to Dr. Gerald Schuchman, an audiologist with Walter Reed's cochlear program, Wiggins's was the first such implant in a person injured in combat.

Specialist Wiggins was awarded the Bronze Star Medal with Valor, as well as numerous other awards for valor. Both men were honored with the Purple Heart and the Army Commendation Medal with Valor.

Coker and Wiggins, along with former Sergeant Major of the Army Jack Tilley, were seated at Del Smith's table at the Awards

EVERGREEN FLEW MEDICINE, FOOD AND OTHER SUPPLIES TO ETHIOPIA AS
PART OF THE "OREGONIANS HELPING ETHIOPIANS" CAMPAIGN.

Dinner when Ed McMahon, the master of ceremonies, introduced them. As spotlights pointed them out, the entire room erupted in a spontaneous standing ovation.

Specialist Wiggins recalled that "I couldn't really hear a lot of what was going on but you didn't really need to with the show they put on. It was very patriotic. All of a sudden Jereme stood up and the spotlight came on him. Del saw me still sitting and he 'picked me up' and everyone started clapping. Then everyone else stood and continued clapping. It was very emotional. I think everyone who could reach us was hugging us and shaking our hands. Ed McMahon came over and said 'Hi' and thanked us for our service."

Del Smith subsequently honored the two men further by offering to underwrite their college education and by giving them both jobs with Evergreen in McMinnville.

In the meantime, the two veterans and Sam White, Senior Vice President in Evergreen's Washington, DC office, met with the Horatio Alger Association staff to put together a scholarship fund for other veterans of the current wars. George Argyros, the United States Ambassador to Spain, donated $6 million to get the scholarship started and soon after others followed. Within a few weeks, the Horatio Alger Military Veterans Scholarship Fund had grown to over $10 million. Coker and Wiggins assisted in getting information about the program to their contacts within the service.

It was shortly after the Horatio Alger dinner that Sam White made his first trip to Walter Reed, accompanied by Coker and Wiggins.

"Perched on top of a hill in northern Washington, DC is a beautiful campus," Sam White said of Walter Reed. "It's a large sprawling facility with perfectly manicured lawns and military-style hedge rows. It is here that I am reminded of the high price for the freedoms we enjoy in the United States. Nothing could have prepared me for what I was about to see. I could hardly comprehend the true meaning of 'sacrifice' as I walked the halls of Walter Reed. I am initially struck by the almost fraternity-like support network in the center."

As they settled down in the cafeteria area of the Mologne House to discuss employment opportunities at Evergreen, another young man joined them. "His face was distorted, his speech was slurred, and his mind was quick to comprehend but slow to react to our conversation," White recalled.

"Sam, our friend here got his face smashed in. . . they had to totally rebuild his face, but he'll be alright." Jereme explained.

"I'm honored to be in the presence of men like these," White says. "They tease each other about their 'stories,' and I laugh at all the appropriate times, but I tell myself, 'don't pretend to understand,' and I feel so inadequate. They laugh. They support each other. They play jokes on each other, like hiding their friend's prostheses during the morning hours and telling him to 'hop over and get it yourself' when he awakes. I guess this is the true meaning of tough love. Many of them are frustrated that they can't return to combat to be with their friends. They know hardship and fear like I will never know. They are brothers in arms and friends for life."

"Sitting at that cafeteria table at Walter Reed, I realize how misguided my perception of a war hero really was," Sam White recalls. "I pray and thank God for soldiers like these; men and women who have given more than I could ever know so that my family and I could have hope for a better and safer tomorrow. I think to myself, 'These are war heroes.' I'm blessed that Evergreen gave me this experience because I believe I now understand, a little better, what a war hero truly is."

A few weeks after the Awards Dinner, the two veterans were aboard Del Smith's Gulfstream IV when he hosted former President George Herbert Walker Bush on a ride between Washington and Maine. During the flight, the four men had occasion to get to know one another.

On May 16, President Bush penned the following handwritten note:

Dear Del,

First, I write to thank you for our round-trip flight on your lovely G-IV. It made a tough schedule work for me.

Second, and most important, I want you to know how truly impressed I am by what you have done with your life. The business success properly speaks for itself. You are universally admired for that. But your being one of a "thousand points of light" says even more.

As I thought about what you are doing for those 2 soldiers I must confess some tears flowed. And there is so much more. So this comes not only with my gratitude, but also with my profound respect.

Your new friend,
George Bush #41

ABOVE LEFT: SUSIE GRAVES IS A SEVENTEEN YEAR VETERAN EVERGREEN
EMPLOYEE, AND HAS BEEN INSTRUMENTAL IN THE COORDINATION OF THIS
BOOK. SHE HAS WORKED IN ADMINISTRATION FOR EIA AND EVERGREEN
TRADE, AND SINCE 1999, HAS WORKED FOR EVERGREEN INTERNATIONAL
AVIATION AS EXECUTIVE ASSISTANT TO MR. SMITH. ABOVE RIGHT: TOM
PITZER OF EVERGREEN INTERNATIONAL AIRLINES. IN 2007, THE FEDERAL
AVIATION ADMINISTRATION AWARDED EIA THE DIAMOND AWARD OF
EXCELLENCE FOR PARTICIPATION IN THE FAA'S AVIATION MAINTENANCE
TECHNICIAN AWARD PROGRAM. OPPOSITE TOP: JOHN KIESLER, A VETERAN OF
MORE THAN THREE DECADES OF SERVICE WITH EVERGREEN HELICOPTERS, INC.
OPPOSITE BOTTOM: THE EVERGREEN INTERNATIONAL AIRLINES
ENGINE TEAM. FROM LEFT TO RIGHT, TRENT TAYLOR, JEAN BUREAU,
ERIC MOORMAN AND CLINT JEFFREY.

Epilogue:

THE BEST IS YET TO COME

by Delford M. Smith

Thebese past forty-five years have been very special ones for Evergreen. We have always resolved to perform safely and reliably in every endeavor we have undertaken. We have sought to make our quality services tangible to our customers at a most economical cost.

While we have great pride in our accomplishments, we know we must focus on the future. Evergreen will continue to play a pivotal role in the economic stability and development of the aviation and commerce industries throughout this century. The challenge for Evergreen in the new millennium is to maintain the entrepreneurial spirit that made us what we are today. We are determined that our role be one of leadership, quality standards, and commitment to our customers, business associates, and employees.

MARIA AND DEL SMITH DURING ONE OF MANY HUMANITARIAN MISSIONS.

We will resolve what we ought and perform without fail what we resolve. Every job we perform and every mission we undertake impacts the lives of many individuals and the success of numerous business endeavors. We assume our responsibility to be sure the results are positive for our customers, lenders, vendors, and our team.

Employees are Evergreen's greatest assets, and all of our progress and accomplishments are the result of a sincere team effort. All recognition is to be shared by the entire Evergreen team who has devoted time and talent to making this company the success it is today.

We thank each person who has assisted us along our flight path, and we look forward with vision and inspiration to the decades ahead. We believe that peace, goodwill, and prosperity for all are achievable goals.

I believe the best is yet to come!

DELFORD M. SMITH

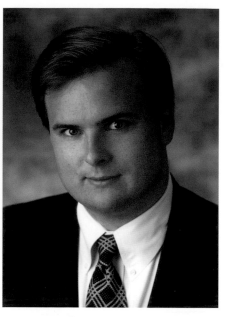

BRIAN T. BAUER

C. BLAIR BERSELLI

A. BLYTHE BERSELLI

MICHAEL A. HINES

JOHN A. IRWIN

DANIEL S. KLUMP

JOHN L. PALO

DAVID B. RATH

RONALD A. SELVY

RANJIT SETH

TIMOTHY G. WAHLBERG

SAMUEL P. WHITE

MICHAEL H. WILHOIT

GWENNA R. WOOTRESS

RAYMOND H. WRIGHT

I salute the leaders who have helped build the Company.
Integrity. Intellect. Initiative. Vision.
— Del Smith

INDEX